AUSTRIA AND THE EUROPEAN UNION
PRESIDENCY:
BACKGROUND AND PERSPECTIVES

Edited by
Kurt Richard Luther and Iain Ogilvie
Keele University

Keele European
Research Centre

First Published 1998
by Keele European Research Centre
Department of Politics, Keele University, Keele, Staffs. ST5 5BG, UK

© Kurt Richard Luther and Iain Ogilvie for the collection;
individual chapters the contributors.

Camera ready copy provided by Kurt Richard Luther and Iain Ogilvie
Printed in Great Britain by Herald Printers (Whitchurch) Ltd., Shropshire.

ISBN 1-899488-16-2

Keele European
Research Centre

CONTENTS

LIST OF TABLES

LIST OF FIGURES

LIST OF ABBREVIATIONS

ATS	Austrian Schilling
B-VG	(Austrian) Federal Constitution - *Bundes-Verfassungsgesetz*
CAP	Common Agricultural Policy
CEEC	Countries of Central and Eastern Europe
CSCE	Conference on Security and Co-operation in Europe
CFSP	Common Foreign and Security Policy (of EU)
COREPER	Committee of Permanent Representatives (to EC)
DM	German Mark - *Deutsche Mark*
EBRD	European Bank for Reconstruction and Development
EC	European Community
ECB	European Central Bank
ECOFIN	Council of Economics and Finance Ministers (of EU)
EFTA	European Free Trade Association
EMU	Economic and Monetary Union
EMU	European Monetary Union (*sic*)
EP	European Parliament
ERM	Exchange Rate Mechanism
ESC	Economic and Social Committee (of EU)
ESCB	European System of Central Banks
EU	European Union
EURO XI	Council of EU member states participating in EMU
FCO	Foreign and Commonwealth Office (of UK)
FDI	Foreign Direct Investment
FPÖ	Freedom Party of Austria- *Freiheitliche Partei Österreichs*
GDP	Gross Domestic Product
GDR	(former) German Democratic Republic
GNP	Gross National Product
IGC	Inter-Governmental Conference
MEP	Member of the European Parliament
NATO	North Atlantic Treaty Organisation
OECD	Organisation for Economic Co-operation and Development
ÖVP	Austrian People's Party - *Österreichische Volkspartei*
SPÖ	Social Democratic Party of Austria - *Sozialdemokratische Partei* Österreich (until 1991: Socialist Party of Austria - *Sozialistische Partei Österreichs*)
UN	United Nations
UNICE	Union of Industrial and Employers' Confederations of Europe
VAT	Value Added Tax
VÖI	Federation of Austrian Industry - *Vereinigung der Österreichischen Industrie*
WIFO	Austrian Institute for Economic Research - *Österreichisches Institut für Wirtschaftsforschung*
WK	Austrian Chamber of Business - *Wirtschaftskammer Österreichs*

CONTRIBUTORS

Harald Ettl is Member of the European Parliament for the Social Democratic Party of Austria (1996-). He has been Secretary (1973-84) and is now Chairman (1984-) of the Textile, Clothing and Leather Trade Union, is Vice-Chairman of the Social Democratic group within the Austrian Federation of Trades Unions (ÖGB) (1987-), and Chairman of the Commission for EU Affairs within the ÖGB. He was Federal Minister for Health, Sports and Consumer Protection (1989-92), and is President of the Austrian Consumers Association (1993-). In the European Parliament, he serves on the Employment and Social Affairs Committee, is substitute member of the Committee on Economic and Monetary Affairs and Industrial Policy, and is member of the Sub-committee for Monetary Affairs.

Anna Gamper studied Law at Innsbruck University and now works at the Institute for Research on Federalism in Innsbruck and as an Assistant in the Department of Public Law at Innsbruck University. Her research interests include the principles of Austrian constitutional law and the Austrian federal system.

Katharina Krawagna-Pfeifer is Chief Political Editor of *Der Standard*, Vienna. She was educated at Linz and Paris. She was a permanent freelance correspondent (1974-78) and political correspondent (1979-93) at the *Salzburger Nachrichten* in Linz. She has been in her present position since 1993.

Kurt Richard Luther lectures Political Science at Keele University, UK. He studied Politics and German at Leeds, Mainz and at Plymouth, from where he received his doctorate. His main research interests relate to political parties, consociational democracy and federalism, especially in the German-speaking states. His publications include numerous journal articles and book chapters, as well as *Politics in Austria. Still a Case of Consociationalism?* (London: Frank Cass, 1992), *Austria 1945-95: Fifty Years of the Second Republic* (Aldershot: Ashgate, 1998), and *Party Elites in Divided Societies: Political Parties in Consociational Democracy*, (London: Routledge, 1998). He was recently awarded a Leverhulme Fellowship for work on a project on European right wing radicalism and is currently preparing a monograph on the Freedom Party of Austria.

Peter Mitterbauer is President of the Austrian Federation of Industry. He was educated at the Technical University of Graz and Vienna, receiving a Diploma in Mechanical Engineering in 1968, subsequently undertaking further postgraduate studies and professional training in the USA. He joined the family-owned company - the Miba Group - in 1969, and has since held various executive posts. He has been Chairman, President and Chief Executive Officer of Miba AG since 1986, and has served as President of the Federation of Austrian Industry since 1996.

Eva Nowotny is the Ambassador of the Republic of Austria to the United Kingdom. She was educated at the University of Vienna in modern European history. She received a doctorate (on Metternich and England) from the University of Vienna in 1968, where she subsequently held an Assistant Professorship (1969-73). She joined the diplomatic service in 1973, serving in the Departments of Press and Information and of Legal Affairs (1973-5), as First Secretary in the

Cultural Institute of the Austrian Embassy in Cairo (1975-78), and as Counsellor in the Permanent Mission of Austria to the United Nations (1978-83). During her time at the UN, she was the Vice-President of the Special Political Committee of the 36th General Assembly. In the period 1983-92, she was Foreign Policy Adviser to the Austrian Federal Chancellor, Franz Vranitzky. She has served as Ambassador to France (1992-97) and has been Ambassador in London since February 1997.

Thomas J. Nowotny is Assistant Professor of Political Science at the University of Vienna and Senior Adviser and Political Counsellor at the European Bank for Reconstruction and Development in London, with principal responsibility for monitoring political developments in the transition countries of Central and Eastern Europe. He has been senior adviser to the OECD Centre for Co-operation with Countries in Transition (1993-97), Head of the Department for Political Planning (*Grundsatzabteilung*) of the Austrian Ministry of Foreign Affairs (1983-93), and private secretary to the then Austrian Chancellor, Bruno Kreisky (1970-75). He has written numerous books and articles, including *Central/Eastern Europe and Transitology*; *Globalisierung, die europäische Linke und New Labour*; *The Transition from Communism and the Spectre of Latin Americanisation*; *Ist Demokratie natürlich? Zur Entwicklung der Reformstaaten Zentral- und Osteuropas*; and *Aber was macht der Dumme schon mit dem Glück? Politische Leadership durch Bruno Kreisky*.

Iain Ogilvie is Lecturer in International Relations at Keele University, UK. He was educated at Edinburgh and Keele Universities. His PhD research was on anti-EU parties and the mobilisation of anti-European sentiment; his current research interests include current developments in European integration, political parties, British politics - in particular British foreign policy and the UK's relationship with the EU - and Greek-Turkish relations.

Peter Pernthaler is Professor at Innsbruck University, Austria and Director of the Institute for Federal Research there. He gained his Professorship in 1963, and subsequently worked as an academic adviser in the Office of the Federal Chancellor (Constitutional Department). From 1966 until 1968, he held a chair at the *Hochschule für Bodenkultur*, and since then has been Professor at Innsbruck. In addition to a series of special investigations, his work includes monographs on important aspects of constitutional and administrative law, as well as on political science and on a general theory of the state. Professor Pernthaler has been Director of the Institute since 1975, and was Dean of the Faculty of Law at the University of Innsbruck 1979-81. He has also held Visiting Professorships in Australia and Canada in 1982 and 1983. Since 1996, he has been a member of the Austrian Academy of Sciences.

Wolfgang Schüssel is the Austrian Vice-Chancellor and Federal Minister for Foreign Affairs. He was educated at the University of Vienna, where he graduated Doctor of Law in 1968. He was secretary of the Parliamentary Austrian People's Party (ÖVP) from 1968-1975. He was General Secretary of the Austrian Economic Federation (*Österreichischer Wirtschaftsbund*), one of the ÖVP's constituent organisations, from 1975-1991. Dr Schüssel has been a member of the Austrian Parliament since 1987; being Deputy Leader of the parliamentary ÖVP from 1987-1989, Federal Minister for Economic Affairs 1989-1995, and Vice Chancellor and Minister for Foreign Affairs since 1995. He has also served as Leader of the ÖVP since April 1995. In addition to his parliamentary activities, Dr Schüssel has written numerous books and other publications, including *Ideen, die geh'n*; *Staat laß nach*; *Mehr Privat - weniger Staat* and *Bildungsplanung und Hochschulexpansion.*

Hannes Swoboda is a Member of the European Parliament for the Social Democratic Party of Austria (SPÖ) and a former member of the Vienna State Government. Educated at the University of Vienna in Law and Economics, he received an LLD and MA (Economics) in 1972. He has held various positions in the Vienna Chamber of Labour (including Head of the Department of Municipal Policies, with a special focus on economic policies for urban issues, health, housing and related areas - 1976-86), in Local Government (including Majority Leader, Social Democratic Group in the Vienna State Parliament and City Council - 1986-88; and Member of the Vienna State Government - 1988-96), and in the European Parliament (Vice-President of the Socialist Group in the EP, Spokesman on Foreign Affairs of the Party of European Socialists, Head of the Austrian Social Democratic Delegation in the EP, Member of the Committee on Transport and Tourism and Member of the Committee on Foreign Affairs, Security and Defence Policy). He is the SPÖ's Federal Spokesman on Educational Affairs, and is a member of the Federal and State Executive Committees of the SPÖ.

Gertrude Tumpel-Gugerell is Executive Director of the National Bank of Austria (*Österreichische Nationalbank* - ÖNB). She graduated from the University of Vienna in 1975 with a Master's degree in economic and social sciences, and received a doctorate in 1981. She joined the Economics Department of the National Bank in 1975, worked as the economic policy adviser to the Minister of Finance and served as member of the Supervisory Board of *Österreichische Länderbank AG* (1981-4). At the ÖNB, she has been Deputy Head of the Economics Division (1985), Comptroller General (1986-92), Director of Area Corporate Planning and Management (1992-7), and Chief Executive Director of the Economics and Financial Markets Division (1997-). Since 1990, she has represented the ÖNB in the economic and social sciences research institutes and has, since 1996, been in charge of co-ordinating the Bank's preparations for EMU.

Gregor Woschnagg is Director-General for Economic and Integration Policy in the Federal Ministry for Foreign Affairs, Vienna. He was educated at the Universities of Vienna, Grenoble and Cambridge, and undertook postgraduate studies in European Law and Economics at the College of Europe in Brugge, Belgium. He entered the Department of Economic Integration of the Foreign Ministry in 1966, and has served within the Austrian Permanent Mission to the UN (1968-73), in the Austrian Embassy in Cairo (1973-5), as Director for Press and Information in the Ministry for Foreign Affairs (1975-81), and as Austrian Ambassador in Nairobi and Permanent Representative to the UN organisations in Kenya for Environment (UNEP) and Town Planning (HABITAT) (1981-86). Since 1986 he has been in the Ministry for Foreign Affairs, Vienna, as Director of the Secretariat General (1986-7), as Director for Economic Integration (EFTA-EC) (1987-93), as Deputy to the Director-General for Economic and Integration Policy (1993-6), and in his current post.

ACKNOWLEDGEMENTS

This book arises from an international conference held on 3 June 1998 at Chatham House in London to mark the occasion of the Austrian Presidency of the European Union. The conference was organised by the Austrian Embassy, London, the Royal Institute of International Affairs and the Keele European Research Centre (KERC) at Keele University. It was made possible by the generous financial assistance provided by Austrian Airlines, Bank Austria, the Austrian National Bank, the Federation of Austrian Industry (VÖI), VA Technologie AG, Böhler Uddeholm, and the University Association for Contemporary European Studies (UACES). We thank them all most sincerely.

All of these organisations, the staff of the Austrian Embassy, the conference panel members and the conference delegates, ensured a most enjoyable and stimulating event, which provided an extremely useful preview of the Austrian Presidency. We would therefore like to express our appreciation to the organisers, sponsors, speakers and participants. In particular, we should single out the Director and staff of the Royal Institute for International Affairs (especially Diana Davies and Philippa Challen) for their professional organisation of the conference.

The Austrian Embassy and KERC agreed it would be good to produce a volume based on the conference and to have it available as soon as possible - and in any event whilst the Austrian Presidency was still underway. Anyone who has ever been involved in seeking to meet such a tight schedule will know how difficult (and fraught) such an undertaking can be. We nonetheless took on the challenge and though we found it hard work, we were gratified by the invaluable assistance we received from various quarters. Without it, we would not have been able to keep to our schedule of having the finished product available within just over two months of the conference.

There are a number of people who have helped make this possible. First, we would like to thank the contributors of the individual chapters, who not only provided us with their manuscripts promptly, but also responded to our queries swiftly. This helped to make the editorial process much less stressful than might otherwise have been the case. Second, we are very grateful to Mr. Berhard J. Holzner and Hopi Media of Vienna for granting us the right to reproduce two photographs taken during the conference. Third, we are grateful for the assistance of Professor Michael Waller and Kath McKeown, of Keele European Research Centre, for their assistance and advice. The production of this book was made much simpler by the professional, patient and friendly manner of Barrie Humphries and his staff at Herald Printers. We would also like to thank our families, friends and colleagues for being patient and understanding throughout the editorial process.

Finally, the advice and support provided by the Austrian Embassy in London was inestimable. Without it, this project would have been impossible. We particularly owe a huge debt to the Austrian Ambassador, HE Dr. Eva Nowotny, who has supported and encouraged us from the outset, and to her staff. Mr. Michael Rendi, First Secretary at the Austrian Embassy, in particular, has provided stalwart guidance throughout this project.

Kurt Richard Luther
Iain Ogilvie
Keele
July 1998

FOREWORD

Eva Nowotny

On July 1st, 1998, Austrian assumed the Presidency of the EU for the first time. The Austrian Embassy in London wanted to mark this occasion with a special conference at the Royal Institute for International Affairs. That conference took place on 3 June 1998, at Chatham House in London. I would like to express, first and foremost, my gratitude to the Director of Chatham House, Sir Timothy Garden, and his staff, who with customary and seemingly effortless efficiency and co-operation made this conference possible. My thanks also go to all the sponsors of the event for their generous support, and to Dr. Kurt Richard Luther from the Department of Politics at Keele University, who not only provided valuable assistance with the planning of the conference, but also took on the additional task of editing and preparing the conference papers for publication. This volume is the result of that process and I welcome this valuable contribution to the literature on both the EU Presidency and on contemporary Austria.

Austria takes over the Presidency at a truly significant moment in the development of the European Union, when three issues of far-reaching importance have to be tackled in order to ensure that the Union moves smoothly into a phase of deeper and accelerated integration: firstly, the successful eastward enlargement of the Union; secondly, the pursuit of much-needed internal structural and institutional reform in order to enable the EU to cope with the pending changes in its size and scope; and, thirdly, the pressing need to resolve the 'democratic deficit' - efforts to make the European citizen feel more comfortable with the workings of the Union, with its capacity for problem-solving and with the democratic legitimacy of its decisions.

These are, in my opinion, the great challenges that the EU has to face today and in the near future, and form a crucial element of the responsibility of the Presidency. I am therefore very pleased to note that this volume reflects this emphasis on the three priority areas I have mentioned, as well as providing analysis (in Dr. Luther's introductory chapter) of post-war developments within Austria, as well as of the background to, and history of, Austria's involvement with Europe and European integration.

Professor Thomas Nowotny's contribution analyses the first policy priority - eastern enlargement of the EU. He focuses on its history, some possible effects on existing members, and Austrian attitudes and policy to enlargement. By outlining the history, economic structure and current political stability of the enlargement region, and discussing Austria's relationship with this region, both in the distant past and in the period 1955-1998, this chapter is a valuable contribution to understanding current Austrian perspectives on the enlargement debate. It places these perspectives in context by analysing the trade patterns, public opinion attitudes and domestic political debates that have influenced this policy development.

Dr Hannes Swoboda's contribution complements Professor Nowotny's analysis with an examination of Austria's current relationship with the rest of Europe. His chapter explores the nature of the domestic debates surrounding this relationship and its future after EU enlargement. It also outlines a potential strategy that Austria could employ to meet the challenges that such expansion implies. That strategy involves a realistic programme of integration of neighbouring states into the EU system: by rethinking the accession timetable, by allowing flexible periods of transition and adjustment to enlargement, by introducing aid measures for those regions most affected by enlargement, and by raising the status of the European Conference. Dr Swoboda's contribution to this volume thus seeks to offer a practical framework for the future development of policy.

The second priority - some of the internal reforms which form part of the future agenda of the EU - are discussed in the contributions by Harald Ettl, Peter Mitterbauer and Dr. Gertrude Tumpel-Gugerell. Mr Ettl's examination of the Austrian system of social and economic partnership points out how effective this system has been in enabling Austria to resolve complex economic disputes in its domestic arena and thus to achieve considerable economic success. He also argues that it has been a key factor in the facilitation of domestic political consensus. According to Mr Ettl, membership of the European Union provides Austria with both challenges and opportunities. On the one hand, Austria needs to adapt to a transnational political and economic environment which may have an impact on existing Austrian institutions and practices. On the other hand, however, the European Union may be able to import elements of the successful Austrian model to achieve a similar degree of consensus on socio-economic questions at the European level.

Mr. Mitterbauer offers a different perspective on the future role of social partnership and this contrast reflects the lively and interesting debate which took place at the conference. The argument advanced by Mr Mitterbauer centres on issue of labour market flexibility and on the desirability of transferring the Austrian model to the European level. It outlines the more modest future role which he believes social partnership ought to play both within Austria and at the level of the European Union. Finally, this chapter enumerates some of the main proposals of the Federation of Austrian Industry regarding the priorities that ought to be pursued by the European Union during Austria's Presidency and beyond.

Dr Tumpel-Gugerell's chapter examines the Austrian National Bank's perspective on Economic and Monetary Union (EMU). It first describes the Bank's plans for preparing the Austrian economy and political institutions for the transition to EMU. Thereafter, it raises some interesting issues - and some potential solutions, that EMU may imply, and discusses the importance of the success of EMU for the wider European economy. Together these three contributions highlight the current domestic and European debates about the future development of the EU, the effects of Economic and Monetary Union, and discuss possible strategies of institutional reform.

The third priority of the Austrian Presidency that I mentioned above relates to improving the participation of citizens in the process of European integration. This is a topic that is also examined in three contributions. These are the chapters by Luther and Ogilvie, Pernthaler and Gamper, and by Krawagna-Pfeifer. In the first of these, Luther and Ogilvie provide empirical information to trace the development of Austrian public opinion attitudes to the European Union. The data they use cover attitudes to both membership *per se* and to some central Union policies and activities. This chapter not only provides a survey of current public opinion in Austria, but compares the Austrian situation with that pertaining with on the one hand the other states of the 'fourth wave' (Sweden and Finland), and with the EU15 average values on the other.

The chapter by Professor Peter Pernthaler and Anna Gamper provides a useful outline of the nature of Austrian federalism and then considers the ways in which Austria's federal structures and procedures have responded to and been influenced by Austria's accession to the European Union. By offering some thoughts on the tensions between Austrian federalism and European integration, this contribution provides insight into the future relationship between different levels of governance. Their main conclusion is an argument for stronger direct representation of the Länder and local communities in the organisations and decision-making processes of the European Union, as the only way to create a what they term a 'really democratic and federal' European Union.

Dr Katharina Krawagna-Pfeifer, however, challenges this conclusion. Her essay is a reply to the Pernthaler/Gamper thesis that the constituent units of EU member states (e.g. the Austrian Länder) should play a more direct and integral part in EU decision-making structures and processes. She argues that, in an era of globalisation and given the decline of the 'nation-state', the sub-units of government in EU member states are increasingly unable to perform their traditional functions of governance, and may even become irrelevant, as European integration further develops.

Last but not least, the contribution by Vice-Chancellor Dr. Wolfgang Schüssel elucidates the Austrian government's priorities for the agenda of the Austrian Presidency of the EU, whilst Ambassador Dr. Gregor Woschnagg's chapter highlights some practical considerations regarding the challenging task that will have to be faced in the administration of the Presidency. Both chapters are accompanied by extracts from the interesting question-and-answer sessions held after the authors' respective speeches at Chatham House on 3 June 1998. These extracts help ensure that this volume reflects the interesting debates that occurred at the conference. Indeed, all the chapters in this book add to the ongoing debate about the future direction of the Union and its member states, which I feel is vital.

Given the complexity of the machinery with which each Presidency must work, and the short, if intensive, tenure of each Presidency, it is almost impossible to pursue all of one's priorities in a focused and co-ordinated manner and guarantee their fruition in the longer term. The current Austrian Presidency will have to deal with the three major Union priorities I have outlined above. Firstly, our Presidency will have to continue the pre-accession work with the prospective members of the next enlargement, which was started under the British Presidency. Secondly, we will have to put legislation in place to enable the effective operation of the mechanisms of EMU, and lay the foundations of an effective transition to the single currency. Thirdly, the Austrian Presidency will have the task of starting and pursuing substantive negotiations on 'Agenda 2000' - the reform of the Union's policies and institutions, including reform of the CAP, as well as regional and structural funds and related budgetary matters.

In addition, the Austrian Presidency intends to place special emphasis on the burning issue of employment, with the aim of placing a code of 'best practices' in the fight against European unemployment before the European Council of December 1998. Austria will also host, in October 1998, a special summit of Heads of State and Government, the aim of which will be to discuss the future of the EU, its further democratisation and the related issue of subsidiarity. In this context, the Austrian experience, detailed in various places in this book, of federalism and the constitutional delineation of competencies between different levels of government may prove to be valuable to our EU partners.

Successful leadership requires what Machiavelli called *'virtu'* and *'fortuna'*. Given the challenges and opportunities I have outlined, the Austrian Presidency will require both of these traits - dedication to our demanding agenda and good luck - in order to pursue our priorities effectively, and to maintain the progress of European integration, so that, when we hand the Presidency over to Germany in 1999, we can be assured that our tenure of the Presidency has been both effective and successful.

All of these issues were comprehensively explored and discussed at the Chatham House conference and examined from different perspectives. I hope and expect that this publication will illustrate the scope of our Presidency's agenda and will serve as a useful aid for the interested reader to follow and understand developments during this challenging and potentially rewarding period.

Part 1

AUSTRIA AND EUROPE

1

FROM WEST EUROPEAN PERIPHERY TO THE

CENTRE OF EUROPE?

Kurt Richard Luther

1.1 Introduction

Austria joined the European Union (EU) on 1 January 1995, and just over three years later, on 1 July 1998, took over the EU Presidency from the United Kingdom. Externally, the six month Presidency offers Austria an opportunity to enhance its European credentials and diplomatic visibility. Internally, Austria's governing parties presumably hope that the sight of their leaders presiding over EU business will help assuage popular concerns regarding aspects of European integration and might possibly even enhance their prospects at the general election due in the autumn of 1999. Yet the Presidency will not necessarily be an unmitigated blessing. For one, Austria's speedy transition from the status of one of the newest members of the 'club' to that of chairman thereof means that the country's political and administrative elite face a steep learning curve. (See Chapter 6 of this volume by Gregor Woschnagg.) Second, the intrinsic nature of the Presidency and the packed schedule of inherited EU business arguably leave the Austrians relatively little scope for major new policy initiatives of their own. Third, as Foreign Minister Wolfgang Schüssel notes in his contribution to this volume, EU presidencies are inherently vulnerable to being overtaken by unforeseen events. Finally, it is likely that Austria's main opposition party will still seek to mobilise public anxieties about issues such as the potentially adverse affect of the EU's proposed eastern enlargement upon Austria's labour market against the governing parties. Predicting the course of EU business during Austria's tenure of office and how the Presidency will impact upon Austrian domestic politics is thus a risky undertaking.

Fortunately, that is not the aim of this chapter. Instead, it is to provide an overview of the development of key aspects of Austria's post-war domestic politics and foreign policy position. It is hoped that this will help explain the context not only of Austrians' current attitudes to the problems and prospects of European integration, but also the priorities which the Austrian government has set out for its Presidency.[1] This chapter will first identify some of the main domestic and foreign policy challenges facing the country in the first decade after World War II and the distinctive manner in which the political elites responded to them. Thereafter, it will consider the period from

---

[1] For a more detailed empirical assessment of Austrian attitudes, see chapter 2 of this volume.

1955 until the 1980s, with a view to establishing the extent to which the structures and techniques adopted by the post-war Austrian elites were successful in resolving the challenges the country had faced. Third, the chapter will outline Austria's path since the late 1980s when, in the midst of profound change at home and abroad, Austria pursued its application for EC membership. The central elements of the elite debate regarding membership will be identified and the outcome of the popular referendum which preceded accession will be discussed. The chapter will conclude by highlighting some of the main issues that will be of concern to Austria during the tenure of its Presidency of the EU and beyond.

1.2 Austria's post-war challenge: bridging divisions

1.2.1 Domestic and geo-political divisions

The prospects for the re-establishment of Austrian democracy after World War II were inauspicious. The country had not only been governed under four very different regimes in the preceding five decades,[2] but had just suffered its second profound military defeat since the 1914-1918 war and was again experiencing severe economic and social dislocation. Moreover, it had a legacy of deep and ultimately pathological internal political division between its exceptionally extensive and mutually hostile *Lager* (political subcultures, or camps),[3] who in 1934 had even fought each other in a short civil war. In addition, Austria was now faced with a second division and one that was potentially just as life-threatening; for not only was its territory partitioned between the four occupying Allied powers, but the country itself straddled Europe's major geo-political division: the deepening 'fault-line' generated by the Cold War.

Yet fifty years later, when it joined the EU, the Austrian Second Republic could look back on decades of political stability and economic achievement, with Austrian living standards ranking amongst the highest not only in Europe, but in the world.[4] As we have argued elsewhere,[5] Austria's progress in mastering its internal divisions was not achieved by a fundamental recasting of governmental institutions, for unlike Germany, Austria re-adopted its ill-fated inter-war constitution.[6] Nor were the key political actors replaced; the establishment of the Second Republic was largely undertaken by the same parties - and indeed by some of the same individuals - that had

---

[2] These were the Habsburg Dual Monarchy, which collapsed in 1918; the 'First Republic', of 1918-34, which has been dubbed 'the state nobody wanted' (Andics 1968); the authoritarian clerico-corporatist dictatorship of the self-styled *Ständestaat* (1934-38) and finally, the Nazi regime of 1938-1945. For a detailed account of the First Republic, see Tálos *et al.* (eds.) (1995).

[3] These comprised on the one hand the mainly rural Catholic-conservative Christian Socials and on the other, the overwhelmingly urban and proletarian Social Democrats. There is an enormous literature on the crucial role Austrian parties have played in moulding the post-war political system. See for example Pulzer (1969a and 1969b), Müller (1994) and Luther (1992 and 1998b).

[4] See section 1.2.3 below, the contributions to this volume by Thomas Nowotny (chapter 3) and Gertrude Tumpel-Gugerell (chapter 9) and Lauber (1992).

[5] See for example Luther/Müller 1992b and Luther 1998a.

[6] For an evaluation of the formal powers and actual working of governmental institutions, see Müller (1992) and Dachs *et al.* (1997).

been involved in setting up the First.[7] Moreover, though their political ideologies were somewhat attenuated, the post-war *Lager* were fundamentally the same as in the First Republic, as were their party organisations.[8] As for Europe's geo-political division, that too was largely gone and though the credit for this cannot be attributed to Austria, the transformation of this second division has also had a profound impact upon Austria's domestic politics and international position.

1.2.2 Constructing bridges

The success of Austria's second experiment with liberal democracy and the position it was to adopt in respect of Europe's geo-political divide has much to do with the very different manner in which the country's twofold divisions were approached by the Austrian political elite.[9] The fundamental feature of that approach was the eschewal of the confrontational orientation associated with Austria's inter-war politics in favour of a strategy of bridging divisions by political co-operation and 'accommodation'.[10] This soon manifested itself on the economic front; though defeated Austria was once again in dire economic straits, the Allies chose not to opt for a punitive reparations regime akin to that imposed after World War I, but instead sought to stimulate reconstruction via the Marshall Plan. For its part, the Austrian elite quickly moved to nationalise many large industrial enterprises,[11] thereby providing the Second Republic with one of the largest nationalised industry sectors of any Western country. This not only facilitated state economic planning, but also provided the governing parties with a large source of political influence and potential patronage, secure access to which necessitated institutionalised political co-operation.

The latter took three main forms. First, from 1944 to 1966, the two major parties (Socialist Party of Austria, or *Sozialistische Partei Österreichs* - SPÖ; and the Austrian People's Party, *Österreichische Volkspartei* - ÖVP) co-operated in a series of 'grand coalitions', which controlled the overwhelming majority of votes and parliamentary seats and reached decisions according to the principle of mutual veto. Second, the parties institutionalised *Proporz*, an extra-constitutional, but nonetheless pervasive system of proportional allocation of posts and other state resources between the governing parties, in rough proportion to their relative electoral strength. Third, co-operation led to the genesis of what became known as 'social partnership' (*Sozialpartnershaft*), an almost archetypal system of neo-corporatist intermediation.[12] Together, these structures proved very successful not only in promoting post-war economic reconstruction, but also in achieving a high degree of consensus between the hitherto very antagonistic forces of labour and capital. In due

---

[7] See Weinzierl (1998) and Knight (1998).

[8] See for example Wandruszka (1954), Simon (1957) and Luther (1992).

[9] The role (initially) adopted by the Allies was of course also important, as will be acknowledged below, but it is not our prime focus in this chapter. For a discussion of the impact of the superpowers, see for example Rathkolb (1998).

[10] Within the comparative political science literature, post-war Austria is often cited as an archetypal example of a 'consociational democracy', that is to say, a political system characterised by the *prima facie* paradoxical co-existence of on the one hand subcultural fragmentation and on the other elite 'overarching' elite co-operation and system stability. See for example Luther/Müller 1992a and Luther/Deschouwer 1998, as well as the academic literature on consociationalism cited therein.

[11] Many had been in the hands of the German Reich and their nationalisation was thus undertaken not so much for ideological reasons, but in order to avoid them falling into the hands of the occupying powers (especially the Soviets). See Müller (1985).

[12] See the contributions to this volume by Harald Ettl (chapter 7) and by Peter Mitterbauer (chapter 8), as well as Gerlich/Grande/Müller (1985), Gerlich (1992) and Bischof and Pelinka (1996).

course, this in turn enabled the Second Republic to enjoy much higher levels of popular legitimacy than its inter-war predecessor.

There were strong political factors promoting accommodation. The post-war elites' commitment to an exclusively democratic mode of problem resolution had been greatly enhanced by the persecution which a number of them had experienced at the hands of the Nazi regime. Nazism and military defeat had also narrowed the party system's ideological spectrum. On the left, the Communist Party of Austria (*Kommunistische Partei Österreichs* - KPÖ) was delegitimised by Soviet occupation of eastern Austria until 1955, and subsequently by communist repression in adjacent Hungary and Czechoslovakia. Furthermore, whilst the Allies' anti-fascist consensus militated against a revival of the anti-democratic extreme right, the experience of incorporation into Nazi Germany had for the overwhelming majority of Austrians discredited pan-Germanism and thus - at least by default - helped prepare the ground for the gradual development of a stabilising common Austrian national identity which the First Republic had demonstrably lacked.[13]

In addition to these internal economic and political factors, co-operative elite behaviour was also promoted by the existence of a significant external threat. Until 1955, Austria was subject to Allied occupation, a situation increasingly resented by its population. There was a universal desire to get rid of the foreign forces, whose presence became potentially ever more ominous, as the Cold War division of Europe ossified. It was widely accepted that to achieve withdrawal of Allied troops and independent statehood, it was necessary for Austria's rival political elites to show a united front externally. This took the form of the grand coalition government's bipartisan approach to foreign policy, the greatest success of which was undoubtedly the State Treaty of May 1955. It secured the withdrawal of Allied troops, re-established Austrian statehood and was in October 1955 followed by the Act of Neutrality.

The State Treaty restricted Austrian sovereignty in a number of military matters (Articles 12-19), whilst Article 4 forbade 'political and economic union' with Germany, making membership of the nascent European Economic Community (EEC) impossible. Though the Act of Neutrality committed Austria to permanent neutrality, it was never understood to require neutralism - i.e. equidistance between the partners to the Cold War. Austria thus became a member of the United Nations in December 1955 and in 1956 joined the Council of Europe. It also took a leading role in creating the European Free Trade Area (EFTA). Austria's Western orientation was also evident from its response to the Hungarian crisis of 1956 and the Prague Spring of 1968. In sum, Austria was unable to enter the North Atlantic Treaty Organisation (NATO), or to sign up to the Treaty of Rome and thereby actively participate in shaping West European integration, but both economically and politically, it was still clearly Western. Yet given its historic ties to many of the Soviet satellite countries of Eastern Europe, it was also able to provide a useful bridge across Europe's East-West divide.

Austria's traumatic and internally fragmented development during the first half of the 20th century meant its people lacked recent events which could serve to promote an overarching national identity, by uniting them in a sense of common achievement. The State Treaty, however, was greeted with near universal popular euphoria and it is thus hardly surprising that the foreign policy watershed of 1955 came to form a cornerstone of that fledgling identity. Though the Act of

---

[13] See Bruckmüller (1998) for details on the post-war development of Austrian national identity.

Neutrality in truth constituted a concession to the Soviets, with whom Austria had been conducting intense and prolonged negotiations, Article 1 proclaimed permanent neutrality to have been decided by Austria 'of her own free will'. The Act was presented to the public as a source of Austrian distinctiveness and pride, and rationalised as providing Austria with a unique role in helping bridge international divisions. This mythologised view of Austria's international mission is but one element of a series of 'constituent myths' of the Second Republic, which promoted an Austrian self-perception perhaps best encapsulated in the notion that Austria constituted an 'island of the blessed'.[14]

Though that designation may be regarded as somewhat self-righteous, it encapsulates a significant objective characteristic of post-war Austria. Compared to the First Republic, the Second was demonstrably more successful in bridging the profound historic antagonisms between Austria's subcultures. Moreover, after 1955, its was relatively quickly able to assume a positive and respected international position. Accordingly, the successful and mutually reinforcing bridging of both external and internal divisions came to be closely intermeshed with Austrians' sense of their collective identity, as did neutrality and institutions of domestic political accommodation such as social partnership. The growth of Austrian national identity is shown in Table 1.1, though it is worth adding that these aggregate figures disguise considerable differences, such as those between the supporters of the main party groups. In 1964, for example, 56 per cent of SPÖ supporters and 53 per cent of ÖVP supporters felt Austria was a nation, whilst only 22 per cent of the supporters of the traditionally German-national Freedom Party of Austria (*Freiheitliche Partei Österreichs* - FPÖ) held that view. By 1987, however, the differences had become much less pronounced and the figures were 82, 75 and 77 per cent respectively.[15] The implications for Austria's subsequent debates regarding EC (and especially NATO) membership of the central role which neutrality came to play in Austrian national identity will be returned to below (see section 1.3).

Table 1.1   The development of Austrian national identity 1964-1993 (%)

	1964	1970	1977	1980	1987	1989	1990	1992	1993
Austrians are a nation	47	66	62	67	75	79	74	78	80
... are slowly beginning to feel like a nation	23	16	16	19	16	15	20	15	12
... are not a nation	15	8	11	11	5	4	5	5	6
no response	14	10	12	3	3	3	1	2	2

Source: Bruckmüller (1998, p.93)

1.2.3 The transformation of divisions

By the 1970s, Austria was flourishing. The economy had made great progress: economic growth during the 1970s averaged 4 and unemployment only 1.9 per cent. A major factor contributing to

---

[14] For critical accounts of some of the Second Republic's constituent myths, see Bischof and Pelinka (1997), or the discussion by Menasse (1992) of what he terms Austria's 'either and or' mentality.

[15] Bruckmüller (1998: 90 and 93)

this success was the bipartisan economic policy pursued by Austria's consensus-oriented political elites. Often described as 'Austrokeynesian', it was a very successful mix that comprised *inter alia* a hard currency policy, the promotion of investment and savings, the depoliticisation of incomes and the stabilisation of demand by deficit spending.[16] A more recent factor was the 1972 agreement with the EEC to lower customs barriers, which had greatly strengthened Austria's trading relations with EEC member states. Despite the setbacks due to the 1970s oil price shocks, Austria's economy continued to fare much better than those of most other West European countries: inflation averaged only 6.1 and never exceeded 9.5 per cent per annum.

There was also progress in terms of overcoming the divisions between Austria's rival subcultures, the lives of the members of which had hitherto largely been encapsulated within their respective *Lager* organisations. The considerable psychological barriers that had existed between them had weakened. In part, this was due to growing prosperity and economic security, but it was also a consequence of the sight of decades of accommodation between the political representatives of the *Lager*. For it was hardly credible for those elites - who had co-operated in government for so long - to still maintain that their coalition partners constituted a threat to democracy, which could only be guaranteed by the constraining influence of grand coalition government. Indeed, such assertions were disproven at the latest after 1966, when Austria moved to single-party rule.

As the degree of mutual hostility between the subcultures declined, the electoral slogans used by the rival parties became less apocalyptic, and the political 'temperature' of Austrian politics dropped. The major parties' electoral appeals were also no longer directed exclusively at mobilising 'their' clientele, but were instead gradually seeking to win over the growing (albeit initially still very small) pool of floating voters, as well as to 'poach' the voters of the rival subculture. One of the earliest signs of declining political rigidity at the mass level was an increase in floating voters. Indeed, at the core of the political success of Kreisky's SPÖ, was its capacity to forge an electoral coalition between those floating voters and stalwart socialist partisans. The result was over a decade of SPÖ rule, during which a fair degree of modernisation of Austrian society took place.[17]

Whilst *Proporz* and social partnership were still very much in evidence, the developments outlined above had some years earlier brought an end to the third and most visible feature of Austrian elite accommodation: grand coalition government. Single-party ÖVP government (1966-70) gave way to a series of SPÖ governments (1970-83). This was considered by some as indicative of the success of accommodation, in that the latter had made oversized coalitions superfluous. On the other hand, it would be wrong to assert that the altered structure of government had resulted in a profound change in the substance and manner of decision-making in Austrian politics. Since social partnership was if anything even more influential (especially in respect of wages and prices), the end of grand coalition government can to some extent be regarded as having transferred consensual decision-making from the political to the corporatist arena, where despite not being a part of the national government, the opposition ÖVP remained very influential, along with its associated interest groups.

---

[16] For a clear exposition of the theory and practice of Austrokeynesianism, see Lauber (1992). On the strategic position of the economies of small states such as Austria, see for example Katzenstein (1979 and 1985).

[17] For an evaluation of the 'Kreisky Era', see Bischof and Pelinka (1994)

The Austria of the 1970s was also characterised by a fair degree of self-confidence in the international arena. The public's perception of Austria's unique and important foreign policy mission was enhanced by Kreisky, whose policy of 'visit diplomacy' (*Besuchsdiplomatie*) to the Eastern European states was just one way in which he helped promote détente between Eastern and Western Europe. More significantly, however, Kreisky extended Austria's self-ascribed role of mediator in international divisions from a European to an increasingly global perspective. Austria's 'active foreign policy' embraced issues such as the Arab-Israeli conflict. It caused Austria to be at the forefront of the attempts on the part of the neutral and non-aligned (N+N) countries to provide the superpowers with good offices, and resulted in Austria assuming an important role in the CSCE (Conference for Security and Co-operation in Europe) process. Moreover, Austria sought played what for a small country was quite a significant role in the United Nations. This included hosting a number of UN activities, as well as the fact that Austria's subsequently controversial Federal President, Kurt Waldheim, served two terms (1971-81) as the UN's General Secretary.[18]

Yet at the latest by the early 1980s, the domestic and international arenas became less rosy for Austria. On the domestic economy front, growth slowed (1981: 0.3 per cent), unemployment increased (1983: 4.5 per cent) and habitual budget deficits came home to roost, particularly in the form of a rapidly expanding public debt. It also became increasingly clear that a significant proportion of Austria's numerous public sector industries had become uncompetitive. In part, this economic slow-down was due to factors beyond Austria's control, but the exceptionally high level of state (and thus party-political) control of the economy did not help, nor did the related practice of *Proporz*. On the contrary, though the latter had undeniably initially helped legitimise the vulnerable post-war state, it now became associated in the mind of the public with overstaffing, inefficiency and a seemingly endless series of corruption scandals. Moreover, the consequence of years of social partnership and 'Austrokeynesianism' included a very generous set of welfare state benefits, which critics increasingly considered to be financially unsustainable in the long-term. Growing concern regarding the economy's structural problems and the unpopularity of the SPÖ's proposals for addressing the budget deficit by raising taxes (the '*Mallorca-Paket*') contributed to the SPÖ's loss of its electoral majority at the 1983 election, which marked the end of the 'Kreisky Era'.

From 1983 to 1986/87, Austria was ruled by a 'small' coalition government between the SPÖ and the FPÖ. It was headed until 1986 by Fred Sinowatz and from June 1986 by Franz Vranitzky.[19] However, it was not until the re-establishment in 1987 of the 'old' SPÖ-ÖVP grand coalition, in which the SPÖ could share with the ÖVP the political odium of introducing unpopular measures, that major progress was made on the economic front. The SPÖ moved towards the economic agenda which the ÖVP had developed whilst in opposition, accepting (and indeed promoting) privatisation and deregulation. Some uncompetitive industries were restructured, but others were sold off, or closed down. In short, the Austrokeynesian consensus that had united the parties until the late 1970s, with its commitment to full employment at almost any price, was gradually replaced by a new economic policy consensus: one which was decidedly more market-oriented and predicated upon the perception that Austria cannot buck the international market.

---

[18] For a recent English language analysis of the development of Austrian foreign policy during this period, see Kramer (1998).

[19] For a critical evaluation of Austria's first 'small coalition', see Pelinka (1993)

Changes in the global economy have of course enhanced the vulnerability of all national economies, not just those of small states such as Austria. They were, for example, a significant factor behind the 1985 Cockfield Report, which presaged the EC's 1986 adoption of the Single European Act (SEA) and measures designed to culminate in the establishment by 1992 of a single European market. In turn, that decision placed Austrian policy-makers in a dilemma. Given the significance for the Austrian economy of the European market, Austria was *de facto* obliged to shadow the single market policies of the Community. Yet as a mere associate, it was unable to have a say in the formulation of those policies. From the mid-1980s, Austria therefore witnessed a growing debate - albeit for some time largely confined to the political class - as to what its future relationship to the EC should be. Initially, EC membership was supported solely by the FPÖ and ÖVP, with the SPÖ split. But the arguments in favour of breaking ranks with EFTA and becoming a member of the Community grew stronger. They maintained that Austria's economic future would be more secure if it were to join and be enabled to influence the direction of EC policy, however modestly. The end of the Kreisky Era in 1983 militated in favour of Austria's move back from a global to a more regional policy agenda. That move was certainly supported by, for example, the SPÖ's Peter Jankovitsch, the last foreign minister of the 1983-87 SPÖ/FPÖ coalition. With the appointment in January 1987 of ÖVP leader Alois Mock as foreign minister of the new SPÖ/ÖVP grand coalition, Austrian foreign policy was headed by someone with a strong personal and political commitment to the prioritisation of the regional dimension of Austria's external relations. At the risk of oversimplification, Austria had 'rediscovered' Europe.

1.3 Europe rediscovered ?

1.3.1 The Austrian elites' pre-accession debate

From the outset, it was the ÖVP (and the ÖVP-dominated Länder of Western Austria) that constituted the driving force for Austrian accession to the EC. As early as December 1985, whilst the ÖVP was still in opposition, it had issued a statement in support of accession. Upon entering Vranitzky's coalition government, Vice-Chancellor Alois Mock worked to promote that policy. The ÖVP's stance was not predicated upon grass-roots pressure, but was leadership-led and strongly supported by the party's business interests, especially by the Federation of Austrian Industry (*Vereinigung Österreichische Industrie* - VÖI), which in May 1987 issued a very strong statement in support of Austria's accession.[20] Initially, the ÖVP's arguments were couched mainly in terms of the likely economic advantages for Austria. Thus it was argued that access to EC markets by export-oriented firms such as those represented in the VÖI was essential for Austria's future economic prosperity. The development of the EC's single market was presented by the ÖVP as being essentially about deregulation, a prospect that was welcomed especially by Austrian big business, which hoped that it would help reduce the power within Austrian economic policy-

---

[20] For the VÖI's current position, see the contribution to this volume by its President, Peter Mitterbauer, in chapter 8. During 1987, the Conference of Länder Governors (*Landeshauptmännerkonferenz*) also issued a call for the federal government to pursue accession. For a discussion of the position of the Länder in respect of Austria's EU membership, see the contribution to this volume by Peter Pernthaler and Anna Gamper (chapter 3), as well as Weber (1996).

making of organised labour. Yet as the debate proceeded, sceptical voices within the ÖVP and its allied groups began to make themselves heard. They pointed to the possible disadvantages of membership, including the likely adverse impact upon the more sheltered branches of Austria's economy, such as public monopolies (e.g. salt, tobacco and alcohol); the retail sector; construction; transport and the professions. Second, farmers were very concerned about the impact of EC membership upon the levels of their subsidies and their capacity to compete with large-scale producers elsewhere in the EC. Third, a number of business groups expressed concern about whether Austrian industries could compete with the often much larger enterprises in the post-1992 Europe. Notwithstanding these internal disputes, in January 1988 the ÖVP passed a formal motion calling for Austrian accession, on condition that neutrality be retained.

Whilst the initially largely unequivocal support of the Catholic-conservative *Lager* for full EC membership came to be qualified by the internal concerns spelled out above, the opposite tendency was apparent within the socialist *Lager*. At the outset, there was some support for EC membership within the SPÖ leadership and from other socialist organisations, such as parts of the Austrian Trade Union Federation (*Österreichischer Gewerkschaftsbund* - ÖGB). Yet many other parts of the socialist camp were extremely sceptical. At best, there was a willingness to accept participation in the single market, but not at the cost of accession. The types of concerns held by these persons and groups related to matters such as neutrality, as well as to welfare and environmental standards. In the more left-wing circles, there was fundamental opposition to what was regarded as the capitalist club of the EC. The strength of opposition within the socialist camp caused the party leadership to adopt a softly-softly approach. Some considerable time therefore elapsed before pro-EC membership orientations grew amongst both the wider leadership and functionary groups, as well as among the general membership. It was not until April 1989 that the party executive passed a motion supporting membership and even then, that motion sought to accommodate lingering scepticism within the party by insisting not only upon the retention of neutrality, but also of Austria's social and environmental standards.

The advantages that the pro-EC members of the SPÖ hoped would accrue from membership were numerous. First, it was asserted that increased price competition would bring about price reductions. This would, it is argued, lead not only to a *de facto* increase in workers' residual income and thus in their purchasing power, but also to greater economic activity. Second, it was alleged that membership would secure future economic growth, which was essential for ensuring the maintenance of Austria's social policy benefits. Third, the party leadership held out the prospect of a decline in the wage gap between Austria and Germany, as the booming southern German economy became more accessible for Austrian labour. Fourth, membership would, it was maintained, ensure Austria's continued access to the wider European market, which might otherwise become more difficult. Fifth, it was suggested that EC membership would lead to modernisation of the country. In other words, Brussels would help ensure the achievement in Austria of the kinds of policy reforms that the entrenchment of domestic vested interests had hitherto prevented. Examples included agriculture, industry and small business.

The Greens were the party most consistently opposed to EC membership. The central thrust of their opposition was concerned with what they perceived to be the likely adverse impact upon Austria's environment. First, they argued that such advances as had been achieved in tightening up Austria's environmental protection legislation would be undermined by the application of lower EC standards. This would be an unavoidable consequence of the EC's single market regulations, which (even if there were some temporary derogation) would in the long term not permit Austria to retain and further develop its higher standards. In addition, there would be the force of market competition: the pursuit of growth at any cost, rather than selective, sustainable growth. The Greens' second major concern related to what they saw as the likely traffic implications for the Austrian environment of the enormous increase they expected EC-membership to bring in transit traffic, especially by heavy-goods vehicles. As a result in large measure of environmental campaigning in the 1980s, Austria had decided to impose restrictions on the flow of in particular lorry traffic, which appeared to have had some considerable success in reducing noise and emission pollution. However, the Greens maintained that the EC would be highly unlikely to countenance the retention of such restrictions if and when Austria acceded to the Community. The short-term consequence would be a loss of those hard-fought advances, whilst in the longer term, the traffic situation would become even worse than it had been before. In addition to these ecological issues, the Greens also articulated opposition based on concerns about the EC's alleged excessive centralism and its 'democratic deficit', issues which grew in importance as the contours of the Maastricht Treaty started to become clearer.

Historically, Austria's national-liberal Third *Lager* (represented since 1956 by the FPÖ) had been the most steadfast advocate of Austria joining in the European integration process. Critics had often argued that this was driven merely by a pan-Germanic desire for closer links with Germany, but in reality, the FPÖ's support for closer European integration embraced a wider range of motives. For one, the FPÖ felt membership would remove the restrictions on Austria spelled out in the State Treaty and thus enhance Austrian sovereignty. A second and related consideration was their support for Austria's greater integration into the West. Third, the FPÖ argued that EC membership would enable the Austrian economy to benefit from the opportunities offered by the single market. Finally, it must be pointed out that the FPÖ's support for EC membership had from the outset also been closely related to its prime domestic political agenda: to achieve change in many of the key institutional features of Austria post-war consensual politics. The FPÖ objected not only to grand coalition government, which they regarded as a marginalsiation of oppositiion rights, but also to *Proporz* and social partnership, which it alleged had resulted in excessive party-political influence in the socio-economic realm. The FPÖ hoped that EC membership would reduce corporatist influence and strengthen economic liberalism. Though as an opposition party it was predictably critical of the government's handling of the issue, on the 29 June 1989 it joined the parliamentary ÖVP and SPÖ in voting for Austria's membership application

During the early 1990s, however, the FPÖ's policy changed and since about 1993 has been virtually reversed, largely as a result of the efforts of the party's electorally extremely successful populist leader, Jörg Haider. A few remaining independent spirits within the FPÖ continued to argue publicly for accession, but the overwhelming majority of the party dutifully towed the new Haider line that although the party remained committed to European integration, membership on the terms negotiated by the government was unacceptable. In effect, the party had moved to outright opposition. Though the party did have some genuine substantive concerns,[21] the predominant view amongst observers is that the transformation of the party's EC policy was

---

[21] For a good overview of the FPÖ's substantive arguments, see thre party's weekly newspaper, the *Neue Freie Zeitung*, Nr. 23, 8 June 1994, pp.13-18, which contains extracts from contributions by FPÖ members including Haider to the parliamentary debate of 4 May 1994.

predicated upon its perception that it could gain domestic greater political advantage from opposing the coalition government's plans, rather than by supporting them. It therefore mobilised the existing anxieties and economic insecurities of the population by reference to issues such as the increased presence and role of foreigners. Thus the party held up the spectre of mass foreign immigration and rising unemployment, the '*Ausverkauf der Heimat*', i.e. of post-accession Austria being unable to restrict the sale of Austrian land to foreigners, and of threats to Austria's high food hygiene standards. In a nutshell, the FPÖ's vehement opposition to the governing parties, foreign policy was primarily a function of the party's opposition to the structures and techniques used by Austria's post-war elite to build accommodating bridges over the country's domestic political divisions.

The governing parties' decision to apply for EC membership was certainly motivated by economic considerations, but it was also a thoroughly political decision. On the one hand, they hoped EC membership would help the country out of the apparent immobilism in domestic economic policy that had grown up parallel to the in itself very successful corporatist system. On the other hand, accession was regarded as a logical expression of the *de facto* economic integration of Austria with, and its political commitment to, the West. In the early stages of discussions regarding a possible membership application, the most significant concern related to the issue of neutrality. For one, the Austrian public had come to internalise the myths surrounding the genesis of neutrality and saw it as an intrinsic and very valuable part of Austria's distinctive identity (see above). It would therefore be necessary for Austrian voters to be reassured that EC-membership was compatible with retaining neutrality. Second, the State Treaty limitations upon military and economic union with Germany were still in force and since the East-West division of Europe still appeared to be a more-or-less permanent fixture, and notwithstanding the changes that were occurring in the Soviet Union since Gorbachov's assumption of power in 1985, it was not clear for some time how the Soviets - who were, after all, formally still a guarantor power of the State Treaty - would respond to the proposal that Austria accede to the EC. In the event, a few months after the formal submission of Austria's membership application, but well before detailed membership negotiations could get underway, there was a momentous and completely unexpected change in Austria's external environment: the fall of the Wall and the *de facto* end of the Cold War.[22] The transformation of the geo-political division that had governed Austria's external environment had at least two important implications for Austria's accession debate. First, it reduced the overall salience of the neutrality issue. Second, it in effect removed any possibility that the Soviet Union would be able to postpone (lat alone veto) accession.

Yet these changes had even greater implications for Austria. The meaning of 'Europe' was about to undergo a radical change, providing Austria with the opportunity to abandon the position of West European peripherality it had perforce occupied since 1945, in favour of one of much greater centrality in the emerging 'new Europe'. In other words, it was not just Austria that rediscovered Europe, but - as a consequence of the events of 1989 and thereafter - Europe that had rediscovered itself. This fundamentally altered the context of the membership negotiations. Initially, it strengthened the position of the proponents of membership, not least because they argued that Austria had to ensure that it was not excluded from West European developments and

---

[22] The possibility that the Soviet Union might seek to be obstructive had of course declined considerably in late 1988, with the Soviet foreign minister's enunciation of the 'Sinatra doctrine': that the East European states could 'do it their way'.

left in limbo with the more anarchic situation of the Former Soviet Union and its previous satellite states. In the longer term, however, the same basic fears were to have a negative impact on the Austrian public's attitudes to the EU (and to their governing parties), since the EU's subsequent policy of eastern enlargement appeared to threaten to re-open the potential for significant labour migration from the east.[23]

Austria's membership negotiations proper started in February 1993 and ran alongside those of other applicant EFTA states, which had decided to follow Austria's lead (Sweden, Finland and then Norway). By the end of 1993, agreement was reached between Austria and the EU on most of the important questions and a compromise formula devised regarding the issue of neutrality. The intense final membership negotiations took place during the first two months of 1994 and reached their culmination after a marathon 70 hour session that was the subject of saturation coverage by the Austrian media. It resulted in an agreement concerning the regulation of issues of special sensitivity for Austria such as agriculture, the question of transit traffic, environmental standards and the purchase by non-Austrian EC citizens of second homes in Austria. News that the outstanding issues had finally been agreed came late in the evening of 1 March 1994 and engendered a euphoric response. Upon its return to Austria, the negotiating team was greeted on the tarmac of Vienna airport by Chancellor Franz Vranitzky, congratulated by President Thomas Klestil and feted by the overwhelming majority of the media as the 'heroes of Brussels'. In May 1994, the agreement was approved by the European Parliament and the Austrian National Council. Since membership of the EU implied a change to fundamental principles of the Austrian constitution, the law on accession had to be submitted to the Austrian public for its approval, or rejection.

1.3.2 The Austrian people decide: the referendum of 12 June 1994[24]

Though we now obviously know that Austria voted yes in the EU membership referendum, it is worth recalling that this outcome was by no means a foregone conclusion. The prospects of a 'yes' vote were not helped by protracted debates within existing EU states over the Maastricht Treaty. In addition, Austrians felt exceptionally exposed to the dramatic events taking place in eastern Europe since 1989 and whilst this in part increased support for EU membership, the failure of European efforts at mediation in the bloody conflict taking place across Austria's southern border in former Yugoslavia provided ammunition for those who argued that Austria needed a different strategy, possibly based on its historic role as a bridge between Western and Eastern Europe.

Accordingly, for quite some time, those expressing support for the idea of EU membership were a minority of those polled, as can be seen in Figure 1.1. That figure also allows one to establish the extent to which changes in the public's attitude to accession coincided with key external events, or with key stages of the accession process. These include late 1988 and early 1989, when the public discussion of the possible implications for neutrality was launched. A second followed the collapse of East European states in late 1989. In addition, there is a clear positive response to the end of then negotiations process in March 1994. Overall, it is clear that

---

[23] See the discussion elsewhere in this volume about Austrian attitudes (chapter 2) and the contributions of Thomas Nowotny (chapter 4) and Johannes Sowboda (chapter 11).

[24] For a detailed analysis of the referendum campaign and outcome, see Pelinka (1995)

there was a gradual decline in the number of undecided and a concomitant increase in not only the supporters of membership, but also - at least until late 1993 - in the proportion of opponents. Indeed, an opinion poll held in September 1993, indicated that the outcome of a referendum was still too close to call.[25]

Figure 1.1   Austrian attitudes to EC/EU membership 1987-1994

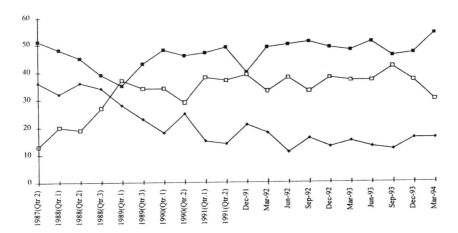

Notes: Source of data for 1987 - Qtr.2 1991: Fessel & GfK representative surveys of 1,000-1,500 persons; subsequent data: ISMA, as reprinted in *Profil*, 28.3.1994, p.22. Given the different sources, the figures have perhaps to be treated with more caution than normal and are reproduced here for indicative purposes. Legend: ■ For; □ Against; ◆ Undecided.

If one examines the profile of membership supporters in, for example, the summer of 1991, one finds that it came predominantly from civil servants and white-collar workers (62 to 36 per cent); from the self-employed and professionals (57 to 39 per cent); from persons with a 'materialist' disposition (63 to 33 per cent); from trade union members (66 to 33 per cent); from the politically interested (62 to 35 per cent) and from those who felt economically secure, or optimistic (64 to 36 per cent). By contrast, the opponents of membership included disproportionately high numbers of Green supporters; farmers (65 to 31 per cent against); pensioners (50 to 43 per cent); 'post-materialists' (52 to 44 per cent); non trade union members (45 to 49 per cent); politically less interested Austrians (50 to 44 per cent) and the economically insecure, or fearful (58 to 38 per cent). FPÖ supporters were marginally more in favour than SPÖ voters (65 to 63 per cent) and only 53 per cent of ÖVP supported membership, whilst Green partisans were 31 per cent for and 66 per cent against accession. Indeed, if one looks at party-political changes during the 1987-91 period, one finds that the opponents to EU membership amongst SPÖ, ÖVP, and Green voters increased

---

[25] For a more detailed analysis than is possible here. see Plasser and Ulram (1995)

from 11 to 32, 12 to 38, and from 26 to a massive 65 per cent respectively. Interestingly, the rise amongst FPÖ partisans was as yet much more modest (18 to 25 per cent), presumably since the party not yet undertaken its policy switch.

Once the referendum campaign started in earnest after March 1994, the governing parties (SPÖ and ÖVP) predictably both campaigned for a yes vote, as did the key social partnership institutions associated with them such as the VÖI and the ÖGB. However, it is worth noting that there were divisions within the ÖVP. The successful negotiations were closely associated in the public mind with former ÖVP leader Alois Mock, who was now touring the country arguing passionately for a 'yes' vote, but certain groups within the ÖVP were decidedly lukewarm, or even openly hostile, to accession. These included farmers, as well as provincial party groups such as that of Tyrol, where in large measure because of the local political salience of the transit traffic issue, Governor (*Landeshauptmann*) Weingartner openly advocated a 'no' vote. Alone amongst the opposition parties, the Liberal Forum (*Liberales Forum* - LiF), a five person parliamentary party that had broken away from the FPÖ in February 1993, in large measure because of the latter's increasingly xenophobic line, campaigned in favour of membership.

Among the factors that probably helped determine the outcome of the referendum were the determined government information campaign that preceded it, as well as the fact that the overwhelming majority of the Austrian print and electronic media were favourably disposed to a yes vote. By contrast, those opposing EU membership not only lacked media access, but were also internally divided. Apart from a number of disparate minor groupings, the no campaign comprised in the main an unlikely combination of the left-wing Greens (some 87 per cent of whose party conference delegates had in May 1994 voted against membership) and the right-wing FPÖ. At the latter's extraordinary party conference of April 1994, 86 per cent of delegates had supported Haider's tactical line on membership: continued commitment in principle to European integration, but rejection of the deal on offer. Both the Greens and FPÖ largely used the arguments they had already articulated (see above). The main difference was that the FPÖ now conducted an extremely emotional campaign, extending its arguments to include issues such as the alleged threats posed by the Schengen Agreement (a weakening of immigration controls and thus a facilitation of organised crime); monetary union (a 'softening' of the hard Austrian Schilling) and lower EU environmental standards (a weakening of Austria's food hygiene regulations).

> Using slogans such as 'Austria first', the FPÖ deliberately played the card of Austrian nationalism. At times, its campaign degenerated into farce, such as when Haider argued that EU-membership was a Masonic conspiracy that would result in the poor being sold contaminated food, in lice extracts being inserted into yoghurts and in Austria being overrun by Islamic culture.[26]

After the referendum result was known, most observers argued that the excesses of the FPÖ campaign had ultimately proved counter-productive. At the time, however, there was considerable concern, especially within government circles, that the FPÖ's campaign might yet suffice to tip the scales against a 'yes' vote.

---

[26] Extract from Luther (1995: 128).

As we know, that did not happen. There was a high turnout (82.4 per cent), exactly two thirds of whom cast their ballots in favour of Austria joining the EU. Surprised pollsters advanced a number of theories to explain why they had not predicted the high 'yes' vote.[27] These included the high proportion of waverers (46 per cent), the large number of persons who only decided which way to vote in the last few days (29 per cent) and the fact that nearly half of those who had intended to vote 'no', but eventually voted 'yes' switched in the last week.[28] Ogris concludes, on the basis of an IFES panel survey conducted from March 1993 to May 1994, that only the votes of farmers and those working in industries likely to be directly affected by EU-membership were shaped by personal economic interest.[29] Those of the majority were governed more by abstract considerations related to economic stability, the labour market, the environment and peace. He contends that, as the arguments of the pro-membership group came to dominate public discourse, a band-wagon effect took hold.

If one examines the characeristics of those who voted for and against accession, one finds that votes were cast very much in accordance with the concerns articulated during the debate (see above). Thus there was relatively little regional variation, save in Burgenland (74.6 per cent) and in Tyrol (56.4 per cent), where concerns about the effects of increased heavy goods vehicle traffic through was greatest. There were also few dramatic differences in the voting patterns of different social groups. Thus support for EU membership was higher (70 per cent) amongst the over-60s and lower amongst the under 30s (55 per cent), whilst men were somewhat more likely to vote in favour than women (70 per cent versus 62 per cent). Greater variations were established in respect of respondents' attitudes. Support for membership was especially high amongst economic optimists and those who expressed trust in MPs and the government. Of these groups, 77 and 83 per cent respectively voted 'yes'. The greatest differences predictably related to party-political orientation. The highest proportion of 'yes' voters (75 per cent) was to be found amongst LiF supporters, closely followed by SPÖ supporters at 73 per cent. Of those expressing a preference for the FPÖ, or the Greens, only 41 and 38 per cent respectively voted for EU membership.[30]

1.3.3 Austria post-accession: redundant bridges?

The governing parties were understandably elated by the size of the vote for EU membership (as were the governments of the applicant countries yet to hold their referendums). The SPÖ and ÖVP were also very hopeful that they would, at the general election of 9 October 1994, reap the benefit of the public's overwhelming endorsement of the terms they had negotiated with Brussels. In particular, it was expected the ÖVP would be able to capitalise on the high profile role Mock had played.[31] Yet that is not what happened. Instead, the election resulted in a further increase in the share of the vote achieved by the Greens (plus 2.5 points to 7.3 per cent) and especially by the FPÖ (plus 6.1 points to 22.5 per cent). Conversely, the SPÖ and ÖVP were reduced to their lowest ever

---

[27] For a detailed evaluation of the referendum, see Pelinka (1995)

[28] Plasser and Ulram (1995)

[29] Ogris (1995: 22)

[30] This paragraph is taken from Luther (1995: 129) which reports figures taken from Plasser and Ulram (1995, Tables 7-10).

[31] The SPÖ was of course aware of this and Chancellor Vranitzky thus firmly rejected the suggestion that signing the accession treaty and representing Austria at European Union summits was the constitutional prerogative of President Klestil (an ÖVP nominee).

joint share of the vote. Indeed, they failed to achieve the two thirds share of parliamentary seats that was necessary to ratify the various acts required to allow Austria to proceed with the accession process, though in the event, they were able to rely upon receiving the necessary support from the LiF. Moreover, as discussed in greater detail in the next chapter of this volume, the positive attitude of the Austrian public towards the EU has since dwindled.

There are a number of possible explanations of why the public's support has declined. For one, Austria's determination to meet the Maastricht criteria for monetary union required it to engage in a series of budgetary consolidation measures that proved unpopular. Second, during the course of the referendum campaign, the governing parties made in part very optimistic forecasts concerning the economic benefits which membership would bring. Many of these benefits, including job security, lower consumer prices, no tax increases and possibly even tax reductions, have failed to materialise. Third, whilst trade relations with and direct investment of Austrian businesses in eastern Europe, especially in Hungary, the Czech and Slovak Republics and Slovenia increased considerably in the early 1990s (see chapter 4 of this volume), there has in the last couple of years been growing concern about the possible consequences of eastern enlargement. Finally, it is worth recalling that the results of the opinion polls on EU membership also reflect unresolved issues of domestic policy. For as has been argued throughout this chapter, an understanding of Austrians' attitudes to their country's external relations is inextricably linked with Austria's domestic politics.

Both Austria's internal and external politics were initially based on the imperative of building bridges over deep divisions. Domestically, that process was successful not only in ensuring economic prosperity, but also in healing deep-seated political divisions inherited from the First Republic. To that extent, the institutionalised features of domestic elite co-operation - above all grand coalition government and *Proporz*, but to some extent also social partnership - gradually made themselves redundant. This was becoming ever more apparent in the mid-1980s, as new parties emerged onto the political scene and the previously very small opposition party, the FPÖ, opted for a strategy of all out confrontation.

Austria was at this time also starting to experience significant economic problems, many of them structural. This helps explain why in 1987 Austria's two major parties chose to reinstate grand coalition government. [32] Seen from another perspective, however, that choice may be regarded as problematic. For whilst the public continues to 'liberate' itself from the psychological and socio-political ties that used to link so many citizens exclusively to one or other of the erstwhile mutually hostile political subcultures that necessitated bridge-building by Austria's post-war political elites, the latter have since 1987 maintained grand coalition government and arguably done little to reform many of the structures and techniques of their cartelised political accommodation that have become unpopular.[33] As I have argued elsewhere,[34] the political change which has been taking place in Austria since the mid-1980s might thus perhaps be described as asymmetrical. One of the unintended side-effects of the governing parties' decision to revert to the

---

[32] Given these parties' much reduced electoral and parliamentary stength, however, the coalition is not as 'grand' as it used to be.

[33] For an Austrian journalist's somewhat emotive argument along these lines, see Czernin (1997)

[34] See Luther (1998b and 1998c).

Second Republic's traditional method of problem-solving may well thus have been to strengthen oppositional forces.

At the same time, Austria has also experienced a significant shift in its international position. As we have shown, after 1955, Austria pursued a policy of 'active neutrality', which became increasingly global in its focus. From the mid-1980s, however, Austria's perspective has again become more regional. But another important difference needs to be stressed. Whilst the period up to the mid-1980s was in large measure one of bipartisanship in foreign affairs, the Austrian political elite has in more recent years lacked consensus on what Austria's foreign policy - and particularly its security policy - should be. Moreover, that division is being exploited by the populist FPÖ, which is demonstrating great skill in mobilising 'modernisation losers' against the governing parties by the use of issues such as immigration, unemployment and the voters' fears about the possible consequences of enlargement. This is the domestic and foreign policy context of Austria's accession to the Union and its assumption of the EU Presidency on 1 July 1998.

1.4 Conclusion: Austria within Europe

Austria brings to the European Union and to its Presidency a distinctive post-war history. Internally, Austria in many respects is a considerable success story. Despite recent worrying xenophobic developments it remains a country that has achieved a degree of domestic peace and consensus that contrasts very favourably not only with its inter-war past, but also with most other EU member states. It has also transformed its absolute and relative economic position. It is thus hardly surprising that many in Austria feel that some of the techniques used to achieve this success are not only worth retaining for Austria, but could usefully be applied to the EU level also. Examples include an economic policy that sets great store on maximising employment, but also the system of social partnership. Others are less sure, arguing that they have limited utility in the context of a very different global economy. This debate is reflected in the contributions to this volume by Harald Ettl and Peter Mitterbauer on the role of social partnership and the approach that should be adopted to labour policy.

Externally, post-war Austria has regarded itself as having a very distinctive - if not unique - role as a diplomatic bridge spanning the geo-political division between East and West. That role was a product partly of geography and partly of history. The upheavals since 1989 have profoundly altered those East and West divisions. To be sure, they may well not have disappeared and may in some ways indeed have become more threatening (e.g. developments in former Yugoslavia). However, Austria has undoubtedly found itself in need of a fundamental review of its diplomatic and security position. The decision in favour of closer European integration via the EU has already been made and is undisputed within the governing elite. However, the security dimension is still a matter of profound disagreement. For some, the key question is not if, but when, Austria will join NATO. The latter appears to persons of this disposition to be the only viable Western military alliance and essential for Austria's future security. They argue that given the end of the Cold War, it is difficult to see the parties between which Austria needs to maintain its neutrality. For others - and especially those who are closely wedded to the notion of neutrality as a distinctive and valuable feature of Austrian identity, as well as for those who have an historic or ideological aversion to military alliances - the NATO option is if anything even more undesirable than it used to be. On the one hand, they argue Europe is currently still undergoing relatively rapid change, so it is too early for Austria to tie itself to NATO, not least since the latter's future shape is as yet unclear. On the other hand, some maintain that it would be more in Austria's interests to work towards strengthening the CFSP pillar of the EU and to seek to move towards a common European security policy. Broadly speaking, the security issue divides Austrian politics on a left-right dimension; the most avid supporter of NATO membership is the FPÖ, followed by the ÖVP, whilst the most opposed are the Greens. The SPÖ is split, but opponents are at present too strong to enable the leadership to speak out for NATO membership - even if that were what they wished to do.

A second key foreign policy issue - and one that is by contrast clearly much more relevant for the Austrian Presidency - concerns eastern enlargement. In some ways, Austria's position on this topic is clear. In view of not only its historic links with the Eastern European countries, but also the above mentioned 'visit diplomacy' and bridge-building of the post-war period, Austria would be expected to be very much in favour of eastern enlargement and is perhaps exceptionally well placed to promote it. (See the contributions to this volume by Thomas Nowotny, and Hannes Swoboda.) Yet its location adjacent to the very premeable economic 'border' between the affluent EU and the much less developed accession states makes it extremely vulnerable to potentially very adverse economic consequences, not least for its labour market. The Austrian public is aware of this potential and even if it were not, the main opposition party has taken it upon itself to ensure that it is. Accordingly, as the Austrian governing coalition embarks on the EU Presidency, it has to engage in a delicate balancing act. It is very much aware that it is in Austria's long-term interests to move the EU's frontier eastwards, since that will ensure that Austria relinquishes its geo-economic peripherality in favour of greater centrality. Yet governments also have to operate with a short-term agenda, not least because voters often do. Accordingly, it will be interesting to see how Austria's political elite choose to handle the eastward enlargement issue both during and after their Presidency.

Bibliography

Andics, H., (1968) *Der Staat, den keiner wollte. Österreich von der Gründung der Republik bis zur Moskauer Deklaration*, Vienna: Molden.

Bischof, G. and Pelinka, A. (eds), (1994) *The Kreisky Era in Austria*, (Vol 2 of *Contemporary Austrian Studies*), New Brunswick, NJ: Transaction Publishers.

Bischof, G. and Pelinka, A. (eds), (1996) *Austro-corporatism: Past-Present-Future*, (Vol 4 of *Contemporary Austrian Studies*), New Brunswick, NJ: Transaction Publishers.

Bischof, G. and Pelinka, A. (eds), (1997) *Austrian Historical Memory and National Identity*, (Vol 5 of *Contemporary Austrian Studies*), New Brunswick, NJ: Transaction Publishers.

Bruckmüller, E. (1998), 'The Development of Austrian National Identity', in Luther, K. R. and Pulzer, P. (eds), *Austria 1945-95: Fifty Years of the Second Republic*, London: Ashgate, pp.83-108.

Czernin, H., (1997) *Der Haider-Macher. Franz Vranitzky und das Ende der alten Republik*, Vienna: Iberia & Molden.

Dachs, et al. (eds), *Handbuch des politischen Systems Österreichs. Die Zweite Republik*, Vienna: Manz.

FROM WEST EUROPEAN PERIPHERY TO THE CENTRE OF EUROPE?

Katzenstein, P.J. (1979) 'Dependence and Autonomy: Austria in an Interdependent World', *Österreichische Zeitschrift für Außenpolitik*, Vol. 19, No. 4, pp.243-256.

Katzenstein, P.J. (1975) *Small States in World Markets*, Ithaca, New York: Cornell University Press.

Knight, R., (1998) 'The Renner state government and Austrian sovereignty', in Luther, K. R. and Pulzer, P. (eds), *Austria 1945-95: Fifty Years of the Second Republic*, London: Ashgate, pp.29-46.

Kramer, I. (1998) 'Austrian Foreign Policy from the State Treaty to European Union Membership (1955-95)', in Luther, K.R. and Pulzer, P. (eds), *Austria 1945-95: Fifty Years of the Second Republic*, London: Ashgate, pp. 161-180.

Kramer, H., (1996) 'Foreign Policy', in Lauber, V. (ed.), *Contemporary Austrian Politics*, Boulder and London: Westview, pp.151-200.

Lauber, V. (1992) 'Changing Priorities in Austrian Economic Policy', in Luther, K. R. and Müller, W. C. (eds), *Politics in Austria. Still a Case of Consicationalism?*, London, Frank Cass: pp.147-172.

Luif, P., (1988) *Neutrale in die EG? Die wirtschaftliche Integration Westeuropas und die neutralen Staaten*, Vienna: Böhlau.

Luther, K. R., (1992) 'Consociationalism, Parties and the Party System' in Luther, K. R. and Müller, W. C. (eds), *Politics in Austria. Still a Case of Consicationalism?*, London: Frank Cass, pp.45-98.

Luther, K. R., (1995) 'An End to the Politics of Isolation? Austria in Light of the 1994 Elections', *German Politics*, Vol. 4, No. 1, pp.122-139.

Luther, K.R. (1997) 'Die Freiheitlichen', in Herbert Dachs *et al.* (eds), *Handbuch des politischen Systems Österreichs. Die zweite Republik*, Vienna: Manz, pp. 286-303.

Luther, K.R. (1998a) 'From Accommodation to Competition: the "Normalization" of the Second Republic's Party System?', in Luther, K. R. and Pulzer, P. (eds), *Austria 1945-95: Fifty Years of the Second Republic*, London: Ashgate, pp.121-58.

Luther, K.R. (1998b) 'From Moderate to Polarized Pluralism? The Austrian party system in transition', in Broughton, D. and Donovan, M. (eds), *Party System Change in Western Europe*, London: Pinter, pp.118-142.

Luther, K.R. (1998c) 'The Politics of Asymmetrical Change: Austrian Parties During the "Vranitzky Era"', in Bischof, G. and Pelinka, A. (eds). *The Vranitzky Era 1986-1996*, (Vol 7 of *Contemporary Austrian Studies*), New Brunswick, NJ: Transaction Publishers, in print.

Luther, K.R. and Deschouwer, K. (eds), (1998) *Political Elites in Divided Societies: Political Parties in Consociational Democracy*, London, Routledge, in print.

Luther, K.R. and Müller, W.C. (eds), (1992a) *Politics in Austria. Still a Case of Consociationalism?*, London: Frank Cass.

Luther, K. R. and Müller, W.C., (1992b) 'Consociationalism and the Austrian Political System', in Luther, K. R. and Müller, W.C. (eds) *Politics in Austria. Still a Case of Consociationalism?*, London: Frank Cass, pp. 1-15.

Luther, K. R. and Pulzer, P. (eds), (1998) *Austria 1945-95: Fifty Years of the Second Republic*, London: Ashgate.

Menasse, R., (1992) *Das Land ohne Eigenschaften.Essay zur österreichischen Identität*, Venna: Sonderzahl.

Müller, W. C. (1985) 'Die Rolle der Parteien bei Entstehung und Entwicklung der Sozialpartnerschaft. Eine handlungslogische und empirische Analyse', in Gerlich, P., Grande, E. and Müller W. C. (eds), *Sozialpartnerschaft in der Krise. Leistungen und Grenzen des Neokorporatismus in Österreich*, Vienna: Böhlau, pp.135-224.

Müller, W.C. (1992) 'Austrian Governmental Institutions: Do They Matter?', *West European Politics*, Vol. 15, No.1, pp. 99-131.

Müller, W.C., (1994) 'The Development of Austrian Party Organizations in the Post-War Period', in Katz, R.S. and Mair, P. (eds), *How Parties Organize: Adaptation and Change in Party Organizations in Western Democracies*, London: Sage, pp.51-79.

Neuhold, H., (1993) *Internationaler Strukturwandel und staatliche Außenpolitik. Das österreichische Außenministerium vor neuen Herausforderungen*, Vienna: Braumüller

Neuhold, H., (1998) 'Austria in Search of its Place in a Changing World: From Between the Blocs to Full Western Integration?', in Luther, K.R. and Pulzer, P. (eds), *Austria 1945-95: Fifty Years of the Second Republic*, London: Ashgate, pp. 203-223.

Ogris, G., (1995) 'Der Diskussionsprozeß vor der EU-Abstimmung', in Pelinka, A. (ed.) *EU-Referendum. Zur Praxis direkter Demokratie in Österreich*, Vienna: Signum Verlag.

Pelinka, A. (1993) *Die Kleine Koalition: SPÖ-FPÖ 1983-1986*, Vienna: Böhlau.

Pelinka, A. (ed.), (1995) *EU-Referendum. Zur Praxis direkter Demokratie in Österreich*, Vienna: Signum Verlag.

Plasser, F. and Ulram, P., (1995) 'Meinungstrends, Mobilisierung und Motivlagen bei der Volksabstimmung über den EU-Beitritt', in Pelinka, A. (ed.) *EU-Referendum. Zur Praxis direkter Demokratie in Österreich*, Vienna: Signum Verlag.

Pulzer, P., (1969a) 'The Legitimizing Role of Political Parties: The Second Austrian Republic', *Government and Opposition*, Vol. 4, pp.324-344.

Pulzer, P., (1969b) 'Austria', in Henig, S. and Pinder, P. (eds), *European Political Parties*, London: Allen & Unwin, pp.282-319.

Rathkolb, O. (1998) 'Superpower Perceptions of Austrian Neutrality Post-1955', in Luther, K. R. and Pulzer, P. (eds), *Austria 1945-95: Fifty Years of the Second Republic*, London: Ashgate, pp.67-80.

Schneider, H. , (1990) *Alleingang nach Brüssel*, Bonn: Europa Union Verlag

Schultz, M. D., (1992) 'Austria in the International Arena: Neutrality, European Integration and Consociationalism', in Luther, K. R. and Müller, W. C. (eds), *Politics in Austria: Still a Case of Consociationalism ?*, London: Frank Cass, pp. 173-200.

Simon, W. B., (1957) *The Political Parties of Austria*, Columbia University: PhD Thesis.

Supper, M. , (1983) 'Die Rolle der Sozialpartner in der Außenpolitik', in Kicker, R. *et al.* (eds), *Außenpolitik und Demokratie in Österreich. Strukturen-Strategien-Stellungnahmen*, Salzburg: Neugebauer.

Tálos, E. *et al.* (eds), (1995) *Handbuch des politischen Systems Österreichs: Erste Republik 1918-1933*, Vienna: Manz.

Tálos, E and Falkner, G. (eds), (1996) *EU-Mitglied Österreich. Gegenwart und Perspektiven: Eine Zwischenbilanz*, Vienna: Manz.

Wandruszka, Adam (1954) 'Österreichs politische Struktur: Die Entwicklung der Parteien und politischen Bewegungen', in H. Benedikt (ed.), *Geschichte der Republik Österreich*, Vienna: Verlag für Gesellschaft und Politik, pp. 289-485.

Weber, K. (1996) 'Der Föderalismus', in Tálos, E and Falkner, G. (eds), *EU-Mitglied Österreich. Gegenwart und Perspektiven: Eine Zwischenbilanz*, Vienna: Manz, pp.50-66.

Weinzierl, E. (1998) 'The Origins of the Second Republic: a Retrospective View', in Luther, K. R. and Pulzer, P. (eds), *Austria 1945-95: Fifty Years of the Second Republic*, London: Ashgate, pp.3-27.

Zemanek, K. (1984), 'Austria's Policy of Neutrality: Constants and Variables', in Neuhold, H. and Thalberg, H. (eds), *The European Neutrals in International Affairs*, Boulder: Westview, and Vienna: Braumüller.

Zemanek, K. (1991), 'The Changing International System: A New Look at Collective Security and Permanent Neutrality', *Austrian Journal of Public and International Law*, 42

2

PUBLIC ATTITUDES TO EUROPEAN INTEGRATION:

IS THE HONEYMOON OVER?

Kurt Richard Luther and Iain Ogilvie

2.1 Introduction

Austria joined the European Union as part of the fourth enlargement, together with Finland and Sweden. These states, all former members of the European Free Trade Area (EFTA), had various motives for joining. One such motive was the impact on non-members of the increased sophistication of European integration[1]. The intensification, or 'deepening' of integration was marked by the adoption of policies - particularly in the economic sphere - which had had profound effects on those states which had pursued closer links with the European Community (EC), both by formal ties such as Association and European Economic Area (EEA) agreements and, more informally, by the necessity of trading realities and geographical proximity. Indeed, as the chapters by Luther, Thomas Nowotny, and Swoboda in this book make clear, in the early 1990s, Austria sought to re-examine its future geo-political status, commitments and affiliations. This process was chiefly guided by the realities of the *de facto* integration of Austria with the economy of Western Europe, as well as by the new strategic international environment and the perception that membership of the EU might help to induce much-needed domestic reform. Moreover, as Tumpel-Gugerell notes later in this book, the Austrian economy had 'shadowed' - in effect been tied to - the German economy for some time, and was heavily dependent on trade with EU member states, thus reducing the salience of some of the 'traditional' arguments against membership raised in other member states (notably the United Kingdom), which revolved around economic and political sovereignty. Given Austria's particular historical experience, the changed international environment, and the economic necessity of being able to influence the regulatory and trading framework in which the Austrian economy was grounded, it was hardly surprising that Austria pursued membership of the EU, which it saw as the fulfilment of Austria's European 'calling'. Membership would, it was argued, secure Austrian economic interests, provide access to, and representation in, the chief mechanism of European integration and influence world-wide, and provide an 'external shock' in order to modernise Austrian institutions and economic practices.[2]

---

[1] See Pedersen (1994); Preston (1997); and the chapter by Swoboda in this volume.
[2] Preston (1997: 92-3). On the re-orientation of Austria's international role, see Luther's in chapter 1 (esp. pp.9-14).

Given the nature of the motives which animated Austrian involvement with the EU, it is hardly surprising that Austria developed a reputation as 'the European Union's most enthusiastic new recruit'[3], the contemporary domestic debates about the implications that membership may have for Austrian neutrality notwithstanding. Indeed, when the ratification procedures were planned after the negotiations - negotiations that were conducted 'more speedily and more effectively' than those of previous enlargements[4] - Austria was deemed to be the 'safest' applicant, and its referendum was held first (on 12 June 1994). Luther deals with the referendum campaign and result elsewhere in this book, but the clear vote (66.6%) in favour of accession reflected and confirmed the Austrian reputation as the most 'positive European' of the new members. Less than three years later, however, in a discussion entitled 'How much public support is there for the EU?', Nicole Notat placed Austria firmly in the 'Euro-sceptic' camp.[5] Moreover, as Luther notes in the introductory chapter, this growing opposition has become mobilised in domestic politics, where it has become inextricably linked with opposition to the institutional structures and style associated with Austria's post-war strategy of elite accommodation.

That Austria should evolve from 'positive European' to 'Euro-sceptic' within three years of a conclusive popular endorsement of membership, an endorsement called 'generous' by Kaiser,[6] does not reflect a change in the priorities and agenda of the political elite within Austria. Yet it should not simply be ignored. Firstly, liberal democracies require the consent of their peoples, and the lack of it can constrain the effective operation of the relevant political system and lead to political and social unrest. Secondly, this internal conflict over EU membership and the implications that the future development of European integration may have, shows signs of exacerbating existing social, economic and political tensions within Austria, as 'modernisation losers' become increasingly disaffected. Finally, one of the Austrian priorities for its tenure of the Presidency of the EU, as outlined in this volume by Dr Schüssel's contribution, and echoed in Ambassador Eva Nowotny's foreword, is to initiate and carry through measures that will bring the citizen more closely into the decision-making processes of the European Union, and thereby reduce its 'democratic deficit'. Evidence of growing dissatisfaction with Austria's membership of the EU could in principle thus impinge on the democratic legitimacy and efficiency of the political system and have important implications for the successful actualisation of its contemporary domestic and EU agenda.

The aim of this chapter is thus threefold: firstly, to examine Austrian public opinion attitudes to the European Union, in order to ascertain whether there is any empirical evidence that supports the claim that Austria is no longer a 'model' European, or at least has evolved from enthusiastically endorsing membership to a more 'sceptical' position. Secondly, we will compare and contrast Austrian public opinion with that in those member states which joined at the same enlargement - Sweden and Finland - and with the EU average, in order to establish whether the Austrian distribution of opinions regarding the EU is shared by other members, especially those who have had a similar time-period in which to adapt to the opportunities and constraints that EU membership implies. Thirdly, we will look at the domestic structure of attitudes to the EU, by

---

[3] Luther (1995: 129). This characterisation is also made in a variety of analyses of the fourth enlargement, including Jones (1996: 276-8); and in Niedermayer and Sinnott (eds) (1995).

[4] Preston (1997: 107)

[5] Notat (1997: 63)

[6] Kaiser (1995: 449)

analysing the pattern of distribution of opinions among Austrians, using standard demographic categories, in order to point to some possible explanations for the current state of Austrian attitudes to European integration.

2.2 Public opinion and European integration

From the earliest days of European integration, both proponents of the latter and integration theorists have assumed that European publics would 'naturally' approve of membership. They would either do so because of the perceived economic and political benefits that were deemed to accrue from membership of a more powerful regional trading and economic bloc, or would at least acquiesce in it through the constant legitimising agency of the political process.[7] Indeed, Sinnott has claimed that the 'focus of explanation remains on elites, and on structures and processes, both at the international and national levels'.[8] This has certainly been as true for Austria as for the other member states of the EU. And yet, 'public opinion must be taken into account in any analysis of the increasingly complex and dense network of inter-state relations in Europe'.[9]

Furthermore, there has been a growing perception of a 'widening democratic disjunction between the wishes and interests of Europe's political elites and generally held political sentiments'.[10] This is perhaps an understandable consequence of the recent institutional development of the Union and the prospect both of its 'widening' to include Austria's immediate neighbours and of its 'deepening', *inter alia* through the implementation of the single currency and the development of a common foreign and security policy. If Notat and others are correct in their assertion that Austria is now amongst the most 'Euro-sceptic' countries, then one is struck by the fact that the aforementioned disjunction between Austrian elites and masses must be exceptionally large. For evidence would seem to point to what Kaiser calls a 'very marked and stable elite consensus on the desirability of EU membership' that also 'encompass(es) all major interest groups.. as well as the four institutions of Austrian organised corporatism'[11]. Changes in public attitudes to the EU thus have increasing political significance, not least because it was the 'solid 'Yes' vote in the 1994 membership referendum' which allowed 'the (Austrian) government to embark on an active integration policy'[12].

This chapter will firstly seek to scrutinise public attitudes to membership of the EU and to the perceived benefits thereof. Secondly, it will explore attitudes to two topical EU policies - enlargement and the single currency - which have been not only the subject of intense debate within all EU member states, but have been identified as Austrian priorities for their Presidency. Finally, it will briefly look at the data concerning public opinion as to what should be the chief priorities of

---

[7] Sometimes referred to as the 'permissive consensus': see Lindberg and Scheingold (1970); Mathew (1980); and Sinnott (1995), amongst others.

[8] Sinnott (1995: 24)

[9] Sinnott (1995: 11). This is arguably of special significance in 'consociational democracies' such as Austria, which political scientists consisder to have relatively high levels of cartelised elite dominance (Luther/Deschouwer 1998).

[10] Chryssochoou (1994: 3).

[11] Kaiser (1995: 414). This reinforces Luther's point in chapter one (p.18f) about the asymmetrical nature of recent developments in domestic politics in Austria.

[12] Kaiser (1995: 423)

the European Union, and compare these with those outlined by some of the key Austrian political and administrative actors involved in the Presidency.[13]

The successful completion of this task requires access to reliable data. One of the most important, if still highly imperfect, sources of opinion data concerning European integration is that provided by the Commission's 'Eurobarometer' surveys, conducted across EU member states on a twice-yearly basis. One of the advantages of using this survey is that an identical set of questions is asked of representative samples of the population in each country, which then allows cross-national comparisons. Another is that vital questions are repeated at regular intervals, allowing for the study of trends in attitudes towards important issues. Finally, the respondents are broken down into demographic groups, thus enabling further in-depth study of responses. However, we should remember that it is as susceptible to the many faults associated with opinion polling as are all other such surveys. As the 'Eurobarometer' remains the only readily accessible source of cross-national opinion polling data, however, it is a vital source, and it forms the principal empirical basis of this chapter. We will, however, also use some recent domestic survey material in the third section of our analysis, which will enable us to outline some of the ways in which Austrian public opinion was structured on the eve of Austria's assumption of the EU Presidency.

2.3 Attitudes to European integration in Austria, Sweden and Finland

2.3.1 Attitudes to membership

We have already noted that Austria's membership referendum produced the most emphatic 'yes' vote out of the four candidate countries in 1994. Many commentators, however, noted that all three new members of the EU, were importing into the Union a high relatively degree of 'Euro-scepticism',[14] in that their populations contained higher proportions of opponents of membership than existing member states (with the possible exceptions of Denmark and the UK). Existing scholarship on successive enlargements has provided two main insights: firstly that the question of popular support for membership of the EU is more problematic for those member states who joined after the initial 'wave'. Those joining in later 'waves' are more likely to experience internal conflict regarding membership.[15] Secondly, it is argued that opposition to membership gradually declines, as economic and material benefits begin to be felt.[16] Thus one would expect Austria to start from a relatively high level of opposition to the EU, which would decline over time. Figure 2.1a shows the actual development of Austrian attitudes to membership of the EU.[17]

---

[13] See the contributions by Schüssel, Woschnagg and Eva Nowotny in this volume.

[14] See *inter alia* Jahn and Storsved (1995); Aarebrot *et al.* (1995); and Preston (1997).

[15] Inglehart and Rabier (1978); Anderson (1995: 116); but also Preston (1997); McAllister (1997) and Nugent (1994).

[16] Anderson (1995: 116); Sinnott (1995); but also see Jones (1996).

[17] The Figure shows responses to the following question: 'Generally speaking, do you think that (your country)'s membership of the EU is a good thing, a bad thing, or neither good nor bad?'

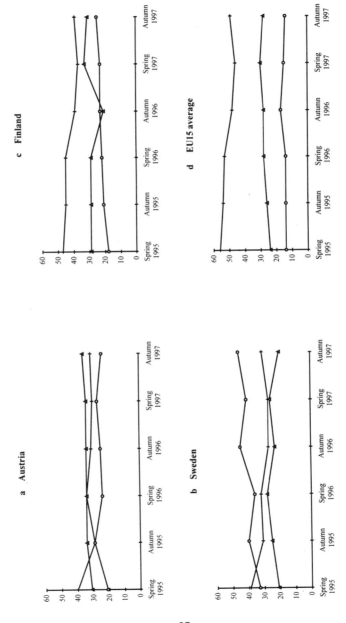

Figures 2.1 a-d   Is EU membership good for your country? (1995-97)

a   Austria

b   Sweden

c   Finland

d   EU15 average

Source: Eurobarometer, Nos. 43-48. 'Generally speaking, do you think that (your country's) membership of the EU is a good thing, a bad thing, or neither good nor bad?'

Legend: Good: +;   bad o;   neither good, nor bad Δ.

There are a number of observations we can make about these data. Firstly, opposition to membership has not declined in Austria. If anything, the proportion of those saying that Austrian membership of the EU was ' a bad thing' has slightly increased - from 21 per cent in Autumn 1995 (the fieldwork for this survey was undertaken in the months following accession) to 24 per cent in the most recently available survey at the end of 1997. Moreover, those who believed that membership was 'a good thing' has steadily declined from 40 to 31 per cent over the same period. Those whose opinion of membership was 'neutral'[18] rose from 31 to 36 per cent.

One would also expect that attitudes to membership would be conditioned by perceptions of the benefits that it was supposed would accrue from membership. This evaluative process is particularly imprint in an analysis of Austrian attitudes, as

> during the course of the (referendum) campaign the governing parties made in part very optimistic forecasts concerning the economic benefits which increases and possibly even tax reductions. (Were) any of these (to) fail to materialise, it (would be) easy to see how this could be used against them.[19]

Figure 2.2a shows the evolution of Austrian perceptions of the benefit that membership of the EU had brought.[20] As one can see, the numbers of people saying that membership of the EU had 'benefited' Austria fell from 44 to 35 per cent, almost exactly mirroring the rise in those claiming that membership had 'not benefited' - from 36 to 43 per cent.

There therefore seems to be some evidence that Austria does not fit into the 'traditional' characterisation of a new member state; opposition to membership hardened in the first three years of membership, while perceptions of benefit declined. Of course, these two facts may be closely inter-related. We argue, however, that since the time of Austria's accession, three additional developments have occurred which may have had a substantial impact on Austrian attitudes to membership of the EU.[21]

Firstly, Austria's largest opposition party, the Freedom Party of Austria (*Freiheitliche Partei Österreichs*, or FPÖ), began to mobilise very effectively around opposition to specific EU-related policies. Secondly, there was a growing perception that popular opinion across the EU member states had 'hardened' against certain EU-related policies, and that outright opposition to membership of the EU had become more 'respectable'. Thirdly, certain policy initiatives that were widely thought to be to be less popular among Austrians, including enlargement and the single currency, came to prominence on the EU's agenda.[22] It is beyond the scope of this chapter to attempt to assess the importance of the role of Jörg Haider's FPÖ on the changing landscape of Austrian attitudes towards the EU, but we will now examine the latter two phenomena. This will be

---

[18] Membership was 'neither good nor bad'.

[19] Luther (1995: 129-30).

[20] The precise question was: 'Taking everything into consideration, would you say that (your country) has on balance benefited or not from being a member of the EU?'

[21] A wider range of possible reasons for recent changes in Austrian attitudes to European integration are disucssed by Luther in chapter 1 of this book (see esp. p.. and p.17-19).

[22] Evidence for this is increased intra-party conflict on EU issues, the genesis and success of 'anti-EU' parties, and various opinion poll evidence from across the member states. For a fuller treatment of this issue, see Ogilvie: *The mobilisation of anti-European sentiment: anti-EU parties in comparative perspective*, doctoral thesis, Keele University, forthcoming.

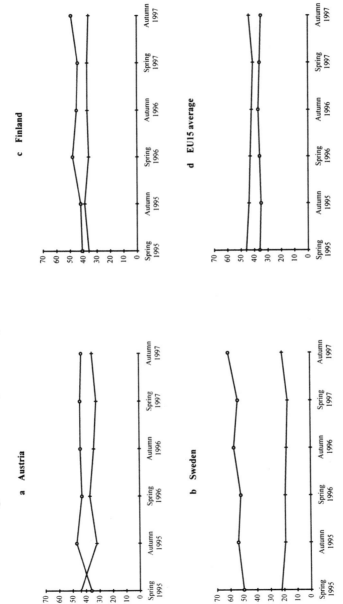

Figures 2.2 a-d   Has your country benefited from EU membership? (1995-97)

a Austria

b Sweden

c Finland

d EU15 average

<u>Source</u>: Eurobarometer, Nos. 43-48. 'Taking everything into account, would you say that (your country) has on balance benefited or not from being a member of the EU?'

<u>Legend</u>: Benefited: +;   Not benefited o.

done firstly by placing Austrian attitudes to EU membership in comparative perspective, and secondly, by examining Austrian attitudes to two contested policy areas - eastern enlargement and EMU - that may have helped condition the wider framing of Austrian public opinion. Figure 2.3 charts Austrian, Swedish and Finnish attitudes to membership of the EU against the EU 15 average.

What we find by examining Figures 2.1a-c is that support for the proposition that membership of the EU was 'good' fell in all three states: in Austria from 40 to 31; in Sweden from 39 to 31; and in Finland from 47 to 39 per cent. As Figure 2.1d shows, this decline in these new member states also mirrored a general decline across all fifteen member states: from 56 to 49 per cent. However, it is in respect of the level of *opposition* to membership that the most interesting relationship occurs. Across the EU15, opposition remained constant at 14 per cent, albeit with a minor increase in the middle of the period, which subsequently subsided, whilst opposition grew in the fourth enlargement states - in Austria from 21 to 24; in Sweden from 33 to 46; and in Finland from 18 to 25 per cent. It would seem that, whereas the chief movement across the EU has been from positive to neutral responses, in the 'fourth wave' states, the prime change has been an increase in the level of opposition.

We can investigate the development of orientations to European integration by asking respondents' whether their country has benefited from membership. The results of recent surveys that did this are contained in Figures 2.2a-d and provide an interesting contrast. Such perceptions stayed stable across the whole EU - in Autumn 1995, 46 per cent said that their country had benefited; and 44 per cent said the same in Autumn 1997. Opposition to this proposition was also stable (36 to 35 per cent) over the same period. Meanwhile, attitudes in Austria provided a marked contrast, since those Austrians perceiving EU membership to be beneficial declined from 44 to 35 per cent (though they were stable in Sweden and Finland). However, when we examine the figures relating to *opposition* to the EU (operationalised in terms of the perception that their country 'had not benefited' from EU membership) we find change in all three 'fourth wave' countries. In Austria, the proportion rose from 36 to 43 per cent, in Finland from 41 to 49 per cent and Sweden by a full 11 points: from 50 to 61 per cent.

2.3.2   Attitudes to the single currency

We will now move on to examine attitudes to a development which has been identified elsewhere in this volume as an issue of vital importance to Austrian interests. Thus Tumpel-Gugerell argues that the successful introduction of the single currency is 'among the central economic policy topics in the upcoming months and years. It also ranks at the top of the agenda of the Austrian EU Presidency'.[23] EMU is also mentioned in the Austrian foreign minister's chapter as a priority issue for his country's Presidency. It is also highlighted by Ambassador Nowotny in her foreword to this book. Accordingly, it would seem clear that the single currency is of central relevance to the framing of Austrian attitudes to the EU, not least because of the assurances made by the Austrian government during the accession debate, referred to above.[24]

---

[23] Tumpel-Gugerell, in this volume.
[24] Luther (1995: 129-30).

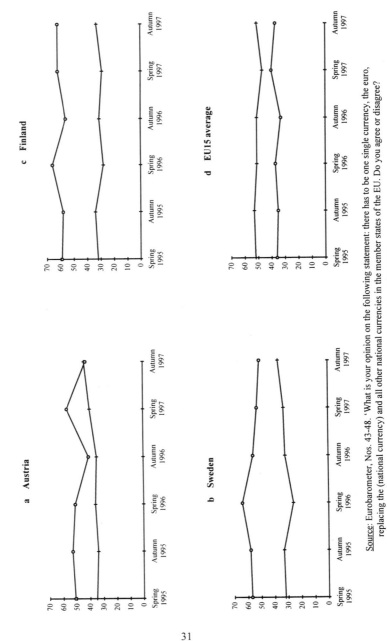

Figures 2.3 a-d   Attitudes to the single currency (1995-97)

Source: Eurobarometer, Nos. 43-48. 'What is your opinion on the following statement: there has to be one single currency, the euro, replacing the (national currency) and all other national currencies in the member states of the EU. Do you agree or disagree?

Legend: Agree: +;   Disagree o.

Figures 2.2a-d shows the development of Austrian attitudes to the introduction of the single currency in comparative perspective, as measured by 'Eurobarometer'.[25] Austria started out at odds with the EU average - being opposed to the single currency by a margin of 51 to 35 per cent, as opposed to the EU 15's support for it by 52 to 36 per cent. This deviation from the EU15 average position was even more pronounced in the other two 'fourth wave' states; the Swedes opposed the single currency by 57 to 32 per cent, and Finns by some 59 to 32 per cent. From Spring 1995 until autumn 1997, the gap between opponents and supporters of the single currency remained fairly stable in Finland, where it ended the period at 62 per cent against and 33 per cent for (Figure 2.3c), and in the EU15: 51 per cent for and 37 per cent against (Figure 2.3d). In Sweden, there was a narrowing of the gap, which in autumn 1997 was exactly the reverse of the average in the EU15, namely, 51 for and 37 per cent against (Figure 2.3b). However, as Figure 2.3a shows, Austrian respondents evidenced a steady rise in support for the single currency over this period (from 35 to 44 per cent), while opposition declined (from 51 to 43 per cent). The result is that for the first time, Eurobarometer 48 (Autumn 1997) was able to report a small plurality in favour of the single currency.

Having reviewed the results the outcome of the polls conducted in the three member states of the 'fourth wave' and compared them to the EU15 average, what conclusions can we draw about the nature and development of Austrian attitudes to European integration? First, it should be noted that these figures suggest that the profile of Austria within the EU 15 has altered, and would seem to provide *prima facie* support for the contention that Austria is now less 'positive' about the EU. Whereas Austria had at the outset almost exactly mirrored the EU average in terms of judgements about the costs and benefits of membership (44-36 as opposed to 46-36 per cent), by the end of the period, Austria had not only more people saying that membership of the EU was not to their country's benefit, but also it also began to mirror the more 'sceptical' profile of the other members of Austria's accession cohort. What is particularly interesting about these data is that, with the exception of its attitudes to the single currency, Austria would seem to have moved away from unconditional support for the EU. Yet it is exactly this growth in support for the single currency - perhaps tied to the motives for Austrian membership in the first place - that make it impractical to generalise about Austrian attitudes to the EU.

It is too early to say whether these trends in public opinion regarding support for EU membership and for the single currency will have wider political implications for Austria and the other member states. What is clear is that the traditional claims about the pattern of public opinion distributions towards membership of the EU after accession have not been supported by these particular data, although it is important to recognise that as yet, we are as yet only able to examine the developments of public attitudes over a very short period of time.

2.4 Austrian attitudes to eastern enlargement

The issue to which we now turn - the potential eastern enlargement of the EU - is one that involves the intersection of the 'national' and the 'European': because of its historical links with,

---

[25] The precise question was: 'What is your opinion on the following statement: there has to be one single currency, the euro, replacing the (national currency) and all other national currencies in the member states of the EU. Do you agree or disagree?'

and geographical proximity to, the candidates for accession, this process affects both the future architecture of the EU and impinges on Austrian national identity and interests. Elsewhere in this book, Thomas Nowotny concludes that

> eastward enlargement is in Austria's vital interest, as it will radically change the political landscape of Central and Eastern Europe for the better. A region that has hitherto been the source of endless conflict will become a zone of stability, a region of economic and cultural dynamism and innovation.[26]

Furthermore, enlargement is not only a central concern in Austria's political discourse due to history and geography, it also implies potential economic costs, especially in increased budgetary contributions to the EU, the potential for expanded immigration, and increased labour market competition. In his contribution to this volume, where he spells out the priorities of the Austrian Presidency, Vice-Chancellor Schüssel, maintains that

> Enlargement is by far the best and most effective instrument to strengthen security in the region. It keeps the nationalist demons at bay. It reinforces the civil society in these countries and stimulates economic and political reforms. It helps to stabilise societies and thus reduces the risks of organised crime and illegal migration. In the long term, the Union will either export stability towards the applicant countries, or it will import instability. No other country has a higher stake in this than Austria.[27]

In view of the above points by Nowotny and Schüssel, one would expect there to be a lively domestic debate about the enlargement process, its speed, its costs, and what transitionary measures are needed to prepare Austria for its challenges. Moreover, given public awareness of both the opportunities and dangers that various contributors to this volume have outlined,[28] and the 'delicate balancing act'[29] that the Austrian government thus has to perform, one might expect that public opinion in Austria would be both volatile and suspicious of speedy enlargement.

Table 2.1 shows the results of an opinion poll, conducted by Euro Initiative in April 1998, in which respondents were told 'In the next few years, five or six Central and Eastern European countries (for example, Hungary, Poland, the Czech Republic, Slovakia and Slovenia) will join the European Union' They were then asked to indicate the extent to which they would in principle welcome this. Less than a third of Austrians would welcome the accession of the Central and East European countries (CEEC) the priorities of the Austrian Presidency. Moreover, enthusiasm is clearly lowest amongst the oldest age cohort, of whom only 24 per cent would welcome this eventuality, and highest among the young (38 per cent). Even more striking is the attitude of the different educational groups. Whilst only 24 per cent of those with a basic education support eastern enlargement, amongst those who have a university degree, or are at least qualifies to study at university, the proportion is 40 per cent.

The Austrians' preferences as between the various potential CEEC member states of the EU are documented in Figure 4.5 in Thomas Nowotny's chapter in this volume. What that figure shows

---

[26] Nowotny, in this volume.
[27] Schüssel, in this volume.
[28] Especially those by Luther, Thomas Nowotny, Schüssel, and Swoboda.
[29] Luther, in chapter 1 of this volume, page 20.

Table 2.1   Austrian attitudes to eastern enlargement (April 1998)

	How welcome would CEEC accession be to you?				Brussels transfers to CEEC states after accession	
	Very	Welcome	Little	Not at all	Justifiable	Unjustifiable
Men	2	27	29	30	32	51
Women	5	25	29	21	24	48
Age						
15-29	2	36	29	17	35	43
30-39	5	26	31	20	26	48
40-49	2	18	36	29	21	54
50-59	5	31	28	20	37	37
60 plus	4	18	24	36	20	60
Education						
Minimal	1	23	24	25	22	44
Secondary	4	27	31	29	29	56
(qualified for) Univ.	10	30	33	15	37	44
Austria	4	26	29	25	28	49

Source: Euro Initiative, representative survey of 1,000 persons, conducted April 1998.

is a distinct 'pecking order'. Hungary is the favourite, with a total of 53 per cent saying they would welcome Hungarian accession, or even welcome it very much, whilst there is a decided lack of enthusiasm for Slovakia, where the analogous figure is 27 per cent.

The survey also asked respondents whether it would be justifiable for Brussels to undertake transfer payments to the CEECs after they had joined the EU. Their answers are summarised in the two right hand columns of Table 2.1 and exhibit many similarities with the responses to the aforementioned question. First, the overall picture is rather unenthusiastic: only 28 per cent think such payments would be justifiable. Moreover, support for transfer payments is positively correlated with respondents' educational levels. Age is again a relevant variable, with the greatest scepticism being exhibited by the oldest age cohort. Yet an interesting tendency, already visible in attitudes to the welcoming (or not) accession, is slightly more pronounced here. At 37 per cent, the 50-59 year olds are the most likely to consider transfer payments justifiable. This is even marginally higher than the level amongst the youngest cohort. Though one must be careful about drawing conclusions from these data, it may be that what we are witnessing here is a cohort effect, with the 'war babies' (socialised during the years after the State Treaty, which assured that Austria was spared inclusion in the orbit of the Soviet Union's satellite states) perhaps exhibiting greater sympathy for the citizens of those countries who were not spared that fate.[30]

---

[30] On Austria's straddling of the Cold War fault line and the State Treaty which ensured the country's independent statehood, see chapter 1 of this volume by Luther (esp. p.6).

Whether or not this hypothesis is correct, the results of this survey (and of another survey conducted at roughly the same time)[31] convey a rather clear message to Austria's opinion formers. If, as the latter consistently assert, eastern enlargement is not only inevitable, but also unequivocally in Austria's long-term economic and political interests, there is still much to be done to convince the Austrian masses of that fact. As yet, the Austrian population also appears decidedly unwilling to countenance providing the kind of economic resources that would (as argued *inter alia* by Thomas Nowotny in this volume) surely be necessary to smooth the accession process.

2.5 Conclusion: is the 'honeymoon' over?

We noted earlier that Austrian public opinion supported EU membership enthusiastically, after the 1994 referendum produced an emphatic and unambiguous 'yes'. Moreover, due to its historical experience and the changed realities of the post-Cold War world, Austria also felt that membership would not only bring economic and political benefits, but would also prefigure the 'return' of Austria into full membership of the West European 'club', fully rehabilitated and with special insight, institutions and practices which may have been applicable to the European level. The evidence contained in the 'Eurobarometer' surveys which we have examined above, coupled with recent developments in domestic politics, in particular in the party system, leads us to make three tentative suggestions about Austrian attitudes to European integration, in the context of falling support for EU membership, and a lessening belief in existence of the benefits it was supposed to bring.

Firstly, we suggest that Austrian popular support for EU membership, and for specific policies, is not, and never has been, unconditional. Arguments in favour of membership were predicated on the assumption that concrete economic advantages would ensue, as we have already mentioned. The absence of these may lead to a shift towards opposition to the EU.

Secondly, whilst the public are becoming more 'sceptical' of the abstract benefits of membership - hence the decline in support for membership - they can be persuaded where tangible benefits from membership can be identified, like for instance over the increase in support - against the wider trend - for the single currency. Thus, a central factor in the future development of Austrian public attitudes to the EU will be the manner in which EU policies are designed, promoted and implemented.

Finally, there remains a great deal of uncertainty about the enlargement process, and the effects this may have for Austria's economic security and on its labour market. Austrians are particularly worried about the speed of enlargement. Under Austria's Presidency, the EU is currently in the early stages of designing measures that will on the one hand facilitate a stable transition period for the future new Eastern European members, and on the other will ensure economic vitally and political stability for those existing member states which are most affected by enlargement. The degree to which Austrians' anxieties about the threats posed by eastward

---

[31] This comprised a random telephone survey of 1,005 persons, conducted during the second half of March and the first half of April 1998 by the *Sozialwissenschaftliche Studiengesellschaft* (SWS) on behalf of the *Österreichische Gesellschaft für Europapolitik*, under the direction of Christian Haerpfer.

enlargement are assuaged will be crucially influenced by the extent to which the EU succeeds in this endeavour - both during the Austrian Presidency and thereafter.

The Austrian Presidency thus comes at a genuinely opportune moment for Austria that may help to address the concerns of the Austrian public, assuming that their Presidency has the usual advantages of Presidencies: those of raising the domestic visibility of the close relationship between the member state and the EU, and of enabling each state to influence and direct the activity of the Union in a manner which allows the vital interests and concerns of that country to be more widely heard and accommodated.[32]

The Austrian government has highlighted six priorities for their Presidency of the EU: EMU, employment, enlargement, Agenda 2000, the environment, and measures related to youth and the family.[33] Though the Austrian public appears to still be somewhat more sceptical overall about the benefits to date of EU membership, it does seem largely to share their government's policy priorities for the Presidency. The extent of agreement between the priorities of the Austrian government and of the Austrian people is of course hardly likely to be fortuitous, but should provide that government with some satisfaction. Thus in a recent 'Eurobarometer'[34], the proportion of Austrians who believed that EMU was a priority was 45 per cent (41 per cent did not). Those who supported measures to combat unemployment amounted to 91. The proportion of respondents who thought that bringing the EU closer to the citizens (Agenda 2000) was a priority stood at 63 per cent. Meanwhile, some 85 per cent supported action in support of the environment. Indeed, these figures were mirrored throughout the Union. It was, once again, only in respect of enlargement that Austrians were not convinced: 57 per cent of Austrians did not agree that welcoming new members to the EU was a policy priority.

So what can we conclude from all this about the attitude of Austrian to European integration? At the referendum of 12 June 1994, the Austrian people voted by a very healthy majority to seal Austria's (polygamous?) marriage with the European Union. They appear to still be quite committed to achieving a stable, prosperous and secure Europe via the European integration process, but they remain to be persuaded that their stability and security would not be endangered by enlargement. In sum, whilst the honeymoon may well be over, divorce is not seriously on the agenda.

Bibliography

Aarebrot, F., Berglund, S. and Weninger, T., (1995) 'The view from EFTA', chapter 14 of Niedermayer, O. and Sinnott, R., (1995) Public opinion and internationalized governance, Oxford: OUP, pp 344-67.

Anderson, C., (1995) 'Economic uncertainty and European solidarity revisited: trends in public support for European integration', in Rhodes, C. and Mazey, S., (eds.) *The State of the European Union: Building a European Polity?*, pp. 111-33, Boulder: Lynne Rienner.

---

[32] See O Nuallain (1985)
[33] See Schüssel in this volume.
[34] 'Eurobarometer' 48 (autumn 1997), table 3.7

Chryssochoou, D., (1994) 'Democracy and symbiosis in the European Union: towards a confederal consociation?', in *West European Politics*, vol. 17, no. 4, pp 1-14.

European Commission (1995-7) *Eurobarometer*, bi-annual reports, numbers 43-48.

Falkner, G., (1996) 'Enlarging the European Union', chapter 13 of Richardson, J., *European Union: power and policy-making*, London: Routledge, pp. 233-46.

Inglehart, R. and Rabier, J-R., (1967) 'Economic Uncertainty and European Solidarity: Public Opinion Trends', in *Annals of the American Academy of Political and Social Science*, 440.

Jahn, D. and Storsved, A-S., (1995) 'Legitimacy through Referendum?: the nearly-successful domino-strategy of the EU Referendums in Austria, Finland, Sweden and Norway', in *West European Politics*, vol. 18, no. 4, pp 18-37.

Jones, R., A., (1996) *The politics and economics of the European Union*, Cheltenham: Edward Elgar.

Kaiser, W., (1995) 'Austria in the European Union', in *Journal of Common Market Studies*, vol. 33, no. 3, pp. 411-27.

Kaiser, W. *et al*, (1995) *Die EU-Volsabstimmung in Österreich, Finnland, Schweden und Norwegen: Verlauf, Ergebnisse, Motive und Folgen*, Institut für höhere Studien (Reihe Politikwissenschaft), March.

Lindberg, L. and Scheingold, S., (1970) *Europe's Would-Be Polity, Englewood Cliffs: Prentice Hall.*

Luther, K. R., (1992) 'Consociationalism, Parties and the Party System' in Luther, K. R. and Müller, W. C. (eds), *Politics in Austria. Still a Case of Consicationalism?*, London: Frank Cass, pp.45-98.

Luther, K. R., (1995) 'Austria in light of the 1994 elections' in *German Politics*, vol. 4, no. 1, pp. 122-140.

Luther, K.R. and Deschouwer, K. (eds), (1998) *Political Elites in Divided Societies: Political Parties in Consociational Democracy*, London, Routledge, in print.

McAllister, R., (1997) *From EC to EU: an historical and political survey*, London: Routledge.

Niedermayer, O. and Sinnott, R., (1995) *Public opinion and internationalized governance*, Oxford: OUP.

Notat, N., (1997) 'Social progress holds the key to the EU's popularity' in *How much popular support is there for the EU?*, Brussels: Philip Morris Institute for Public Policy Research, April, pp. 56-64.

Nugent, N., (1994) *The government and politics of the European Union*, 3rd edition, Basingstoke: Macmillan.

O Nuallain, C., (ed.) (1985) *The presidency of the European Council of Ministers: impacts and implications for national governments*, Beckenham: Croom Helm.

Pedersen, T., (1994) *European Union and the EFTA countries*, London: Pinter.

Preston, C., (1997) *Enlargement and Integration in the European Union*, London: Routledge.

Sinnott, R., (1995) 'Bringing public opinion back in', chapter 2 of Niedermayer, O. and Sinnott, R., *Public opinion and internationalized governance*, Oxford: OUP, pp. 11-32.

AUSTRIAN FEDERALISM AND THE EU:

NEW CENTRALISM VERSUS FEDERAL REFORM ?

Peter Pernthaler and Anna Gamper

3.1 Introduction

Much of the academic and topical debate concerning the nature of European integration and the challenges it poses for the constitutional, administrative and political structures of the member states of the Union has focused on the alleged threat to the nation state and to the traditional distribution of state sovereignty. Yet European integration also implies changes to the manner in which political and administrative power has hitherto been exercised within the member states and in particular to the established powers of their substate units. This is especially true for federal states, where the constitutionally entrenched rights of the constituent territorial units are susceptible to being undermined.

The aim of this chapter is to consider the nature of Austrian federalism and the ways in which federal structures and procedures have responded to and been influenced by Austria's accession to the European Union. Given the paucity of English language literature on the Austrian federal system, however, this chapter will first outline the historical origins and key institutional features of Austrian federalism. Thereafter, it will consider the concerns of the Austrian Länder (states) immediately prior to and during accession. Third, we shall highlight some of the challenges faced by the Länder since Austria joined the European Union, before offering some final thought on the tensions between Austrian federalism and European integration.

3.2 The origins and key structures of Austrian federalism

3.2.1 The history of Austrian federalism[1]

In 1919, after the end of the Austro-Hungarian monarchy, the Republic of Austria was founded simultaneously in Vienna and in the constituent Länder of the new state.[2] The central government

---

[1] Though the monarchy was not absolutely devoid of federal elements, the historic development of Austrian federalism has to be conceived as a process mainly of this century. See Ermacora (1976: 27 ff).

tried to establish Austria as a unitary state, whereas the autonomously created Land governments sought a federal system based on the Swiss model. On account of the strength of the forces promoting centralisation, the Federal Constitution (*Bundes-Verfassungsgesetz*, or B-VG)[3] that came into force on 1 October 1920 contained but modest federal (i.e. Land-oriented) elements; only in 1925, when the distribution of competencies and an administrative reform were enacted,[4] was federalism established as an important feature of the Austrian Constitution.

After World War II, an attempt to unitarise Austria failed, so the federation was re-established in October 1945. During the period of Allied occupation (1945-1955), the federal system was undermined by the introduction of new centralising elements, especially by the Fiscal Constitution Act (*Finanz-Verfassungsgesetz*) of 1948.[5] After Austria had regained sovereignty in 1955, this centralisation process was continued and even intensified in respect of the education system and broadcasting services, as well as via a reduction in the autonomy of local communities. Since 1964/65, the Länder have repeatedly called for a federalising reform, but their demands have been only partially achieved.[6] Austria's accession to the European Union seemed to offer an opportunity to undertake a general structural reform of Austrian federalism, but this has to date also not been achieved.[7]

3.2.2 Key structural features of Austrian federalism[8]

The federal principle is laid down in Art 2 B-VG.[9] According to the Constitutional Court,[10] the federal principle consists of three substantive elements: the distribution of competencies; Länder participation in federal legislation and administration; and Länder constitutional autonomy. Federal theory adds further dimensions, such as Länder financial autonomy, equality of federal and Land legislation and administration, internal self-determination of the Länder, or of institutions of co-operative federalism. Each of these elements will now be outlined briefly.

a) The distribution of competencies between the federation and the Länder[11]
The rules concerning the division of competencies between the federation and the Länder are numerous and spread widely throughout the Federal Constitution, its amendments and supplementary legislation. Judicial power is an exclusively federal competence, but legislative and administrative competencies are distributed between the federation and the Länder. This is done in four main ways.

---

[2] See Ermacora (1976: 40 ff) and Pernthaler (1979).

[3] For general information regarding Austrian constitutional law see Walter/Mayer (1996); Adamovich/Funk/Holzinger (1997) and Öhlinger (1997a).

[4] BGBl 1925/268. See Werndl (1984: 26 ff).

[5] BGBl 1948/45. See Pernthaler (1984: 119 ff).

[6] See Pernthaler (1980); Berchtold (1988) and Thanner (1997: 275 ff).

[7] See Pernthaler (ed.) (1997).

[8] See Weber (1980: 87 ff).

[9] See Mayer (1997: 2 ff).

[10] The leading case was VfSlg 2455/1952.

[11] See Funk (1980); Werndl (1984); Pernthaler (1989) and Adamovich/Funk/Holzinger (1997: 278 ff).

First, there is a range of matters in respect of which legislative and administrative competencies reside solely with the federation (esp. Art 10 B-VG).[12] More than 100 important functions belong to this main type. They include foreign policy, the judiciary, civil and criminal law, trade law, labour law, banks, industry, federal road and rail transport, mining, weapons, forests, water supply, hydropower, most matters regarding the protection of the environment, health, social security, employment, education services (except elementary, professional and some matters of agricultural education), national economy and fiscal policy, radio and television, law of association, assembly, food, unfair competition, public security and all police forces and armed forces.

Second, some matters are subject to federal legislation and Land administration (esp. Art 11 B-VG).[13] Only few matters belong to this type. Examples include nationality, traffic regulations on roads and non-frontier rivers and lakes, as well as housing. Third, there are matters where the Federation issues general legislation and the Länder are responsible for supplementary legislation and for administration (esp. Art 12 B-VG).[14] Here again, only few matters belong to this category, e.g. basic social welfare, hospitals, land reform, electricity, school buildings and maintenance of schools (except universities and other higher education institutions) etc.. Where the federal legislator declines to establish binding principles, the Länder are free to legislate.

Finally, there is a residual category of matters over which the Länder retain exclusive legislative and administrative rights (Art 15 B-VG).[15] Formally, this includes all matters that are not specified as federal competencies ('residual' or 'general competence' of the Länder). But since most important functions have been specified as federal by the constitution (directly or constructively), there are only few matters left to this type. Examples include building legislation, town and country planning, some environmental protection matters, hunting, fishing, some agricultural matters, youth and children welfare issues, sport, tourism, local government, local police, land transfer, preservation of landscape and of natural heritage and nursery school regulation.

In their activities, the Länder are in practice not, however, wholly restricted to the few matters over which they retain exclusive legislative and administrative competence. Instead, they are entitled to support and to subsidise any activity - regardless of whether it constitutes a federal or a Land competence - and can use all legal institutions and forms of private law or non-governmental administration to this end (Art 17 B-VG).[16] This constitutional principle can be seen as a counterweight to the severe centralisation of competencies that exists in Austria and is of great practical importance for the regional and political independence and self-determination of the Länder - especially the richer western Länder and Vienna.

---

[12] See Mayer (1997: 15 ff).
[13] See Mayer (1997: 55 ff).
[14] See Mayer (1997: 64 ff).
[15] See Mayer (1997: 80 ff).
[16] See Binder (1980); Korinek/Holoubek (1993) and Mayer (1997: 105 ff).

b) Länder participation in the federal legislative process

The Austrian federal parliament is divided into two houses, both of which have the right to initiate bills: The members of the National Council (*Nationalrat*)[17] are directly elected by universal adult suffrage, whereas those of the Federal Council (*Bundesrat*)[18] are indirectly elected by the Land parliaments. The National Council is constitutionally and political much more important than the Federal Council. For one, the federal government is responsible only to the National Council. Moreover, the latter alone has the right to decide on the federal budget and to conduct committees of inquiry. Finally, if the Federal Council rejects a bill passed by the National Council, the National Council may override that veto, unless Land competencies are concerned That is to say, the consent of a two-thirds majority of the Federal Council is needed only for bills which reduce Land competencies.[19]

c) Land governments[20]

The constitutions of seven Austrian Länder provide for membership of the Land government (*Landesregierung*) to be proportional to the strength of the parties in the Land parliament (*Landtag*).[21] Land governments are thus proportionally elected by Land parliaments. Only the Land governor (*Landeshauptmann*) needs to receive majority support from the Land parliament, though the effect of this latter principle may itself of course militate in favour of coalition-based Land governments. The Land governor is responsible for all delegated federal administration[22] and therefore has great political and administrative power. The 'Conference of the Land Governors' (*Landeshauptmännerkonferenz*) - an informal meeting of the Land governors - is one of the most important centres of co-operative federalism and practical political power in Austria.

Since the system we have just described means that all major Land parties are represented in Land government, the dominant type of political process in Land governments is the system of so-called 'consensual democracy'. Notwithstanding this fact, majority decisions sometimes prove necessary and this leads to the somewhat paradoxical situation that although they remain formally represented in the government, smaller Land parties can simultaneously act as opposition parties.

d) Land parliaments[23]

The practical importance of Land parliaments is usually very low. This is partly due to the fact that the Länder have only minor legislative competencies, but is also a consequence of the system of proportional government. In practice, parliamentary control of government is very weak, as every party - except very small ones - is represented both in parliament and government. Land parliaments therefore degenerate into a sort of discussion-club, in which numerous political petitions to the federal and Land governments are drawn up, but political decisions or laws are hardly ever made.

---

[17] See Walter/Mayer (1996: 136 ff).
[18] See Kathrein (1983); Kathrein (1986: 337 ff) and Schambeck (ed.) (1997).
[19] See Art 44 para 2 B-VG.
[20] See Fallend (1997: 847 ff).
[21] At the time of writing, one of these Länder (Salzburg) is in the process of abolishing this constitutional rule.
[22] See below I.2.e.
[23] See Wolfgruber (1997: 833 ff).

e) Federal and Land administration[24]

Federal administration is organised in two different ways. First, there is a system of so-called 'direct federal administration' (*unmittelbare Bundesverwaltung*), undertaken by special federal authorities located in the Länder, or by federal ministries. This type of administration is constitutionally restricted to specific matters and in practice rather exceptional. Examples include the federal armed forces; public security; financial, postal and railway authorities; the supervision of banking; universities and federal roads.

Second, the Federal Constitution (Art 102 B-VG) provides that the standard type of administration is the so-called 'indirect federal administration' (*mittelbare Bundesverwaltung*), which is delegated to the Land governor and is to be performed by Land authorities at their own expense ('delegated federal administration').[25]

The first level of delegated federal administration is called 'district authority' (*Bezirkshauptmannschaft*), which is the general public administration authority for nearly all branches of federal and Land administration at the first level. At the second level, authorities are divided as follows: The Land governor is responsible for the delegated federal administration; the Land government, as a collective entity, is responsible for Land administration. Only in few cases of national importance does the law provide a third level of delegated federal administration hierarchically located above the Land governor and supervised by the federal minister. A governor who does not act according to the federal minister's directions may thus be prosecuted at the Constitutional Court.

Land administration (*Landesverwaltung*) is organised at two levels. These are district authorities as the first and Land governments (*Landesregierungen*) as the second level. The administrative agency at the second level of Land administration is called the 'Office of the Land Government' (*Amt der Landesregierung*) and this Office also serves the Land governor in fulfilling his tasks as an executive of delegated federal administration.

The typical structure of the administration at the first two levels is the so-called 'mixed administration' (*gemischte Verwaltung*). Both federal and Land tasks are carried out by Länder administrative agencies, which gives the Länder great political and administrative influence. The structure of administration is organised in a manner which ensures that different branches and aspects of public administration are co-ordinated by and integrated into one agency. This system is very unusual in federal states; it was introduced in 1925, when the country was under the economic pressure of both inflation and the conditions imposed in connection with the loans provided by international banks.

Due to this system of combined federal and Land administration at the first two levels, Austrian administration is quite uniform and concentrated. It returns to the Land governments some of the influence they have lost on account of the centralised distribution of competencies. As will be seen later in this text, the Länder have for some time been calling for indirect (delegated) federal administration to be completely turned over to their own administration. The concern that caused them to raise this demand relates to what they regard as the undesirable directive and supervisory power of federal ministers in respect of delegated federal administration (including the

---

[24] See Walter/Mayer (1996: 219 ff and 310 ff) and Öhlinger (1997a: 208 ff).
[25] See Weber (1987).

impeachment of the Land governor) and the fact that Länder have to bear the costs of the delegated federal administration although the competence is formally still federal.

f) Local communities[26]

Local government is guaranteed by the Federal Constitution as an autonomous and democratic system of self-government by the local communities. Its tasks are specified by the Federal Constitution in two ways, namely, by both by means of a general clause of competencies and by an enumeration of specific matters, which are legally defined as belonging to this general clause (Art 118 B-VG).[27]

The general clause of local competencies is determined by the principle of subsidiarity.[28] All matters of exclusive or predominant interest of the local community which may be performed by the local government within its own borders and with its own administrative capacity are within the competence of local communities. Some competencies are enumerated, e.g. local elections, civil services, local police, local traffic, roads, emergency and general rescue services, fire protection, local building regulations, town and country planning, etc..

Each individual local government competence must be confirmed by law. A local government may file an appeal to the Constitutional Court to decide whether a specific law is consistent with the constitutional rights of communities. Besides, local communities have unlimited power to act as private law subjects and subsidise all matters.

Local governments are proportional governments as provided by the Federal Constitution; but in many towns the mayor has to be backed by a coalition, because he has to be elected by the majority of the local council. The mayor has a predominant position, since he organises the administrative offices and is responsible for delegated Land administration. The political importance of local governments varies considerably and depends upon the size and economic powers of the communities, as well as the special traditions of the different Länder.

Large towns (i.e. those exceeding 20,000 inhabitants) and some historically important towns have been given a special status by a city-statute. These statutory cities have all the competencies of local governments and also operate as district authorities at the first level of federal delegated and Land administration. The capital Vienna is not only a local government but also a Land, which means that in Vienna the local authorities act as Land authorities.

For special purposes there are also associations of communities, which are organised either according to public law or private law. They run special public services, such as the water supply, sewage system, waste disposal, traffic and energy-supply. However, they also act as local administration agencies for small communities.

---

[26] See Oberndorfer (1971); Gallent (1978) and Neuhofer (1997: 866 ff).

[27] See Mayer (1997: 313 ff).

[28] See Pernthaler (1996: 290).

g) Constitutional autonomy of the Länder[29]

As has been already mentioned in this text, the Austrian federation was founded by the voluntary accessions of the Länder that were - and still are - autonomous and indestructible Länder with original powers of their own, including their constitutional autonomy. Due to that fact, Land constitutions recognise this right of 'internal self-determination'. This constitutional autonomy is limited only insofar as the Federal Constitution determines the contents of Land constitutions. Beyond those precisely formulated restrictions, however, the Land constitutions are not bound by any general rules or principles of the Federal Constitution.

h) The principles of federal fiscal relations[30]

In Austria, federal fiscal relations are settled not in the Federal Constitution itself, but in a special Fiscal Constitution Act[31] and in a special Tax Sharing Law (*Finanzausgleichsgesetz*),[32] which operates only for a limited period, currently from 1997 to 2000. The financial constitutional system is very clearly set out, with the Länder and communities treated as lower territorial units that are, strictly speaking, only forms of local government at different levels and with different competencies.

The power to assign and share taxes is not reserved to constitutional law, but left to ordinary federal legislation. Federal law has to assign taxes within an abstract constitutional framework of nine types of shared or exclusive forms of tax allocation. The most important types of taxes are exclusive federal taxes, exclusive Land taxes, taxes divided between federal, Land and local governments and exclusive local taxes.

As the Länder have no important taxes of their own, their main revenues come from sharing joint federal taxes in a tripartite system together with local governments, their shares being fixed by federal law. The tax yield is modified by a great number of transfers, such as grants, contributions and cost sharing payments between the governments. In addition there exist numerous non-official cost-sharing arrangements between the federal, Land and local governments to finance special projects or to subsidise private expenditures. The main reason for this unofficial cost-sharing is that Land and local governments want to have certain types of federal expenditures within their territories and that the Federal government 'sells' these services at the price of sharing the costs of politically attractive projects. There is also a substantial reverse flow from Land and local funds to the federal government by means of unofficial financial settlements. This 'grey financial settlement' (*grauer Finanzausgleich*)[33] is regulated by private law agreements and instruments, or by political gentlemen's agreements between governments.

The effect is that Austrian Länder are completely dependent on the federal government as far as their finances are concerned. Notwithstanding the fact that in practice there have always been tripartite negotiations before the adoption of a new tax sharing law that led to political agreements about the tax sharing for the respective period, the bargain positions of the federal government and

---

[29] See Pernthaler (1986: 477 ff) and Marko/Poier (1997: 817 ff).
[30] See Matzner (ed.) (1977) and Pernthaler (1984: 119 ff).
[31] BGBl 1948/45.
[32] BGBl 1996/201.
[33] See Pernthaler (1984: 31 ff).

the 'lower' governments are very unequal. Länder and local communities have no alternative but to accept the determination of fiscal relations by the federal government.

i) Co-operative federalism[34]

Co-operative federalism is a very important feature of Austrian federalism. In uniting the political power of the Länder and in co-ordinating Land administration to counter centralising tendencies, it improves the otherwise weak legal position of the Länder and creates a political power that helps countervail the federal government's overwhelming legal powers.

Some of the instruments of Austrian co-operative federalism have formal legal bases, whilst others are partly informal. Examples of the latter include political and administration agreements and institutions. Each year, heads of Land governments and senior Länder officials meet at a total of over 500 conferences. Some are held at regular intervals, whilst the scheduling of others is determined by the current political agenda. These inter-Land conferences are prepared and the necessary information circulated to the Länder by extra-constitutional institutions and agencies specifically set up for this purpose, the most prominent of which is the 'liaison office' (*Verbindungsstelle der Bundesländer*) of the Länder in Vienna. The most important political institution of Länder co-operation is the Conference of Land Governors, which has regular quarterly meetings, as well as irregular extraordinary meetings called to discuss special issues. There are also two institutions of local governmental co-operation: the Austrian Federation of Towns (*Österreichischer Städtebund*) and the Austrian Federation of Communities (*Österreichischer Gemeindebund*), both of which are mentioned in the Federal Constitution (Art 115 para 3 B-VG).

The most important legal forms of co-operation are the formal public law treaties between federal and Land governments or among the Länder themselves (Art 15a B-VG),[35] and all sorts of private law agreements between the three levels of government. By these legal instruments, or by political agreements, a great number of combined programmes have been launched for special public tasks.

Co-operative federalism is of great political importance. In practice, all major changes in the legal, political or financial situation of the Länder or of local governments are negotiated and cannot be carried out without their consent. Yet since there is no possibility of forcing a Land to co-operate and if, as a consequence, a unanimous vote of the Länder cannot be achieved, the federation will be in a stronger position, since it is empowered to use the legal instruments to change federal law, federal tax sharing law and even the Federal Constitution without the consent of the Länder.

In spite of the increasing political power of the Länder, the principal features of Austrian federalism are still the predominant national role of the federal government in the legal, political, economic and financial process, and the dependence of all other governments on federal planning and policy.

---

[34] See Ermacora (1976: 141 ff) and Weber (1980: 221 ff).
[35] See Öhlinger (1978: 7 ff); Burtscher (1988: 137 ff) and Mayer (1997: 102 ff).

j) The trend towards asymmetrical federalism[36]

In principle, the Länder are equal in competencies and in their legal status as indestructible Länder (Art 2 and 3 B-VG). Notwithstanding this formal basic equality, some institutions and constitutional procedures exist which mean that in practice, the legal and economic position of individual Länder varies. The most important legal dispositions concerning this 'differentiated' federal system are sixfold.

For one, the Länder are empowered to pursue all political and administrative goals by means of financial subsidies, or by private legal institutions, regardless of whether or not those policy priorities pertain to matters for which they are formal competent (Art 17 B-VG).[37] This has to be considered a very important compensation for the extremely limited range of formal competencies held by the Länder. Moreover, since there are considerable differences between the political priorities and room for political manoeuvre of the Länder, as well as in respect of their particular economic and budgetary situation, the logical corollary are significant differences in the legal, political and economic situation of the nine Länder.

Second, the Länder also have a wide range of treaty making powers. They can conclude (national) treaties[38] with other Länder and with the federation. Moreover, they can enter into international treaties[39] within the scope of their competencies (Art 15a and 16 B-VG). These powers have resulted in the establishment of a number of special institutions of regional co-operation between particular Länder and of special joint federal and Land agencies. There also exist some transfrontier co-operation agencies between Länder and neighbouring regions of other countries; though up to now they have not been legally based upon the model-treaties of the Madrid (framework) Convention.

Third, important constitutional and legal differences between the Länder are based on international law guarantees of minority protection to the Slovenian and Croatian (language) minorities (ethnic groups) in the Länder Carinthia, Styria and Burgenland.[40]

Fourth, the Länder have the power to establish their own Land constitutions; albeit within the constraints imposed by the Federal Constitution (Art 99 B-VG).[41] As the Länder use this constitution-making power in very different ways, their constitutions differ considerably in respect of their system of government, their institutions of direct democracy and regarding constitutionally guaranteed principles, individual rights, social institutions, bodies charged with ensuring public accountability and in the powers of their respective parliaments.

Fifth, legal differences between the Länder are also based upon their power to implement federal framework laws and to implement European Union directives, recommendations and programmes that fall within the scope of Land competencies (Art 23d para 5 B-VG).[42] Despite this legal authorisation to adopt different legal solutions, in practice, the implementation of federal or

---

[36] See Pernthaler (1992b).
[37] See Binder (1980) and Korinek/Holoubek (1993).
[38] See Öhlinger (1978: 7 ff).
[39] See Burtscher (1988: 143 ff); Thaler (1990) and Hammer (1992).
[40] See Österreichisches Volksgruppenzentrum (ed.) (1997) and Österreichische Rektorenkonferenz (ed.) (1989).
[41] See Koja (1988). Regarding the Land constitutions of the Tyrol and Vorarlberg, see Pernthaler/Lukasser (1995) and Morscher (1991).
[42] See Öhlinger (1997b: 43 ff).

European 'frames' by Land legislation does not differ very much. They are usually the subject of common implementation strategies agreed between the Länder.

Finally, the only constitutional differences between the Länder that relate to their population size concerns the unequal size of their representation in the Federal Council and the federal constitutional regulation of the limits of salaries for political functionaries. Some minor constitutional differences are based upon the special status of Vienna.

3.3 Länder concerns prior to and during accession

3.3.1 Introduction

The Länder have since 1956 been negotiating with the federation in an attempt to get the latter to implement the propositions contained in their various 'demand programmes' (*Forderungsprogramme der österreichischen Bundesländer*), the objective of which is to achieve a significant structural reform of Austrian federalism.[43] The efforts of the Länder have to date been only partially successful. Certain constitutional amendments implementing Länder demands have been achieved, (in 1974, 1983, 1984, 1987, 1988 and 1990). However, during the same period, the Länder were confronted by antagonistic tendencies of centralisation and stagnation. The discussion about federal reform was revived by the idea of Austria's joining the European Economic Area and European Community. Unlike their German counterparts, the Austrian Länder from the outset regarded those accessions as constituting a serious challenge to the federal system.[44] In the following paragraphs, we will concentrate upon five such groups of problems.

3.3.2 General Problems

Surprisingly, that the Länder were from the outset clearly in favour of joining the EU and presented themselves to the federal government as important partners and opinion leaders during this difficult political process. From the beginning, however, the Länder had also indicated how incisively an accession would affect their autonomy: Their few remaining competencies would, they argued, be further curtailed, while direct participation in EU-decision-making-processes would not be possible for them. Even the loss of federal competencies consequent upon EU accession would affect in the main the Länder, as they would lose their constitutionally granted rights of participation in respect of those federal matters. The example of the German Länder plainly showed the functional loss of Land sovereignty - particularly that of the Land parliaments - caused by the organisation and operation of EU decision-making. The Länder therefore demanded effective measures of compensation and unmistakably hinted both at their constitutional right of obstruction in the Federal Council (Art 50 para 1 B-VG) and at the extent to which it would prove politically impossible for the federal government to win over public support for accession should the Länder decide to oppose it. The latter argument was considered the most important, as a referendum seemed to be constitutionally inevitable.

---

[43] See Pernthaler (1980); Berchtold (1988) and Thanner (1997: 275 ff).
[44] See Pernthaler (ed.) (1989) and Burtscher (1990).

3.3.3 The co-operative accession process

On account of this political situation, the federation deliberately involved the Länder in the national process of preparing and implementing accession. Co-operative federalism gained a totally new and very complicated dimension, to which the Länder were not at all accustomed. Co-operative teams at the Federal Ministry for Foreign Affairs ('European Integration') and at the Federal Chancellor's Office ('Integration Issues', 'EU-Federalism') minutely analysed the likely effects of accession and the legislation which would have to be enacted by the federation and the Länder. A little later, co-operation was legally enshrined in the so-called 'Council for European Integration Policy' (*Rat für Fragen der österreichischen Integrationspolitik*).[45] Thus the course was set for getting the Länder demands accepted.

3.3.4 The procedure of Land participation[46]

As a compensation for the lack of Land participation in the EU, the Länder were granted a new right of participation in European integration matters. It works like this: the Länder are entitled to formulate 'uniform (common) statements' on European integration matters. Moreover, such statements are in principle binding on federal representatives and should only be overruled where there are 'compelling reasons of foreign or integration policy' (Art 23 d para 2 B-VG).[47] The organisational and procedural reality, however, has turned out to be rather difficult and apt to instigate conflicts. The opinion of the federation was that a 'uniform' (albeit not necessarily unanimous) statement would be indispensable; but how to achieve 'uniformity', was controversial:

The Federal Council believed itself (or its standing sub-committee) to be the proper institutional forum in which such statements should be reached, a belief which was strongly resisted by the Länder and which - according to the Federal Constitution and political reality - it would hardly have been possible to implement. The Länder discussed and in the end rejected the possibility of outvoting a Land; instead they accepted the possibility of voting abstention (for as many as four Länder). Just as controversial was the question of participation by Land parliaments, as opposed to the Land governors, who posses a constitutional right of exclusive Land representation. The compromise solution finally hammered out allocated to the presidents (i.e. chairpersons) of the Land parliaments the right to represent the Länder in the 'Integration Conference of the States' (*Integrationskonferenz der Länder*), but did not grant them voting rights. This consultative body was eventually replaced by the 'Standing Integration Committee of the States' (*Ständiger Integrationsausschuß der Länder*).[48]

The Land participation procedure was legally installed by a complex system, consisting of a constitutional amendment, a federation-Land treaty and a Land-Land treaty.[49] The federation-Land treaty entitles the Länder to further rights of participation in EU-matters (especially representation by their own Land representatives and the possibility of bringing actions concerning Land matters to the European Court of Justice).

---

[45] BGBl 1989/368.

[46] See Pernthaler (1992a) and Unterlechner (1997).

[47] See Unterlechner (1997: 25 ff).

[48] See Unterlechner (1997: 48 ff).

[49] See Unterlechner (1997: 5 ff).

3.3.5 Loss of Land competencies

Austria's accession to the EU meant the loss by the Länder of several competencies to the EU, of which we shall mention five such examples of regional and so-called 'sensitive' - competencies.[50] The first relates to regional economic policy. Under Art 17 B-VG, the Länder are currently extraordinarily dominant regarding economic policy and employment policy. Public procurement is largely under their control and they establish various programmes that help to, for example, stimulate the Land economy and subsidise farming within their Land. The second pertains to Land law and in particular the question of transfer of land to foreigners (Art 10 para 1 subpara 6 B-VG), i. e. the restriction of foreign acquisition of land. Furthermore, the Länder are responsible for regional planning, which means that they have the right to determine and supervise the utilisation of land at the level of communities and Länder. The Alpine Länder are particularly keen to limit the possibility of persons acquiring second homes.

The third area of competence concerns economic law. The Länder have the right to regulate certain types of occupation related to tourism or mountain farming. Examples include mountain guides or ski-instructors. The penultimate competence we shall mention refers to legislation in the environmental and nature conservation areas. Here the Länder have significant remaining competencies,[51] as well as exclusive competencies, especially concerning environmental and nature conservation law.[52] Should the EU establish uniform procedures regarding environmental compatibility , this would cause further shifts of competence detrimental to the Länder. Finally, the Länder are responsible for building and running hospitals and for staff regulations. They are also completely responsible for medical supply in the regional and local area.

3.3.6 Attempts at structural reform of the federal system

In compensation for the diminution of their powers which they would suffer as a consequence of Austria's accession to the EU - or rather to the European Economic Area - the Länder demanded competence changes on two different levels: First, in order to prevent alienation and growing scarcity of land, control over the transfer of building plots should speedily become a matter subject to Land legislation. Thereafter, there should be a fundamental reorganisation of the distribution of competencies within the Austrian federation ('Structural Reform of the Distribution of Competencies', or 'Strukturreform der Kompetenzverteilung').[53] The aim of that reform should be to compensate for the loss of Land competencies by means of transferring to the Länder other competencies, which should themselves not be diminished by the EU in the future.

It proved to be very difficult to implement even the first of these Länder aims. Opposition to restricting land acquisition and to possible Land control over the transfer of building plots was extremely fierce. Furthermore, the Federal Minister of Justice resisted the idea of a further reduction in the federation's civil law competencies. in the end, the Länder had to accept that the

---

[50] See Burtscher (1990).

[51] E.g. see Art 10 para 1 subpara 12 B-VG (heating systems regarding air purification and non-dangerous waste regarding waste economy).

[52] See Art 15 para 1 B-VG.

[53] See Öhlinger (1995: 543 ff); Pernthaler/Schernthanner (1995: 559 ff) and Pernthaler (ed.) (1997).

new competence would depend on a treaty with the federation (concerning the application of civil procedural rules for the transfer of land)

In preparation for the total reform of the distribution of competencies, a committee of experts (*'Strukturreformkommission'*) was installed at the Federal Chancellor's Office. It eventually drafted an abstract, academic general concept of a 'structural reform' concerning the distribution of competencies.[54] However, it did not actually formulate a new distribution of competencies, as this was not considered an academic, but a political question, which could not be solved by the committee.

As the Länder realised that negotiations about a fundamental reform of the distribution of competencies could not be concluded before Austria's accession to the EU, they conceived the notion of a 'political pact', the terms of which would oblige the federation to agree to specific reform demands and competence transfers to be undertaken at a later date. The legal transformation itself would then be negotiated in a more detailed manner after accession. The pact ('Political Agreement on the Reorganisation of the Federation') was signed in 1992 by the Federal Chancellor (on behalf of the Federal Government) and by the chairman of the Conference of Land Governors (on behalf of the Land parliaments). It contained an agreement about the timing of constitutional reform which stipulated that a government bill was to be drafted before the date of the referendum on EU-membership, so that it could be enacted no later than the constitutional amendment concerning Austria's EU-accession. However, though a bill entitled 'Structural Reform of the Federation'[55] was indeed drafted, it proved impossible for parliament to enact it. For at the 1994 general election, the incumbent SPÖ/ÖVP grand coalition[56] lost the necessary two-thirds majority in the National Council[57] and the Länder in the end rejected the compromise formula which the government was obliged to negotiate with the opposition on whose voting support the bill now depended.[58]

The most important and substantive elements of reform contained in the pact were the transformation of the system of 'delegated federal administration' into genuine and autonomous Land administration and the installation of Land administrative courts. Both changes would have been most important, not only for financial and organisational reasons, but also because of the legal implications of an independent administrative judiciary. The reform proposal also envisaged the Land governors no longer being bound by the instructions of the federal government or ministers. Moreover, there would have been an assimilation to the organisational standard of federations such as Germany and Switzerland.

The current coalition government again enjoys a two-thirds majority of seats in the National Council and resubmitted its former structural reform bill at the beginning of the new legislation period.[59] Since then, negotiations between federal and Land governments have been concentrating upon details of the 'grand' reform: They finally agreed on a new co-operative 'consultation

---

[54] See Bundeskanzleramt (ed.) (1991).

[55] RV 1706 BlgNR 18. GP.

[56] It comprised the Socialdemocratic Party of Austria (SPÖ) and the Austrian People's Party (ÖVP).

[57] Constitutional amendments need a two-thirds majority in the National Council, where at least half of the members have to be present (Art 44 para 1 B-VG).

[58] Institut für Föderalismusforschung (ed.) (1995: 17 ff).

[59] RV 14 BlgNR 20. GP.

process'[60] to be applied if legislative or administrative acts of one territorial authority impose financial costs upon other authorities. Other parts of the 'grand' reform project, especially the reform of the system of delegated federal administration, of the distribution of competencies in general and the creation of new administrative courts in the Länder, are still being negotiated and will probably be enacted step by step in the future.

3.4 The Länder after Austrian accession

3.4.1 Introduction

Austria's referendum on EU membership took place on 12 June 1994 and showed an overwhelming majority of the population to be in favour (66.6 per cent). As a result, the special constitutional act of accession to the EU could be published[61] and, since 1 January 1995, Austria has been a member of the EU.

The losses of Länder competencies caused by Austria joining the EU seemed to result in a collapse of Länder autonomy. In view of the already very limited range of Land competencies, accession must clearly be regarded as having constituted a total revision[62] of the Federal Constitution, as it had essentially diminished the federal principle.[63]

But though the federal principle was considerably modified by accession, it was not completely abolished. This means that the basic structures of Austria's federal system, as described by this paper, are still valid and working within the context of European law and the 'European Constitution'. Although there are some faint structures of a new European federalism[64] growing in the legal organisation and practical policy of the EU, federalism is legally and politically based mainly upon the internal structure of the member states. Without a clear and sufficient national constitutional base, European regionalism[65] - also as a transnational co-operation process - cannot work properly and cannot answer the new challenges of open European and global markets.

3.4.2 Land Participation and Implementation Procedure

When seeking to assess the role of Austria's Länder in European affairs, there are two main aspects one might consider. The first concerns the extent to which they are permitted to participate in decision-making (and policy formulation) processes in respect of European issues. The second relates to their role in implementing the laws and regulations that derive from those decisions. The following paragraphs will outline the position with respect to each of these two aspects.

---

[60] See Weiss (1997: 153 ff) and Hengstschläger (1997: 196 ff).

[61] BGBl 1995/65.

[62] Art 44 para 3 B-VG.

[63] See Öhlinger (1988: 19 ff); Burtscher (1989: 29 ff) and Burtscher (1990).

[64] See Huber/Pernthaler (eds.) (1988) and Pernthaler (ed.) (1997).

[65] See Huber/Pernthaler (eds.) (1988); Strejcek/Theil (eds.) (1996); Pernthaler (1996: 312 ff) and Wally/Panosch (1997: 178 ff).

The participation of Austria's Länder in the European process of preparing and making decisions is governed by a special Austrian constitutional procedure.[66] It envisages three different forms of participation. First, Federal agencies and representatives to the EU have to provide the Länder and local government authorities with immediate and comprehensive information about all European projects that refer in any way to Länder competencies or interests. Länder and local government representatives also have the right to inform federal agencies and representatives fully about their views and interests regarding the respective European project (Art. 23d para 1 B-VG). If this project falls within the legislative competence of the Länder, the latter have the right to formulate a 'uniform statement', which is, as has already been mentioned above, in principle binding upon federal representatives and should only be overruled where there are 'compelling reasons of foreign or integration policy'(Art. 23d para 2 B-VG). The Länder, however, have of late been quite reluctant to do so[67] and have instead tended to issue ordinary, non-binding 'common statements' under Art 23d para 1 B-VG.

Second, the Länder may be directly represented in the Council, if the subject of negotiation impacts upon Länder legislation and if the representative, who is nominated by the Länder, is authorised by the federal government to do so. The Länder representative then participates in the Council together with the competent federal minister and is bound to a uniform statement of the Länder, unless there are 'compelling reasons of foreign or integration policy' (Art 23d para 3 B-VG). Up to now, there has been only little Länder representation in the Council, the reason for which might be that Länder legislation has not been involved that often.

Third, the Länder and local governments are represented in the (advisory) Committee of the Regions.[68] Each Land may nominate one representative, whereas the Austrian Federation of Towns together with the Austrian Federation of Communities may nominate three representatives (Art 23c para 4 B-VG).

Länder representatives may also participate in various other committees, if they are members of the respective Austrian delegation: Under Art 8 of the federation-Länder agreement,[69] the Länder may be represented at their own expense if their competencies or interests are concerned. Since their representatives are only permitted to speak if their contribution is approved by the delegation's head, their practical influence has to be doubted. Moreover, the Länder have their own representative at the Austrian Permanent Representation. His task is to inform them about relevant facts and look after their interests in general.

---

[66] Art 23c para 4, 23d para 1-4 B-VG. See also the federation-Lander agreement about participation rights of the Länder and local communities regarding European integration issues (BGBl 1992/775); Pernthaler (1992a); Morass (1994) and Unterlechner (1997).

[67] In 1997, there was only one uniform statement (regarding the emissions of small heating systems), which is far less than in the two preceding years (ca. 20 statements). Unterlechner (1997: 71) believes that binding statements lack the flexibility needed for negotiations in the Council and that the time available for the prior co-ordination procedure between the Länder is too limited.

[68] See Unterlechner (1997: 129 ff).

[69] BGBl 775/1992

Each Land[70] (with the exception of Vorarlberg) has its own representation (*Länderbüro*) in Brussels to present its interests and attend the preparatory procedures in European committees, commissions and administrative bodies. The *Länderbüros* are not statutory bodies, as there is no formal Länder competence in the constitution, but they are nevertheless tolerated by the federation. Whilst the representative at the Permanent Representation has to present the joint interests of all Länder, the *Länderbüros* have to consider the advantages of only their individual Land, and this is the main reason why these rather expensive institutions are maintained.[71]

The second key dimension of Länder involvement in European affairs concerns their role in the implementation of EU regulations. The EU is a union of nation states. Their internal structure as federal or unitary states, as centralised or decentralised systems, does not have any legal effect upon the international law obligations of the member states towards the EU, especially regarding the implementation of European directives, or of other legal regulations. The organisation of the EU in the main also reflects this character as a union of states and shows very few traces of subnational or regional representation in the European Union's decision-making-process or administration.

On the other hand, federal or highly regionalised member states usually have constitutional rules that divide competencies regarding the implementation of European law. Thus in Austria, the Länder are constitutionally obliged to implement European law that pertain to their competencies (Art 23d para 5 B-VG). Accordingly, only in cases where the Court of First instance, or the European Court of Justice clearly states that a Land has not implemented a European legal act adequately or on time, is it permissible for the federal legislator or for the system of federal administration to implement that European law on behalf of the defaulting Land. Even such cases, it may only do so provisionally.

However, the systems of these internal distributions of competencies differ very much from those regarding European competencies, because the former were shaped by member states' specific national histories, or political processes. The consequence is that in federal or regional systems individual European acts are very often implemented by both levels of government.

In Austria, it is therefore frequently the case that nine Land and one federal legislative (or administrative) authority have to implement such individual EU acts or political plans, because the respective European act 'touches' both Land and federal competencies. Since only federal agencies are legally responsible for implementation, they claim some co-ordinating and supervising functions as to the internal implementation process of European law, even if they have no regular constitutional competence or power to act like this in spheres of autonomous Länder jurisdiction. this leads to an extraordinary process of centralising Land competencies that fall within the scope of the competencies of EU legislation or political programming.

---

[70] The Italian Parliament has finally agreed to the fact that the Tyrolean *Länderbüro* represents not only the Austrian Land Tyrol, but also the Italian provinces of Trentino and Alto Adige/Südtirol (Act of 24.4.1998, No. 28: '*Disposizioni per l'adempimento di obblighi derivanti dalla appartenenza dell' Italia alle Communità Europee*').
[71] See Institut für Föderalismusforschung (ed.) (1997: 72 ff) and Unterlechner (1977: 85 ff).

3.5 Conclusion

If the project of 'European federalism' is to have any prospect of uniting Europe, it must be a kind of federalism which is based on a great variety of specific political subsystems and different cultural entities. This kind of federalism must be able to protect ethnic differences as well as to integrate homogeneous nation states; it must be applicable both to strongly regionalised and unitary states. European federalism thus has to be developed into a special type of asymmetric federalism, which should integrate strong local governments as well as regional authorities and the constituent units of federal states. The most important means for safeguarding democracy appears to be to ensure that direct involvement in European integration is not limited only to member states, but includes all those national subsystems also.

The legal and economic institutions of the European Union should seek to achieve a balance between the traditional national values of democratic and social identity on the one hand and the new forms of European freedom and peaceful union on the other. European institutions will therefore certainly have to rely for some considerable time to come on nation states and their specific political systems. It is of vital importance, however, that these states' political subsystems, which are much closer to the citizens, are not only partners in their respective national systems, but also become direct partners in the European integration process.

Are there any grounds for optimism regarding the model frequently referred to as 'Europe of the Regions'? To permit the answer to this question to be in the affirmative, we would need to ensure the existence of appropriate frameworks at two different legal levels. First, there would have to be a clear and sufficient constitutional basis for local and regional governance. Second, at the level of the European Union there needs to be a legal guarantee which secures participation and co-operation between on the one hand European institutions and on the other, subnational political systems, such as regions or local communities. At present, the latter does not seem as well developed as the national constitutional provisions. To be sure, we do have the principle of subsidiarity, the Committee of the Regions, as well as various forms of direct co-operation and partnership between European institutions and regional or local units. In reality, however, these regional elements are far less powerful within European institutions than the member states and their representatives. It therefore seems to be clear that the relative influence of the regions both on and within European institutions and must be increased.

Such considerations are important when one seeks to assess whether European Union membership has improved the position of Austrian federalism, or brought about a new process of centralisation. What we are confronted with is a contradictory and inconsistent 'dual federalism', which has not been constructed on the basis of an integrated theory, but has emerged as a result of two different integration processes. There is only one possible alternative to the structural legal problems which this duality entails, namely, to ensure that, where the autonomous spheres of Land and local government competencies are directly effected by EU institutions and decision-making processes, there is a stronger direct representation of the Länder and local communities in the organisations and decision-making processes of the European Union. This is the only way to create a really democratic and federal European Union.

Bibliography

Adamovich, L. K., Funk, B.-C. and Holzinger, G., (1997) *Österreichisches Staatsrecht I: Grundlagen*, Vienna - New York: Springer.

Berchtold, K., (1988) *Die Verhandlungen zum Forderungsprogramm der Bundesländer seit 1956*, Vienna: Braumüller.

Binder, B., (1980) *Der Staat als Träger von Privatrechten*, Vienna - New York: Springer

Bundeskanzleramt (ed.), (1991) *Neuordnung der Kompetenzverteilung in Österreich*, Vienna: Bundeskanzleramt.

Burtscher, W., (1988) 'Die völkerrechtlichen Aspekte des Forderungskataloges der österreichischen Bundesländer im Vergleich zu bestehenden 'Außenkompetenzen' anderer Gliedstaaten', *Österreichische Zeitschrift für öffentliches Recht und Völkerrecht*, Vol. 39, No. 2, p. 137.

Burtscher, W. (1989) 'Auswirkungen eines EG-Beitrittes auf den bundesstaatlichen Aufbau Österreichs - materielle und institutionelle Aspekte' in Pernthaler, P.(ed.), *Auswirkungen eines EG-Beitrittes auf die föderalistische Struktur Österreichs*, Vienna: Braumüller, pp. 29-59.

Burtscher, W., (1990) *EG-Beitritt und Föderalismus*, Vienna: Braumüller.

Ermacora, F., (1976) *Österreichischer Föderalismus*, Vienna: Braumüller.

Fallend, F., (1997) 'Landesregierung und Landesverwaltung' in Dachs, H. *et al* (eds), *Handbuch des politischen Systems Österreichs. Die Zweite Republik*, Vienna: Manz (3rd edn) pp. 847-865.

Funk, B.-C., (1980) *Das System der bundesstaatlichen Kompetenzverteilung im Lichte der Verfassungsrechtsprechung*, Vienna: Braumüller.

Gallent, K., (1978) *Gemeinde und Verfassung*, Graz: Leykam.

Hammer, S., (1992) *Länderstaatsverträge*, Vienna: Braumüller.

Hengstschläger, J., (1997) 'Der Finanzausgleich im Bundesstaat' in Schambeck, H. (ed.), *Bundesstaat und Bundesrat in Österreich*, Vienna: Verlag Österreich, p.196.

Huber, S. and Pernthaler, P. (eds), (1988) *Föderalismus und Regionalismus in europäischer Perspektive*, Vienna: Braumüller.

Institut für Föderalismusforschung (ed.), (1995) *19. Bericht über die Lage des Föderalismus in Österreich*, Vienna: Braumüller.

Institut für Föderalismusforschung (ed.), (1997) *21. Bericht über dir Lage des Föderalismus in Österreich,,* Vienna: Braumüller.

Kathrein, I., (1983) *Der Bundesrat in der Ersten Republik*, Vienna: Braumüller.

Kathrein, I., (1986) 'Der Bundesrat' in Schambeck, H. (ed.), *Österreichs Parlamentarismus: Werden und System*, Berlin: Duncker und Humblot, pp.337-401

Koja, F., (1988) *Das Verfassungsrecht der österreichischen Bundesländer*, Vienna - New York: Springer.

Korinek, K. and Holoubek, M., (1993) *Grundlagen staatlicher Privatwirtschaftsverwaltung*, Graz: Leykam.

Marko J. and Poier K., (1997) 'Die Verfassungssysteme der österreichischen Bundesländer: Institutionen und Verfahren repräsentativer und direkter Demokratie', in Dachs, H. *et al* (eds), *Handbuch des politischen Systems Österreichs. Die Zweite Republik*, Vienna: Manz, (3rd edn) pp. 817-832.

Matzner, E. (ed.), (1977) *Öffentliche Aufgaben und Finanzausgleich*, Vienna: Orac.

Mayer, H., (1997) *Das österreichische Bundes-Verfassungsrecht*, Vienna: Manz.

Morass, M., (1994) *Regionale Interessen auf dem Weg in die Europäische Union*, Vienna: Braumüller.

Morscher, S., (1991) *Das Verfassungsrecht der österreichischen Bundesländer: Tirol*, Vienna: Österreichische Staatsdruckerei.

Neuhofer, H., (1997) 'Gemeinden', in Dachs, H. *et al* (eds), *Handbuch des politischen Systems Österreichs. Die Zweite Republik*, Vienna: Manz, (3rd edn), pp. 866-876.

Oberndorfer, P., (1971) *Gemeinderecht und Gemeindewirklichkeit*, Linz: Institut für Kommunalwissenschaften.

NEW CENTRALISM VERSUS FEDERAL REFORM ?

Öhlinger, T., (1978) *Verträge im Bundesstaat*, Vienna: Braumüller.

Öhlinger, T., (1988) *Verfassungsrechtliche Aspekte eines Beitritts Österreichs zu den EG*, Vienna: Signum.

Öhlinger, T., (1995) 'Das Scheitern der Bundesstaatsreform', *Österreichisches Jahrbuch für Politik '94*, pp.543-558.

Öhlinger, T., (1997a) *Verfassungsrecht*, Vienna: WUV-Universitätsverlag.

Öhlinger, T., (1997b) 'Bundesstaatsreform und Europäische Integration', in Pernthaler, P. (ed.), *Bundesstaatsreform als Instrument der Verwaltungsreform und des europäischen Föderalismus*, Vienna: Braumüller, p.43.

Österreichische Rektorenkonferenz (ed.), (1989*) Lage und Perspektiven der Volksgruppen in Österreich*, Vienna: Böhlau.

Österreichisches Volksgruppenzentrum (ed.), (1997) *Volksgruppenreport 1997*, Vienna: Hermagoras.

Pernthaler, P., (1979) *Die Staatsgründungsakte der österreichischen Bundesländer*, Vienna: Braumüller.

Pernthaler, P., (1980) *Das Forderungsprogramm der österreichischen Bundesländer*, Vienna: Braumüller.

Pernthaler, P., (1984) *Österreichische Finanzverfassung*, Vienna: Braumüller.

Pernthaler, P., (1986) 'Die Verfassungsautonomie der österreichischen Bundesländer', *Juristische Blätter*, Vol. 108, pp.477-487.

Pernthaler, P., (1989) *Kompetenzverteilung in der Krise*, Vienna: Braumüller.

Pernthaler, P. (ed.), (1989) *Auswirkungen eines EG-Beitritts auf die föderalistische Struktur Österreichs*, Vienna: Braumüller.

Pernthaler, P., (1992a) *Das Länderbeteiligungsverfahren an der europäischen Integration*, Vienna: Braumüller.

Pernthaler, P., (1992b) *Der differenzierte Bundesstaat*, Vienna: Braumüller.

Pernthaler, P., (1996) *Allgemeine Staatslehre und Verfassungslehre*, Vienna-New York: Springer.

Pernthaler, P. (ed.), (1997) *Bundesstaatsreform als Instrument der Verwaltungsreform und des europäischen Föderalismus*, Vienna: Braumüller.

Pernthaler, P. and Lukasser, G., (1995) *Das Verfassungsrecht der österreichischen Bundesländer: Vorarlberg*, Vienna: Verlag Österreich.

Pernthaler, P. and Ortino, S., (1997) *Europaregion Tirol*, Bozen: Europäische Akademie Bozen.

Pernthaler, P. and Schernthanner, G., (1995) 'Bundesstaatsreform 1994', *Österreichisches Jahrbuch für Politik '94*, pp. 559-595.

Schambeck, H. (ed.), (1997) *Bundesstaat und Bundesrat in Österreich*, Vienna: Verlag Österreich.

Strejcek, G. and Theil, M., (eds), (1996) *Regionalisation in Österreich und Europa*, Vienna: WUV-Universitätsverlag.

Thaler, M., (1990) *Die Vertragsschlußkompetenz der österreichischen Bundesländer*, Vienna - Köln: Böhlau.

Thanner, T., (1997) 'Bundesstaatsreform und Forderungsprogramme der Bundesländer', in Schambeck, H. (ed.), *Bundesstaat und Bundesrat in Österreich*, Vienna: Verlag Österreich, p. 275.

Unterlechner, J., (1997) *Die Mitwirkung der Länder am EU-Willensbildungs-Prozeß*, Vienna: Braumüller.

Wally, S. and Panosch, M., (1997) 'Europäischer Regionalismus', *Journal für Rechtspolitik*, Vol. 5, No. 2, p.178.

Walter, R. and Mayer, H. (1996) *Grundriß des österreichischen Bundesverfassungsrechts*, Vienna: Manz.

Weber, K., (1980) *Kriterien des Bundesstaates*, Vienna: Braumüller.

Weber, K., (1987) *Die mittelbare Bundesverwaltung*, Vienna: Braumüller.

Weiss, J., (1997) 'Der Konsultationsmechanismus als Instrument zur Reduzierung der Folgekosten gesetzgeberischer Maßnahmen', *Journal für Rechtspolitik*, Vol. 5, No. 3, p.153.

Werndl, J., (1984) *Die Kompetenzverteilung zwischen Bund und Ländern*, Vienna: Braumüller.

Wolfgruber, E., (1997) 'Landtag', in Dachs, H. *et al* (eds), *Handbuch des politischen Systems Österreichs Die Zweite Republik*, Vienna: Manz, (3rd edn), pp.833-846.

4

AUSTRIA AND THE ENLARGEMENT DEBATE:

IS GEOGRAPHY DESTINY ?

Thomas Nowotny

It has been claimed that 1989 brought the 'return of history', the normal flow of which had been held back by the barrage of totalitarian systems as they arose in Europe after 1917, 1933 and 1945. With these obstacles removed, Europe - and especially its Eastern realm - would, it was maintained, revert to what had been the common and well-known pattern before the arrival of totalitarian governance. This is a patently over-simplistic view. One should neither pretend, nor assume, that changes were absent, that economic, political, and cultural developments did not occur in societies located in what one might perhaps refer to as the 'deep freeze' of Communism.

Nonetheless, the events of 1989 and those in the following years have to be seen and analysed against the background of larger, secular trends that reach far back into history. The issue of the transition countries' accession to the European Union, and also Austria's policy towards its eastern neighbours cannot be dissociated from these long-term, historical trends.

4.1 The Region

The states of the region are young. At the beginning of the 19th century, just four covered the area between the Baltic, the Adriatic and the Black Sea: Prussia, Russia, the Ottoman Empire, and Austria. By the end of the 20th century, their number has risen to 24. The building and consolidation of these states was associated with much violence, and as the underlying dilemma still persists, the situation is still fluid today. The principle of the nation state as the exclusive home of one ethnic group (or of a state that at least gives preference, or dominance, to one ethnic group) is in conflict with the reality of a vast inter-mingling of many different ethnic groups. In Central/Eastern Europe, this century has therefore been one of vast 'ethnic cleansing'. One may hope that the worst is over, but - as recent events in Kosovo have reminded us - it would be naïve to assume that all is over.

Even without the added burden of Communism and its historical legacy, the region of Central/Eastern Europe has been less stable and consolidated than the western part of the Continent; and it has tended to 'export' this instability. Various theories of European integration - functionalism, neo-functionalism, institutionalism etc - assume that politics is driven by rational choices and rational expectations; and that most of these goals are economic ones. Citizens would, such theorists have claimed, support integration because it enhances their well-being. But politics centred on ethnic identity are not focused on such economic considerations, but on inclusion and exclusion. They are not rational in the sense understood by the 'functionalist'. Moreover, the distinction between these two modes of politics is of more than merely theoretical relevance. It points to a serious dilemma that has plagued Central/Eastern Europe, where waves of modernisation alternated with lapses into nationalist indolence. The newness of the nation states is linked to the desire to be self-sufficient and unique. European integration, on the other hand, is based upon the assumption that citizens would forfeit their desire 'to belong' in the rational search for greater comfort and security. The enlargement of the European Union is based upon the assumption that the new nations, too, would come to share this goal.[1]

An historic pattern has also returned in the economic 'pecking order' of the countries of Central/Eastern Europe,[2] but it has been affected by the long reign of Communism. In an article written some time ago, Kenneth Galbraith once claimed that, if measured by its economic achievements, Communism had not done too badly. According to Galbraith, the German Democratic Republic (GDR), for instance, could be seen as a successor to old Prussia. This eastern province of the old German Empire had always been a somewhat poorer than Germany's more western and southern regions. At the time of Galbraith's article, the general opinion was that the GDR was just slightly poorer than the German Federal Republic. This was also the view of the United States' Central Intelligence Agency, which believed that the GDR's gross domestic product was close to that of the UK. If that had been the case, the Communist regime would indeed have had neutral economic effects. If this thesis were correct, the GDR would - contrary to communist claims - not have produced more enhanced growth rates than would have been achieved had the country been organised as part of the capitalist system, but it would also not have pushed growth very much below this level. Today, we know that these assumptions were wildly off the mark. Those countries that lived under Communist regimes fell behind economically. If measured against one another, the historic 'pecking order' has been restored in Central/Eastern Europe: Hungary is wealthier than Poland; and Poland is wealthier than the Ukraine. But the gap separating this group of countries from the western part of the Continent has widened. Austrians have certainly not failed to notice this.

The territory that today forms the Czech Republic used to be the most industrialised and economically most advanced part of the old Austro-Hungarian Monarchy. In the period before the two World Wars, the gap between it and Austria widened, with the standard of living being considerably higher in Czechoslovakia than in the First Austrian Republic. By 1990, though, the

---

[1] Thus the policies of present European Union members towards Eastern Central Europe have always been influenced primarily by political considerations. Economic motives were always a distant second. See for instance the recommendations of the European Socialdemocrats (Eatwell, 1995)

[2] Gross domestic product gives quite a good indication of where a country stands in the world. The level and the development of productivity points quite clearly to where it will go in the future. Military power adds very little to this position. Attempts to enhance the position of a nation over and above this benchmark set by the economy - for instance by high spending for the military - has always ended in disaster (as Paul Kennedy (1987) has reminded us). At least in the presnet day, competition between nations is thus won on the battlefield of economic performance. In fact, the Cold War was the first vast and long-lasting confrontation to have been won exclusively by economic means. The Communist Empire collapsed due to its economic inefficiency. Had its wealth grown at a rate of six per cent or more per year, it would arguably still exist.

situation was reversed - very much to the detriment of Czechoslovakia. If measured in purchasing power parity, per capita wealth in Austria was nearly twice as high as in the Czech Republic.[3] (see Table 3.6).

There is a positive aspect to this: being so far behind opens the prospect of catching up rapidly. The European Bank for Reconstruction and Development (where I work) has looked at other regions that have managed to 'catch up' at a fast pace: namely post-war western Europe and East Asia. The European Bank for Reconstruction and Development tried to ascertain which factors were present to permit such rapid economic growth. It found that being relatively far behind was indeed one of them. The others were proximity to important markets, an acceptable infrastructure, and human capital - especially that of skilled labour.

Figure 4.1   Education levels in post-Communist, developing & semi-developed countries

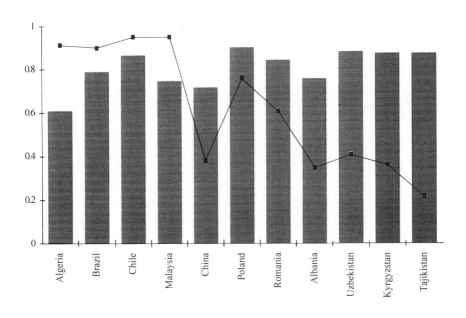

Source: UNDP (1996), *Human Development Report*, Oxford University Press, by kind permission.
Note: The GDP index (line graph) captures each country's ranking in terms of real gross domestic product per capita. The education index (depicted in columns) is a ranking based on first-, second-, and third-level gross enrolment and adult literacy rates in 1993.

---

[3] Czechoslovakia, was, of course an exception. According to Butschek (1993), the average wealth of the various other countries in Central and Eastern Europe has been between 40 per cent and 80 per cent of that of pre-WWII Austria. Today, however, the gap is of course much greater.

As Figure 4.1 shows, the human capital of skilled labour is indeed abundant in eastern Europe, which ranks far above developing or semi-developed countries in this respect. Other factors that would permit a rapid process of 'catching-up' are also present. This might lead one to assume that growth could be fast and even more rapid than growth in East Asia.

The European Bank for Reconstruction and Development does not, however, believe that actual growth will be that vigorous. As the upper figure in the centre-column of Figure 4.2 indicates, growth is not likely to exceed 4.5 percent. Why this difference between a theoretically possible and an actually feasible level of economic growth? In Central/Eastern Europe, growth is held back by institutional deficiencies. It is the latter - and not for instance shortage of capital - which present the most serious bottleneck for future development. This was underlined by the setbacks suffered by Bulgaria, Albania, Romania, Latvia, Lithuania and - to a certain extent - even by the Czech Republic. All of these setbacks were caused by institutional failures. From this, two lessons can be drawn, both of which have a bearing upon the process of accession to the European Union. First, institutional reform and consolidation is a key requirement for accession. This was pointed out to all applicant countries in the 'avis' of the European Commission in July 1997, and also in all of the 'accession partnership' documents that were agreed upon in March 1998. Second, the most crucial contribution the European Union can make to the further advancement of Central/Eastern Europe is precisely in this field of institutional reform and consolidation.

Figure 4.2   Growth potential and prospects in transition economies

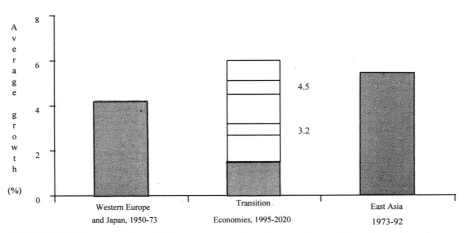

Source: ERBD (ed.) (1997) *Transition Report 1997.* A comparison of 'growth factors' present in two other 'catch-up' periods (post-war Western Europe and East Asia 1960-1980) would have us assume that the transition countries could grow even faster. Institutional deficiencies, however, reduce this potential to an average between 3.2 and 4.5 per cent.

Central/Eastern Europe did not 'return to history' in a time machine, travelling back to the point where Communists seized power. Communism changed these societies profoundly, causing damage which is difficult to repair. Nonetheless, after the fall of Communism, some of the older, historic patterns in economic relations did re-emerge . Up to 1989, trade amongst the Communist countries was quite intense. When measured in the percentages of each country's exports that went to the other members of this Communist sub-region at that time, the Central/Eastern European states had in fact become as integrated as the European Union. This trade pattern of sub-regional integration has disappeared. Central/Eastern Europe has returned to its historic trade pattern with its commercial exchanges being centred upon western Europe.[4]

Table 4.1   **Re-orientation of Central/Eastern European 6 trade exports, 1989-95 (%)**

CEE exports to:	1989	1995
Former CMEA *	47	23
EU-15	35	63
USA	2	2
Japan	1	1
Rest of the World	15	11

* Because of disparities in the methodology used (notably the rouble conversion rate and
   eastern Germany's position), these data should be taken as indicative rather than precise.
Source: Eurostat (1997).

The same holds true for direct foreign investment (FDI, that is to say, investment directly in the 'real' economy and not merely in financial markets). The bulk of such investment comes from western Europe (see Table 4.4). Its volume has grown markedly and it has become an important agent in economic transformation. This is demonstrated, for example, by the especially rapid structural change in Hungary, which leads all other Central/Eastern European countries as a recipient of FDI (if measured in per capita terms). FDI has become an important agent for change, especially in the more advanced transition countries. However, the annual net investment flows are still far below those which these countries require. Thus Begg *et al.* (1990) estimated that level to be of the order of between 100 and 200 billion US $ per annum.[5]

We therefore conclude that the countries of Central/Eastern Europe are drawing closer to the rest of Europe again. However, they start this process from points a considerable distance away from the West, since Communism exacerbated the pre-existing relative disadvantage of the East vis-à-vis the West and has thrown the former countries far back behind the point where they would have been today had Communism not intervened. This 'catching up' is rapid in some fields (for

---

[4] The movement started even before the various trade agreements with the European Union entred into force. One should thus assume that at least a large proportion of this trade would have developed in this direction even in the absence of such agreements. One reason for this fast re-structuring of foreign trade was the decision to opt for a liberal trade regime. To relatively small industrialised countries, no other option was available. Unlike China (Csaba 1994), they could not chose 'autarky'.

[5] As a closer scrutiny shows (EBRD, 1998), the impact of the Asian crisis upon FDI in Central and Eastern Europe was negligible. FDI will continue to be significant, and its volume will increase further.

example trade and investment relations) and slower and very uneven in others. (It seems autonomous to a certain degree, as the pattern of historic Europe re-emerges). But 'catching up' is nonetheless influenced and promoted by politics and policies. Effective and functioning constitutions are essential. In reality, however, institutional performance is uneven, and the further east a country is located, the weaker its record. This increase in institutional inefficiency and failure is reflected in widespread corruption - a phenomenon that if unchecked might jeopardise not only wealth and internal peace but even the survival of the state.

The uneven performance of institutions has enhanced the already existing differences between the transition countries of Central and Eastern Europe. They are currently more marked than at any time in their recent history. This is a fact that simply cannot be disregarded by the European Union, and which is bound to affect European Union policy. We could wish that the European Union would find it difficult to accept this large and growing diversity among Central and Eastern European countries , as such an acceptance implies acceptance too of 'new dividing lines in Europe'. We could prefer that all applicant countries are treated in the same manner. We might think it sensible that membership negotiations should commence at the same time for all applicant countries (the 'start-line model'). At the outset, Austria did indeed favour such an approach. In the end, however, it sided with the European Commission and opted for the model now chosen. It seems unjust to risk the creation of new dividing lines in Europe. But such lines - such differences- already exist. It would have been even more unjust had one ignored them and treated as equal things that are so blatantly unequal.

Figure 4.3   Corruption and physical distance from Brussels[6]

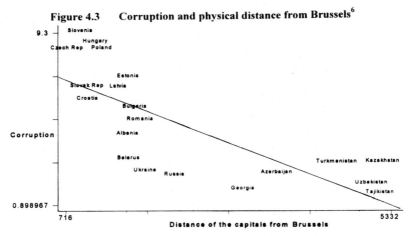

Source: 'The Great Growth Race', *Central European Economic Review*, Vol. 3, No. 10, pp. 8-14. The index is based upon surveys among business people active in the transition countires.

---

[6] The title of the figure is of course a bit 'tongue in cheek'. The relevant and causal factor is cetrainly not distance as such, but the end result of historic processes that have been influenced by geography.

4.2 Austria and the region 1955-1998

Ever since it established itself as a state and nation, Austria has been torn between conflicting foreign and security policy goals. On the one hand, it aimed for a special role in its immediate region and especially among its Central European neighbours. On the other hand, it was conscious of never having marched in the first ranks of wider modernisation. It wanted to close this historic gap, become as 'European' as the West European countries, and thus be accepted as an equal among them. A third constant was Austria's fretting over relations with its powerful neighbour, Germany. The process of nation-building had been one in which Austrians had learned to define themselves as 'non Germans'; as something distinct. It was intended that Austria's foreign and security policy should emphasise that distinction

This inherent conflict between diverging goals did not become an issue in the time immediately after the achievement of full sovereignty in 1955. Attention then was absorbed by some overdue 'housekeeping': normalising relations with Yugoslavia, settling outstanding issues with Germany, coming to an agreement with Italy on the question of the South Tyrol. But this having been done, attention increasingly turned towards the three goals mentioned above. A policy of 'active neutrality' clearly marked Austria out as different from Germany. Co-operation with the West was pushed to the limits of what was possible at a time of continued East-West tension. The results of this strategy came first in the form of the 1973 free trade agreements with the then European Community. In the field of trade, these agreements brought to Austria most of the benefits of full European Community membership.

At the outset, some controversy surrounded Austria's pursuit of the third goal of good relations with its eastern neighbours. Austrians were overwhelmingly anti-Communist, with no marked differences on this matter between the centre-left Social Democrats and the centre-right People's Party. Seeking closer contacts with Communist rulers was not popular. Thus there was some uproar when the then foreign minister Bruno Kreisky visited Hungary in 1959 - the first Western statesman to do so - and called upon prime minister Janos Kádár (the 'butcher' of 1956). Yet long-term interests of the state prompted Austria's politicians to ignore such sentiment. They had to assume that the Communist regimes were here to stay for quite some time and thus it would have been unwise not to meet the desire of (most of) the Central and East European countries (and of course of their people) to have as much contact with the 'West' as their Soviet overlords and 'real existing socialism' permitted. The goals of Austria's 'Ostpolitik' remained unchanged after Kreisky had left government in 1964. The new conservative prime minister Josef Klaus himself took charge of relations with the East and pursued the same policy goals and priorities. As Chancellor from 1970, Kreisky stuck to that course too.

After 1989, there was a belated intellectual backlash against Austria's policies towards its Communist neighbours. Austria's diplomats and politicians were accused of having become too friendly with repressive dictators, and of thus having propped up the decaying Communist empire.[7] I believe that this accusation has the whiff of self-indulgent polemics and is unjustified - not least

---

[7] Examples include Tony Judt's 1996 article in the *New York Review of Books* and a vitriolic article by the Hungarian writer Gaspar M Tamas, which appeared in *Profil* on 27th April 1998.

given Austria's active and effective support for dissidents and other persons persecuted by Communist authorities. But perhaps the story is best told by a remarkable incident: in 1975, when the Helsinki declaration was signed at a summit meeting of the Conference on Security and Cooperation in Europe. In his speech, Chancellor Kreisky departed from the text prepared for him by diplomats. The only Western statesmen to use such clear and unequivocal language, Kresiky said the following:

> This declaration will consolidate co-existence. But it will not put an end to the ideological battle between two opposing and mutually exclusive political systems and doctrines. You gentlemen from the East, you believe that - in the long run - you will win over the democracies. But let me tell you: you are mistaken. It is we who will emerge victorious.

Austria's 'Ostpolitik' was enacted on many levels - political, economic and cultural. It was also supplemented by initiatives of the Austrian *Länder* (the constituent states of the Austrian Federal Republic). One example is the 'ARGE Alpen Adria', a loose partnership between the *Länder* and various regions of bordering countries, which embraced regions of one NATO country (Italy), one neutral country (Austria); one non-aligned country (Yugoslavia); and one Warsaw Pact country (Hungary). The search for areas of practical co-operation also motivated the Central European Initiative (originally the 'Quadrilaterale' between Italy, Austria, Hungary, and Yugoslavia).[8]

Table 4. 2   **Main sources of finance for Central/Eastern European countries and the newly independent states of the former Soviet Union (1990-95)**

	Total Net Flows			Of Which Concession Aid		
	$ million	$ per capita	% of total	$ million	$ per capita	% of total
Bilateral						
Germany	64441	797	59.2	16,809	208	38.9
United States	14,272	55	13.1	8,960	35	20.8
Austria	4,489	568	4.1	1,713	217	4.0
France	4,464	78	4.1	2,947	51	6.8
United Kingdom	3,764	65	3.4	1,948	34	4.5
Japan	2,428	19	2.2	1,665	13	3.9
Netherlands	2,378	156	2.2	1,125	74	2.6
Total: above countries	96,236		88.4	35,167		81.5
Multilateral						
IMF	14,756		40.8	104		1.3
EC	10,350		28.6	6,959		85.7
World Bank/IDA	7,573		21.0	456		5.6
EBRD	2.,18		7.0	122		1.5
Total: above agencies	35,197		97.4	7,641		94.1

Note: The percentages shown are separate for bilateral and multilateral sources, and for total and concessional finance. Bilateral figures include contributions to the EBRD and the European Commission. Source: OECD (1997). (Unfortunately, no OECD figures are available for the years after 1995.)

---

[8] Other motives of the founders were support for ailing Yugoslavia and the desire not to have Germany as the only Western 'player' in the region.

After 1989, the European Union emerged as the main partner of, and actor in, Central and Eastern Europe. Before it became a full member in 1995, Austria had to try to influence these European Union policies from the outside. 'Eastern' issues in fact became quite prominent in Austria's relations with the European Union. Acting in support of French President Mitterrand, and in tandem with him, the Austrian Chancellor Franz Vranitzky, for instance, took a leading role in the establishment of the European Bank for Reconstruction and Development, which today provides substantial assistance in support of the process of economic transformation and renewal. Both Vranitzky and his foreign minister, Alois Mock, were tireless (and mostly frustrated)[9] in their pleas to the European Union to become involved in halting the slide to disaster in former Yugoslavia.

Austria provided ample assistance to the transition countries (mainly to the Central and Eastern European Countries). When one measures such assistance as a proportion of the donor country's GDP, one finds that for a number of years, Austria shared with Germany the distinction of being the most generous provider of such aid.

Notwithstanding all these efforts, the goals of Austria's 'Western policy' and 'Eastern policy' clearly remained to some extent mutually exclusive. Until 1989, the policy of permanent neutrality still limited participation in some European institutions. And the West, for its part, would not have supported all initiatives Austria took in its relations with the East. They might well have been useful to the West (as were many of the Austrian activities in the Conference on Security and Cooperation in Europe, for example), but Austria could only act in the manner it did precisely because it was not fully integrated into the Western camp.

Nonetheless, the forces of autonomous social and economic development slowly pulled Austria away from the East. After WWI, half of its trade had been with what later became the Communist countries. This percentage dropped to 30 per cent on the eve of WWII, and had by the 1950s shrunk to 20 per cent. By 1989, it had dropped to less than 10 per cent. Demographic change in Austria shadowed these economic developments: Both the population and economic dynamism shifted westwards, while the long 'dead' borders with Communist countries (half of all Austrian borders) became economically 'anaemic'.

Austria's own membership of the European Union, and the forthcoming accession of at least the majority of its eastern neighbours will eliminate this age-old dilemma in Austria's foreign and security policy.[10] It is not that new cards will then have been dealt, or that Austria would now be able to re-arrange its priorities. The game as such has changed. The old dilemma of the pursuit of conflicting goals has been superseded. With Austria's eastern neighbours having become members of the same club, and with their participation in common decision-making, the conflict of goals will have ceased to exist. This also pertains to the continuing desire to assert Austria's own identity. In an age of interdependence, this is more readily achieved by participation in such decision-making, than in the vain search for autonomy.

---

[9] One exception was the EFTA industrial fund, which came too late, however, to serve its intended purpose of supporting the central government in Belgrade.

[10] In its July 1991 'avis' on the Austrian membership application, the European Commission specifically pointed to what the Union would gain from Austria's historic and present connections to the region in which it is embedded three years earlier these connections would arguably have been perceived by the Commission as drawbacks

4.3 The impact upon Austria of the current regimes governing relations with the 'accession partnership countries'.

As shown in Table 4.3, trade has been rapidly restructured in the reforming countries of Central and Eastern Europe. This change was supported first by the European Union's free trade agreements, which were followed by association agreements. Austria was one of those to profit most. Its exports to the transition countries increased by 311 per cent in the period between 1989 and 1996. This increase in exports stimulated the economy. Cumulative growth in the period was about 4 per cent faster than it would have otherwise been. Not only was wealth created, but also an additional 56,000 jobs.[11]

Table 4.3   Development of Austria's trade with the transition countries (1996)

	Index (1989=100)		Share of Total Trade	
	Export	**Import**	**% of total exports**	**% of total imports**
East/Central Europe	311.2	241.6	9.6	6.4
Hungary	280.5	244.3	4.0	2.7
Czech R. & Slovakia	508.7	310.4	4.6	2.9
All Transition countries	227.7	204.0	15.4	10.0
World	142.6	188.5	100	100

Source: Eurostat

Table 4.4   Foreign direct investment (FDI) in transition countries' stock (end of 1997)

Origin Country	Total FDI in all Transition Countries		FDI in Central/Eastern Europe		
	Mio US$	**% of total**	**Origin Country**	**Mio US$**	**% of total**
USA	11,710	21	Germany	6,938	21
Germany	8,783	15	USA	6,668	20
Netherlands	3,756	7	France	2,914	9
France	3,646	6	Austria	2,823	8
Austria	3,570	6	Netherlands	1,946	6
Switzerland	3,174	6	Italy	1,568	5
UK	2,322	4	Switzerland	1,184	4
Italy	1,840	3	UK	770	2
Others	17,944	32	Others	8,772	26
Total	56,744	100		33,583	100

Source: Austria Ministry of the Economy (ABT. X/A/2, Spring 1998).

---

[11] According to Economic Minister Johann Farnleitner, *Die Presse,* 28.04.98.

Austria's economy is largely based upon small and medium-sized enterprises. With some spectacular exceptions, few had previously dared to venture abroad and to set up production facilities in other countries. Yet they have now seized the opportunity provided by the opening up of the east. In terms of volume, Austria is the leading investor in two of the applicant countries (Slovenia and Slovakia). Overall, it holds fourth place, providing $2.8 billion, that is 8 per cent of all FDI in the Central and Eastern European countries Table 4.4). This puts it far ahead of, for example, the United Kingdom. (2 per cent). For the Austrian economy, this was the first sustained and broad diversification achieved by moving abroad. It reflects not only the desire to conquer new markets that have the advantage of being geographically close, but is also a response to the challenges of globalisation. It permits outsourcing of some more labour-intensive production processes and a diversification of suppliers and customers.

As already been mentioned above, western Austria had ever since WWII developed more dynamically than the eastern part of the country. The intensification of economic relations with Austria's eastern neighbours now provided a stimulus to the eastern part of Austria and especially to the region around Vienna. Indeed, the city authorities were very optimistic as to the positive impact which the opening of the eastern frontiers would have on the development of the city. As yet, not all of these hopes have proved to be well founded. Yet at least the decline in population has been halted and quite a number of transnational companies have chosen Vienna as the headquarters for their operation in Central and Eastern Europe. The city's attraction lies not only in its geographic location (Vienna is to the east of Prague and Ljubljana), and its physical infrastructure (with good traffic connections in all directions), but also in the advantage of its great concentration of supporting services specialised in serving the east. Examples include banks, accountants, lawyers, and research institutes.

To claim that Austria's relations with its eastern neighbours have 'much improved', is to expose the vacuity of diplomatic language. In fact, relations have come to resemble those with other European democracies in that they too have to a large extent escaped diplomatic control and guidance They now rest upon a much broader bureaucratic and social base. Common participation in institutions like the Council of Europe and - for some of them - in the Organisation for Economic Cooperation and Development adds a solid element of businesslike multilateralism.

The question of NATO enlargement and its consequences for Austria is dealt with elsewhere in this volume. Nonetheless, it should be mentioned here as something that has already transformed, and will continue to transform, Austria's relations with its eastern neighbours. There is no immediate threat in the region that would call for a reaction that only NATO and NATO members could provide. But, as new NATO members, those countries will participate in decision-making from which Austria is excluded. This will certainly help to shift relations more in the direction of those between equal partners, which in the past they were not. Resentment over what was perceived as Austria's patronising attitude was not wholly without foundation.

4.4 The likely impact upon Austria of eastern enlargement

As shown in Tables 4.3 and 4.5, the economic opening of the East has resulted in a rapid expansion of Austria's exports to the region. Austria has certainly been one beneficiary, but the main beneficiary has been Germany. Austria continues to be the third largest provider of exports to the

Central and Eastern European countries (after Italy which retains second place), yet the share of both Austria and Italy in overall European Union exports to the Central and Eastern European countries has dropped, together with the shares of everyone else. Only the share of Germany has increased. It now provides more than half of all European Union exports. Moreover, one should assume that this development will continue, albeit at a slower pace.

Table 4.5   Shares of main EU exporters to CEE countries, 1989 and 1995

| | % of EU-1 Exports to CEE-6 | |
	1989	1995
Germany	36.05	51.43
Italy	15.53	11.75
Austria	9.79	7.87
France	9.83	5.84
United Kingdom	7.79	5.47
Netherlands	5.51	3.72
Other	25.30	21.79
Total	100.00	100.00

Source: IMF and Grabbe/Hughes (1997)

Eastern importers have already substituted western suppliers for eastern suppliers. No further stimulation will come from that corner. The trade regime with the European Union already in place provides for an asymmetric removal of tariffs and quotas (with the exception of agricultural products). Those on the European Union side have all been lifted. Some of those on the side of the Central and Eastern European countries are still in place, but all should have been removed by the year 2001. The removal of these few remaining barriers might provide some added stimulus to Austria's exports, but not much. As far as the trade regime governing imports from Austria is concerned, the accession to the European Union of some candidate countries will therefore only marginally improve the trade regime that will be in place after 2001, since by then free trade will have been established in any case.

The main factor facilitating further expansion of Austrian exports is the continued economic growth of the region. It will be higher than the European average (see Figure 4.2); and it is likely to be accelerated by membership of the European Union (and by the processes involved in moving towards membership). But it is difficult to provide an exact forecast of this added growth. Whatever it might be, the effects of membership or prospective membership are certainly much smaller than the effects resulting from the general 'catching up'. To sum up: while Austria's exports have profited from the general opening up of the East, the accession of Central and Eastern European countries to the European Union will add very little over and above that which can be expected if European Union membership does not materialise for the Central and Eastern European countries.

The biggest change in the trade regime that European Union membership would bring is in the field of agricultural products. At present, all the candidate countries (with the exception of

Hungary) are net importers of agricultural goods. But they have considerable spare capacity in the agricultural sector. Their accession would increase the arable surfaces of the European Union by 50 per cent. Furthermore, in the Central and Eastern European countries, prices for agricultural staples are between 50 and 80 per cent of what they are in the European Union. Raising these prices to European Union levels would have many negative effects. It is for this reason that the European Union's 'Agenda 2000' calls for a further reform of the Common Agricultural Policy (CAP). One key element of reform would be a further decrease in the prices of agricultural products. They would therefore move closer to the present prices in the Central and Eastern European countries. This reform of the CAP would have to happen in tandem with enlargement; and is in fact a prerequisite for making accession possible.[12] None of the necessary decisions have yet been taken, and it is therefore difficult to arrive at reliable estimates as to the effects on Austrian agriculture of European Union membership for Austria's eastern neighbours. One thing seems certain: the competitiveness of the agro-food industries - both in Austria and in the accession countries - will be decisive for the end result in the trade flows of agricultural products.

Figure 4.4 Wage differentials between Austria and candidate countries in 1998.
(Average monthly wages before taxes, in Austrian schillings)

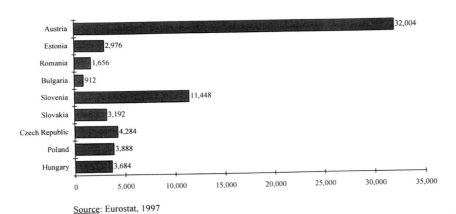

Source: Eurostat, 1997

The most notable impact that accession of the Central and Eastern European countries would have is on the Austrian labour market. It is here that the greatest political problems arise for Austria, as this impact would be massive indeed. One reason is the wide gap in wealth and wages that separates Austria from its eastern neighbours. The income gap, measured in purchasing power parity, is quite large. It will become narrower over the years, but will still be substantial in the year

---

[12] The reforms envisaged would also imply an increase in direct, not product related, payments to farmers. But - at least for a transitory period - farmers in the new member countries would not receive such support.

Table 4.6   Differences in per capita wealth: gross domestic product per head at current US$ in purchasing power parities

	1980	1987	1990	1996	2000	2010	1980	1987	1990	1996	2000	2010
Czech Republic			9526	11128	12732	18847			62	*57	*60	74
Hungary			5,750	6,845	8,154	12,070			37	35	39	47
Poland			4,221	5,882	7,084	10,486			27	30	34	41
Slovakia			7,313	7,914	9,448	13,985			47	41	45	55
Slovenia			9,225	11,045	12,700	18,799			60	57	60	73
Austria	8,593	13,369	16,712	21,395	23,159	28,230	108	107	108	110	110	110
Spain	5,781	9,231	11,856	14,954	16,393	19,983	*73	*74	77	*77	*78	78
Portugal	4,494	7,128	9,372	13,100	14,388	17,539	57	57	61	67	68	68
Greece	5,207	7,606	9,187	12,743	13,996	17,061	66	61	60	66	66	67
EU15	7,927	12,524	15,440	19,333	21,029	25,635	100	100	100	100	100	100

Source: OECD and WWII

72

2010. If we assume that accession will occur somewhere between 2002 and 2005, the income-gap would still be about 50 per cent and therefore roughly 10 per cent larger than the gap that existed for the Iberian countries at the time they became European Union members.

Two factors heighten the problems arising from this disparity. First, the population centres of both Spain and Portugal are far removed from the population centres in the other European Union member countries. Second, and as already mentioned, Table 4.6 measures the gap in terms of purchasing power parities, which is a useful yardstick to assess the potential for permanent emigration: persons who consider leaving their country will compare their present, real wealth with the real wealth they would have in a country they might emigrate to. That is, they would make their comparison in 'purchasing power parities'. But the situation is different when they do not consider true emigration, but remaining resident in their own country and just commuting to work in a foreign country. It is here that geography comes into play. The population centres of the accession countries - or at least some very important urban agglomerations - are very close to the population centres in eastern Austria. For example, Graz can be reached from Maribaor in a car journey of less than one hour; Vienna from Sopron, Gyoer, Znojmo or Brno in less than two hours; the drive between the Slovak capital Bratislava and Vienna takes about half an hour. These are similar to daily commuting times which may people already undertake within their own countries. If commuters from Central and Eastern European countries were to undertake such cross-border journeys, they would continue to pay for most of their living expenses in their (undervalued) local Czech, Hungarian, Slovak or Slovene currency; and they would profit from the low rents, utility costs and food prices in their home countries, whilst their wages would be paid in Euro. When assessing the potential for workers from Central and Eastern European countries to commute to the Austrian labour market, the comparison of wealth at the official exchange rates (and not in purchasing power parity) will therefore provide a better picture; which becomes even starker; as the wage differential becomes even greater, with wages in the accession countries being about 10 per cent (!) of what they are in Austria.

The accession of Spain and Portugal to the European Union in 1987 was not followed by large numbers of Spanish and Portuguese citizens deciding to migrate to other European Union countries. Indeed, the big migration had already occurred in the 1950s and 1960s. Yet for the reasons given above, it would be wrong to infer from this experience that the impact of Austria's eastern neighbours becoming European Union members would have a similarly minor impact upon Austria's labour market. The reason for this relates to another problem that European Union enlargement is bound to cause for Austria. The European Union single economic space provides for the 'four freedoms', among them not only the above mentioned freedom to move from one member country to another in search of work, but also the freedom to provide services in another member country.[13] Were they free to move into Austria after their countries accession to the European Union, the Central and Eastern European providers of such services would, by dint of their very low wage levels - easily out-compete providers located in Austria,

There is concern in Austria that the wage differential will be sharpened by differences in social security contributions - for old age pensions and unemployment insurance, and the like.

---

[13] Service providers in some Czech and Hungarian border towns have already attracted a vast number of Austrian customers - opticians, dentists, hairdressers, car repair shops plus, of course, providers of some less reputable services.

These contributions are very high in Austria and, workers therefore fear that competition would become unfair in a process that they term 'social dumping', that is to say the export of goods and services produced more cheaply as a consequence of such lower standards and, concomitantly, of lower social security contributions.

A similar concern is raised in the field of environmental protection. Here too, the Austrian standards are high and this fact is occasionally reflected in higher production costs.[14] Most Austrians are firmly convinced that they became a beacon of hope for the rest of the world when in 1978 the electorate refused (by a narrow referendum margin) to allow a nuclear power station that had already been completed to go on stream. Moreover, the 1987 disaster at the Ukrainian nuclear power station of Chernobyl confirmed the Austrians in their assessment that theirs was the only realistic national strategy. Austrians fear the nuclear installations located in their neighbouring countries, especially those of ancient Soviet design such as that in Slovak Bohunice. But it is difficult to see how European Union membership could or would change the givens in this difficult dialogue - other than that it could, perhaps, marginally increase Austrian leverage.

Austria is the third biggest net-contributor (After Germany and the Netherlands) to the European Union budget. On the basis of some rather optimistic assumptions (future real economic growth of 2.5 per cent per annum, plus further deep changes in the Common Agricultural Policy; and in the structural funds), the European Commission assumes that contributions will remain at 1.27 per cent of GDP. However, since the accession of the poor Central and Eastern European countries would drag the average European Union GDP downwards, the wealthier countries' contributions would have to increase. This, and the other changes that are likely to come (in respect of structural funds, for example) have led the Austrian Ministry for Finance to assume a consequential increase in Austria's annual net transfer to Brussels from 11 to 27.4 billion Austrian Schilling.

As already mentioned, the European Commission assumes in its Agenda 2000 project that the European Union's structural funds will be reformed. (Were that not to happen, ALL of the territory of the new Central and Eastern European members would become entitled to 'Zone 1' privileges.). The reforms likely to be proposed would imply that the number of existing Target Zones be reduced. This might also affect the only Austrian Target 1 Zone (the Burgenland, which is Austria's Easternmost *Land*). The resulting disadvantages would become sizeable if the eastern parts of Germany (the new *Bundesländer* comprising the former GDR) were to retain their privileged status as Target 1 Zones. This would severely handicap the Burgenland in the competition for inward investment.[15]

As we can see, the immediate advantages that would accrue to Austria from an eastward expansion of the European Union are not that important, whereas the costs and risks Austria would face are sizeable. Seen in the long term, however, the positive effects far outweigh the negative

---

[14] According to a study by Mayhew/Orlowski (1998) the candidate countries would have to spend not less than *half of their 1995 GDP* (!!) to reach the European Union's environmental standards.

[15] It is for this reason, and in fear of the probable consequences of enhanced mobility of both service providers and labour, that the Austrian government submitted a memorandum covering these issues in October 1997. It calls for special support for regions in member countries close to the prospective new members. This support should help to cushion the negative effects of enlargement on the labour market and upon the local economy in general. The first reaction of the Commission was not a very positive one.

ones. The most important gain would be in regional stability, democratic consolidation and institutional modernisation. These positive effects already became evident as the candidate countries anticipated membership and started to prepare for it. One of the conditions, set forth in the 'European Stability Pact', was the normalisation of relations with neighbouring countries, amongst whom outstanding conflicts were to be settled. This specifically also pertains to issues of national minorities, which had in the past been the most prominent cause of unrest in Central and Eastern Europe. The least one can say is that the European Stability Pact and the prospect of European Union membership have added an incentive for the search for compromise on these matters. Treaties such as that concluded between Romania and Hungary - or between Poland and Lithuania - must be regarded as milestones, especially in view of the historic legacy of distrust and hostility; and the sensitivity of the issue of language in the context of states which are relatively young and thus have tended to affirm their character as homelands for one nation, and only one nation.

Figure 4.5   Public satisfaction with democracy in the EU and the CEE countries

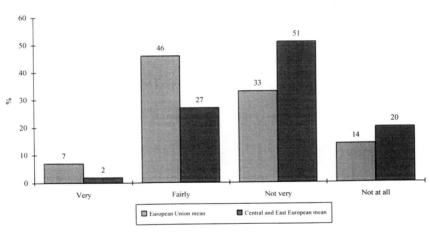

Source: Central and Eastern European Eurobarometer (CEC Report 4/1994) and Eurobarometer (CEC Report 1/94)

A widely used rule-of-thumb for assessing whether democracies have become consolidated relates to whether power has changed twice as a consequence of free and competitive elections. All countries in the first line for accession meet this test. In that sense, their democracies have indeed become 'consolidated', but their democracies are certainly not as firmly secured as those of countries with long and unbroken democratic traditions. The official political institutions are not supported by vibrant political and civic cultures, nor by strongly-held democratic convictions amongst their publics.[16]

Given this situation, the resilience of democratic institutions and practices depends crucially on the international regime in which a country finds itself. The European Union provides a strong tie to - and largely embodies - such an international regime. European Union membership for Austria's eastern neighbours will thus enhance the democratic stability of the region in which Austria is embedded. It also will make Austria wealthier. Eastern Austria, with the capital Vienna, is a natural focus for much of the surrounding area - including the area beyond Austria's eastern, northern and southern borders. The region is rich in human capital, in entrepeneurship; in potential for mobile and flexible medium-sized firms. The local infrastructure is sufficiently developed to support rapidly increased exchanges. The region of and around eastern Austria therefore does have the potential to evolve into an economic (but also a cultural) powerhouse, comparable to the region of the upper Rhine valley or northern Italy. But this presupposes that the existing borders cease to be relevant, and that is something only European Union membership for the neighbouring countries can bring.

4.4 A test of the efficiency of the Austrian political system

The Austrian political system will have to deal with the immediate and mostly negative impact that European Union eastward enlargement will have. But it will have to do so in light of the overall long-term consequences of the enlargement process, which are mostly very positive. This long-term perspective should be the decisive one. Unfortunately, however, politics is a game where the short term often wins out over the long term. If a politician loses elections he is 'out' and then has ample time to philosophise over long-term issues.

Another well-known deficiency of democratic politics is also relevant in this context. A certain development might benefit the vast majority of citizens; but hurt some narrow interests. As the benefits would be widely distributed, they would but mildly affect each one in this vast majority of citizens, while the disadvantages would hit only a few, who would very much resent this. Therefore, vocal special interests often win out over the general interest.

The Austrian political system has been subject to rapid transformation since the beginning of the 1980s. Until then, it had been rather well-equipped to favour the long term over the short term, and general interests over the particular. Parties were all-powerful and thus not easily swayed by the pleadings of narrow interest groups. Voters were not very mobile and thus did not sanction political decisions that trespassed - even if ever so marginally - on personal comfort and interests. One voted for a party not because of what it did, but because of what it 'was' (and what one assumed oneself to 'be'). The representative organisations united under the neo-corporatist umbrella of the system of 'social and economic partnership' (employers, labour and farmers) also

---

[16] It is widely assumed that, for the stability of a democratic regime, consensus on this regime must exist between the various 'elites'. They must agree on the parameters of the political system. Mass support for the regime would be less essential (Burton and Higley, 1989). But it is hard to see how democracy can endure in the long run, if it is supported by the 'elites' only and not by the majority of citizens.

tended to take the long-term view.[17] In a sense, they even acted as joint 'modernisation agencies', and not - as such organisations otherwise tend to do - as embalmers of the status quo.

However, these are things of the past. One reason for the reversal of the old order is simply that Austrians have become wealthier. This has changed their perspective. Being less well endowed with all sorts of possessions, ones looks and strives for a future of greater wealth and security. But once that goal has been reached (and though one is seldom satisfied with what one has) one becomes absorbed by a concern to how consolidate what has been gained. The wealthier one is, the greater one's fear of reverting to a less prosperous state of affairs; and to a level still held by citizens in less fortunate countries. In the case of Austrians (and especially of those living in the eastern part of the country) such fear is nourished by everyday experience. When Austrians travel - let us say for a weekend shopping trip - to Brno or Sopron, as many Austrians do, they find persons with the same surnames, the same looks and roughly the same education, who work just as hard or even harder; than they do and who are nonetheless very, very poor: 'There but for the grace of God go I. Banish the spectre that will haunt me.'

Other important changes are those that have occurred in Austria's political institutions, and especially those affecting the party landscape. Political parties have become weaker. Voters increasingly tend to switch from one party to another. Hitherto, Austria had two larger parties: the Social Democratic Party of Austria (*Sozialdemokratische Partei Österreichs*, or SPÖ) and the Austrian People's Party (*Österreichische Volkspartei*, or ÖVP), which could afford to ignore these volatile voters, as they were few in number. But now their votes have become supremely decisive; Austrian voters now choose between five parties. The organisations that form the pillars of the Austrian 'social and economic partnership' have been affected in a similar way. They too now have to reflect the wishes of their 'customers'; and are no longer in the position of being able to make decisions without any prior consultation.

The single most important development in the evolution of Austria's political system, however, has been the rise of Jörg Haider's *Freiheitliche Partei Österreichs* (Freedom Party of Austria, or FPÖ). In the 1970s and early 1980s, this party had been an agglomeration of small town notables, ex-Nazis, homeless arch-liberals and the like. It was altogether without much influence. That changed under the leadership of Haider. The party greatly increased its share of the vote and now ranks in opinion polls only marginally behind the conservative ÖVP, and about ten percent behind the SPÖ.

Haider's party is unique and successful because it targets one group, and one group alone: the losers of the process of continuing economic change. Haider's predecessors as leaders of the FPÖ had mainly poached on the electoral hunting grounds of ÖVP. By contrast, Haider has made deep forays into the territory of the Left; with the dissatisfied, insecure blue collar worker having become his most prized booty; while on the Right he continues to attract small shopkeepers and disgruntled public sector workers (especially in the police and army).

Both the ÖVP and the SPÖ had of course also represented some of those who had lost out in the process of modernisation. But these groups did not dominate the two parties, which therefore both remained essentially optimistic and forward-looking. The competitive challenge which Haider

---

[17] The most prominent example was perhaps the decision of labour not to press for 'redistribution', as long as employers ploughed their profits back into high and rising investment

poses now forces them to take more seriously the concerns of the insecure, pessimistic and resentful part of the population, which they will otherwise completely lose to Haider.

None of the parties represented in parliament is against European Union enlargement, but Haider has come out most clearly in favour of postponing it to a point in the very, very distant future. For him, the issue is a heaven-sent opportunity. It is amenable to being associated with all the fears and resentments that plague those who have lost out in life, or who feel threatened for other reasons. Thus it is asserted that enlargement would increase crime; the good old Schilling would have to be abandoned in favour of a worthless Euro; strangers would flood into the country and transform Austrian society into a 'multi-cultural' one that could no longer provide a sense of belonging and identity; and - above all - jobs would be destroyed.[18]

How have the other parties reacted? None of them could afford to ignore the issue. In recent (albeit local) elections, the question of European Union enlargement has even become central.[19] Even the Governor (*Landeshauptmann*) of the Burgenland (a Social Democrat) opposed European Union expansion in general and the accession of neighbouring Hungary in particular. For it is clear that his *Land* would have to deal with the most serious consequences of European Union enlargement. But he now has been converted - or so it seems. After having been invited to Budapest by Hungary's Foreign Minister Kovacs, he no longer insists on delaying Hungary's membership and contented himself with stipulating that Hungary should meet all criteria for membership, something Foreign Minister Kovacs promised. (*BBC Monitoring Service*; 16 January 1998).

Even the persons directly responsible for Austria's foreign relations tread very carefully indeed. While confirming 'that there is my view no doubt that we will fully support this historic process', Austrian President Thomas Klestil nonetheless added that it would be necessary to 'prepare enlargement carefully'. 'Transitional periods and other measures will be needed.' (7 May 1997). While being unequivocal in support for the project (of enlargement), Chancellor Viktor Klima for his part added that 'this expansion process must be so carefully prepared to ensure the European Union itself can cope and the new numbers can cope. (Accession) is not a question of dates but of orderly preparation' (*Reuters*, 12 January 1998). Foreign Minister Wolfgang Schüssel recalls that 'there is no alternative to European Union expansion ... The opportunities (it offers to Austria) are greater than the risks', but 'much time will pass anyhow, before these countries will have become members' (*Der Standard*, 30 March 1998). At the start of the Austrian EU

---

[18] It should be noted, though, that one recent attempt to mobilise against the distant and threatening European Union ended in political failure for Haider. A *Volksbegehren* (initiative) against participation in Economic and Monetary Union which he presented to voters in November 1997 was able to gather the support of only 254,077 signatories. Though this figure was high enough to have the text submitted to and discussed in parliament, it constituted a very poor showing in comparison to other such initiatives. In the spring of that same year, for example, the popular initiative against genetically altered food had gathered some 1.2 million signatures.

[19] The situation became quixotic (or tragic - take your pick) in the recent elections for the Land parliament of Lower Austria. *Länder* like Lower Austria hardly have a mandate to shape Austrian foreign policy, yet instead of concentrating on issues they are empowered to decide, the Governor of the incumbent People's Party campaigned on the issue of European Union enlargement (which he opposed); and his Social Democratic rival campaigned on the basis of his opposition to Austria joining NATO. While it thus became clear what they did not want, they were less clear about what they would do if elected. In the event, the People's Party candidate, who opposed European Union enlargement, won handsomely.

Presidency, however, both the Chancellor and his foreign minister have become more decisive in their support for the eastward enlargement of the Union; and so has the Austrian president, Thomas Klestil. For instance, in his inaugural speech in the Fedeeral Assembly [*Bundesversammlung*], he defined enlargement as one of the three major tasks facing Austria.

Partly in response to the challenge posed by Haider, but largely as representatives of Austrian workers, both President Verzetnitsch of the Austrian Trade Union (*Österreichischer Gewerkschaftsbund*) and President Tumpel of the Chamber of Labour (*Arbeiterkammer*) have come out strongly against early enlargement. The latter presented a study by the prestigious Austrian Institute for Economic Research (WIFO, or *Österreichisches Institut für Wirtschaftsforschung*), claiming that each year about 47,000 persons from the Central and Eastern European states would come to seek work in Austria, should they be permitted to do so after their countries become European Union members.[20] While the Federation of Austrian Industry (*Vereinigung Österreichischer Industrieller*, or VÖI) steadfastly supports European Union enlargement, the Austrian Chamber of Business (*Wirtschaftskammer Österreichs*, or WK), which represents small business, was a bit more ambivalent and advocated some protection of service sector enterprises that would otherwise be threatened by extinction through enhanced competition from businesses in towns such as Brno and Gyoer, which are located just across Austria's border with prospective member countries.

4.5 Austria's current policy towards eastern enlargement

Austria will maintain its support for eastern enlargement, but will do so by adding some 'ifs' and 'buts'. These qualifiers will not, however, be of a nature that will jeopardise Austria's basically positive stance. On the contrary, they are simply necessary to carry the project through in the face of Austrian public opinion, the support of which is at best lukewarm , and at worst openly hostile.

Austria will seek some temporary exemptions in respect of the freedom of movement and the right to seek employment in other member countries. A system of gradually expanded quotas could be combined with some derogations. During a transition period of about ten years, such clauses would permit limitations on the freedom of movement of labour in certain sectors of the labour market.[21] Similar clauses could be put in place to smooth adjustment in those services sectors where, in the event of competitors from the East gaining immediate and full access to the Austrian market, existing low wages in the Central and Eastern European countries would result in the wholesale destruction of Austrian firms. As already foreshadowed in its memorandum of October 1997, the Austrian government will also demand that all border regions adjoining the new members should benefit from the same regime. This concerns regions both to the west (including Germany) and to the east of the present frontiers of the prospective new member countries.

---

[20] This study by the WIFO confirms the one mentioned earlier, which had been completed in 1997 by the Austrian Academy of Science

[21] Demographic trends mean that without immigration, Austria's population would naturally decrease. To keep the population stable, 30,000 immigrants would have to be admitted annually. This quota would increase after the 'baby - boom' generation retires from the labour market in around 2010

Concerns over the safety of the nuclear installations in Central and Eastern European countries present a major problem for Austria's political class. Immediately after 1989, it responded with the ambitious - albeit unrealistic - goal of creating 'a nuclear-free Central Europe'. This goal has since been quietly abandoned in favour of the more realistic goal of ensuring 'a high level of nuclear safety'. Public opinion will be very keen to scrutinise the implementation of this policy.

Figure 4.6   How Austrians view eastern enlargement

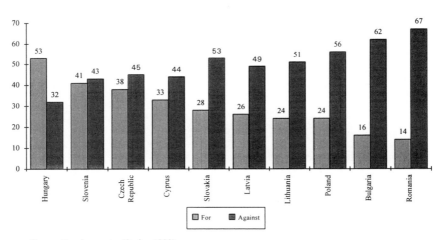

Source: Eurobarometer (Spring 1998).

The accession of Austria's eastern neighbours to the European Union threatens to further augment the already sizeable heavy goods traffic that passes through Austria on the country's roads. The European Union's transport policy is evolving in a direction desired by Austria. One of its prime goals will be to encourage the substitution of road traffic by transportation via rail and water (also in the form of 'combined traffic'). Austria will ask that this evolving scheme be immediately applied to the new member countries and that a full liberalisation of road transport be avoided.

Transitionary agricultural regimes will also have to be found. As envisaged by the European Commission, agricultural support by the European Union for the new members should not be in the form of subsidies to individual farmers, but through measures that promote the structural reform of their agricultural sector.

Austria wishes its present share of contributions to the European Union budget to remain unchanged at 2.6 per cent of the overall budget, and opposes that proportion being raised as a consequence of eastward enlargement[22] If - as seems necessary - institutional arrangements are reformed to adapt them to the much larger number of members states the European Union will in future embrace, Austria wishes to maintain the principle of 'one Commissioner per country'.

As can be seen, Austria has very specific and very substantial interests to protect in the negotiations with the Central and Eastern European candidate countries. But the period in which it will hold the European Union Presidency (the second half of 1998) is not the most appropriate one in which to put these concerns into the limelight. A good European Union Presidency is not one that pushes its respective national agenda, but one that acts as the servant of common interest and as the promoter of the process of integration. This also applies to enlargement, a process which Austria has to advance. Yet even if it were inclined to disregard this obligation, Austria would have few opportunities to do so, as the European Commission and the accession candidates are now engaged in what is called the 'screening of the *acquis* (*communautaire*)'. This merely comprises the scrutiny of the extent to which the common rules of the European Union have been integrated into the legislation and administrative practice of the applicant countries. Austria will report on the results of this process at the Vienna European Union summit in December 1998.

Once the screening is completed, the issue of Austria's concerns will have to be addressed. There is a danger that the pressure of domestic politics could force Austria's representatives into what could be seen as an obstructionist position. Great care has to be taken to avoid such polarisation, which could start to feed on itself and get out of political control. All sides should therefore be aware of the necessity to preserve flexibility. While Austria will have the most serious problems with eastward enlargement, it will be far from the only one having such problems. Powerful voices in Germany have articulated concerns similar to the Austrians'.[23] Not all 'hot potatoes' will have to be touched by Austria first.

But these are tactical considerations. They should not obscure the basic fact that the European Union's eastward enlargement is an historic necessity. It is inevitable. Even if it wanted to, Austria could not prevent it. Moreover, it of course basically does not want to prevent it. Eastward enlargement is in Austria's vital interest, as it will radically change the political landscape of Central and Eastern Europe for the better. A region that has hitherto been the source of endless conflict will become a zone of stability, a region of economic and cultural dynamism and innovation.

BIBLIOGRAPHY [24]

Agh, A., (1996) 'From Nomenklatura to Clientura' in Pridham, G. and Lewis, P., (eds.) '*Stabilising Fragile Democracies*, New York, pp.44-68.
Almond, G. and Verba, S., (eds.) (1980) *The Civic Culture Revisited*, Boston: Little Brown.

---

[22] Germany goes even further. It wants to reduce its quota

[23] This has, for example, been done in a moderate way by the Bavarian Minister President, Edmund Stoiber, and more bluntly by his CSU party colleague, Mr. Gloss, who maintained that 'expansion should come at a later date' (*Frankfurter Allgemeine Zeitung*, 12 May 1998).

[24] Additional sources consulted for this chapter include journals and magazines, wire services, data-banks and, finally, a number of internal Austrian documents.

Ash, T. G., (1993) *In Europe's Name: Germany and the Divided Continent*, New York.

Begg, D. *et al.*, (1990) *The East, the Deutschmark and EMU, Monitoring European Integration - The Impact of Eastern Europe*, London: Centre for Economic Policy Research.

Bertelsmann-Stiftung Forschungsgruppe Europe, (eds.) (1997) *Kosten, Nutzen und Chancen der Osterweiterung für die Europäische Union*, Gütersloh.

Bundeskanzleramt Sektion IV, (1996) *Konzept für die Ostzusammenarbeit des Bundeskanzleramtes*, Vienna, January.

Bundeskanzleramt, (1996) *Europa 1996 - Auswirkungen einer EU Osterweiterung, Studie verfasst vom WIFO*, WIIW, Wien: Institut für Höhere Studien.

Bundesministerium für auswärtige Angelegenheiten, (1998) *Außenpolitischer Bericht 1997*, Vienna: Manz Verlag (as well as all such reports for the preceding years)

Bundesministerium für Finanzen, (1997) *Study on the effects of EU expansion on the Austrian net contributions to the EU budget*; as quoted in "trend", 12/97, p.38.

Burton, M. and Higley J., (1989) 'The Elite Variable in Democratic Transition and Breakdown', *American Sociological Review*, February, pp.17-32.

Butschek, F., (1993) 'External Shocks and Long Term Patterns of Economic Growth in Central and Eastern Europe', in Good, D. (ed.) *Economic Transformation in East and Central Europe*, New York, pp. 27-42.

Csaba, L., (1995) 'China - Mitteleuropa; Reformstrategien im Vergleich', in *Europäische Rundschau*, Vol. 24, No. 4, pp. 15-27.

DeFontenay, P., Gomel, G. and Hochretier, E., (1995) *Western Europe in Transition: the Impact of the opening up of Eastern Europe and the Former Soviet Union*, Washington DC: IMF.

Eatwell, J. *et al.*, (1995) *Transformation and Integration - Shaping the Future of Central and Eastern Europe*, London: Institute of Policy Research

European Bank for Reconstruction and Development, (1997) *Transition Report 1997*, London.

European Commission, (1995) *White Paper on the Preparation of the Associated Countries of Central and Eastern Europe for Integration into the Internal Market*, Brussels: CEC, June.

European Commission, (1997) *Agenda 2000*, Doc.: 97/6, Strasbourg.

European Commission, (1998) *Accession Partnership Documents for the 11 Candidate Countries*, Brussels, March.

Fassmann, H. and Hintermann, C., (1997) *Migrationspotential Ost- Mitteleuropa*, Vienna: Verlag der Österreichischen Akademie der Wissenschaften.

Gaertner, H. (1996) *Souveraenität, Staat und Nation in einer sich verändernden Welt*, Laxenburg: Österreichische Institut für Internationale Politik, Arbeitspapier 13.

Gehrlich, P. *et al.* (eds.), (1992) *Regimewechsel, Demokratisierung und politische Kultur in Ost-Mitteleuropa*, Vienna.

Grabbe, H. and Highes, K., (1998) *Enlarging the EU Eastwards*, London, Royal Institute for International Affairs.

Haerpfer, C. and Wallace, C., (1998) *From Euphoria to Depression, Changing Attitudes towards Market Reform and Political Reform in the Czech Republic in Comparative Perspective 1992 - 1998*, Vienna: Institut für Höhere Studies, Sociological Series, No 27.

Helmstedt, K., (1998) *Ausländische Direktinvestitionen in den Oststaaten, 1997*, Wirtschaftsministerium, Abteilung X/A/2, Vienna.

Holzmann, R. and Neck, R., (eds.), (1996) *Ostöffnung: wirtschaftliche Folgen für Österreich*, Vienna.

IBRD, (1996) *World Development Report 1996 - From Plan to Market*, Washington.

Inotai, A., (1997) 'Wirtschaft', in Bertelsmann-Stiftung Forschungsgruppe Europe, (eds) *Kosten, Nutzen und Chancen der Osterweiterung für die Europäische Union*, Gütersloh.

Institute for East-West Studies, (1996) *Coming to Terms with Accession*, London.

Kennedy, H., (1987) *The Rise and Fall of Great Powers*, New York.

Kramer, H., (1998) 'Austrian foreign policy from the State Treaty to European Union membership (1955-95), in Luther, K.R. and Pulzer, P. (eds.), *Austria 1945-95: Fifty Years of the Second Republic*, Aldershot: Ashgate, pp.161-180.

Landesmann, M., (1995) *The Pattern of East-West Integration: Catching up or Falling Behind?* WIIW Research Paper 212, Vienna.

Linz, J. and Stepan, A., (1996) *Problems of Democratic Transition and Consolidation - Southern Europe, South America, and Post-Communist Europe*, Baltimore.

Mangott, G., (1996) *Autoritäre Demokratie und instabile Identitäten*, Laxenburg: Österreichisches Institut für Internationale Politik, Arbeitspapier 1996.

Mayhew, A. and Orlowski, W., (1998) *The Impact of EU Accession on Enterprise Adaptation and Institutional Development in the EU-Associated Countries in Central and Eastern Europe*, European Bank for Reconstruction and Development, January, (manuscript).

Morass, M., Leitgeb, M. and Holnsteiner, E., (1995) *Europa 1996. Auswirkungen einer EU-Osterweiterung auf die zweite und dritte Saeule*, Vienna: Bundeskanzleramt.

Mizei, K. and Rudka, A., (1995) *From Association to Accession*, New York: The Institute for East-West Studies.

Nowotny, T., (1996) 'The Transition from Communism and the Spectre of Latin-Americanisation', *East European Quarterly*, Autumn, pp. 69-91.

OECD, (1998) *Aid and other Resource Flows to the Central and Eastern European Countries and the Newly Independent Sates of the Former Soviet Union (1990-1995)*, Paris.

Olson, M., (1965) *The Logic of Collective Action; Public Goods and the Theory of Groups*, Cambridge, Mass..

Radice, H., (1995) 'The Role of Foreign Direct Investment in the Transformation of Eastern Europe', in Ha Joon Chang, and Nolan, P. (eds.), *The Transformation of the Communist Economies - Against the Mainstream*, London: Macmillan.

Ringen, S. and Wallace, C., (1997) 'Social Reform in East-Central Europe: New Trends' in *Transition*, Vol III, Prague.

Schmitter, P., (1993) *Some Propositions about Civil Society and the Consolidation of Democracy*, Vienna, Institut für Höhere Studien, September.

Swoboda, H., (1998) *Thesen zur Osterweiterung der EU*, Vienna: Die Sozialdemokratische Parlamentsfraktion, (manuscript).

Szomolanyi, S. and Gould, J., (1997) *Slovakia's Problems of Democratic Consolidation*, Bratislava.

Ulrich, C., (1994) 'The Growth of Crime in Russia and in the Baltic Region', in *RFE/RL Research Report*, 3/23, June 1994.

UNICEF, (1998) *Central and Eastern Europe in Transition, Regional Monitoring Report*, Florence.

Wallace, C., Choumliar, O. and Sidorenko, E., (1997) *The Eastern Frontier of Western Europe: Mobility in the Buffer Zone*, Vienna: Institut für Höhere Studies, Sociological Series, No. 12.

Walterskirchen, E. and Dietz, R., (1998) *Auswirkungen der EU Osterweiterung auf den österreichischen Arbeitsmarkt*, Vienna: Wirtschaftsforschungsinstitut.

Weidenfeld, W., (ed.) (1996) *Mittel und Osteuropa auf dem Weg in die Europäische Union, - Bericht zum Stand der Integrationsfähigkeit 1996*, Gütersloh: Bertelsmann-Stiftung.

Part 2

PERSPECTIVES ON THE

AUSTRIAN PRESIDENCY

5

THE PRIORITIES OF THE AUSTRIAN PRESIDENCY *

Wolfgang Schüssel

5.1 Introduction

Let me start out by saying how delighted I am that I have the opportunity to present a preview of the forthcoming Austrian EU Presidency. I feel that for me, the Presidency will probably constitute on the one hand one of the most hardworking periods and on the other hand one of the most exciting times of my professional career.

When I entered the Austrian Federal Government on 24 April 1989 and became Minister for Economic Affairs, the Iron Curtain was still in existence. Though I am a native of Vienna, my then constituency was located in the northern part of Lower Austria, in the so-called *Waldviertel*, which is near the Czech border. I vividly remember the minefields, the machine guns and that, economically, this part of Austria was a dead end. The situation was very different from that which pertains today.

After 1989, I was closely involved in Austria's application to join the European Union and conducted the negotiations for the construction of the European Economic Area, introducing the EU-internal market regime for the participating EFTA countries. Since Austria's accession to the European Union on 1 January 1995, I have concentrated all my energy on Austria's active and constructive participation in the European Union. I have stressed on many occasions that in view of our role as an equal partner in the European Union, we should not be afraid to tackle the difficult and controversial questions which must be solved in the European Union as we approach the new millennium.

5.2 The legacy of the British Presidency

Assuming the Presidency of the Union is never an isolated event. Presidencies succeed each other, and it is every Presidency's obligation to keep the ship on course and to hand it over unharmed to the next helmsman six months later. We Austrians are fortunate to have the United Kingdom as our

---

* This chapter comprises two elements. The first is the speech delivered by the Austrian Vice-Chancellor and Minister of Foreign Affairs in London on 3 June 1998, on the occasion of the conference on 'Austria and the European Union Presidency', on which this volume is based. The second consists of extracts from the subsequent question-and-answer session and press conference. Only stylistic and linguistic editorial changes have been made.

87

predecessor in this role and I consider it a privilege to succeed a supremely experienced navigator like Robin Cook (whom I might perhaps refer to as 'Captain Cook') at the helm of the Union. He has been obliged to steer the Union through very troubled waters and he has done so with great energy and remarkable success.

We are looking back at what has to date been a momentous year under the British Presidency. First, the enlargement process has been successfully launched. Second, the decision on the participants in the third stage of EMU was taken. Third, there has been a good start to the Agenda 2000 debate. Fourth, in foreign policy proper, Algeria and Kosovo remain continuing challenges. Fifth, we have seen the impossible made possible: there has been a break-through in the peace process in Northern Ireland. Sixth, Robin Cook has done everything he could to reopen the dialogue between the Union and Turkey, albeit not with the result he deserves and everybody in the Union wants.

As for the tragic and highly explosive current events in and around Kosovo, Robin Cook has presented the Union's position with clarity and firmness. This is certainly one of the major challenges that the Austrian Presidency will face. We are aware of how important the transatlantic dimension is for a positive development in this war-torn region and we believe the Union has a specific responsibility for the stability of the Balkans. Thousands of Kosovo Albanians have already fled their homeland and we are threatened with a further escalation. At the moment, we estimate that around 15,000 soldiers from the Yugoslav Army and about 30,000 policemen are in the region. We are again faced with ethnic cleansing. It is my firm conviction - and I share that conviction with Robin Cook - that the Bosnian tragedy must under no circumstances repeat itself in Kosovo.

5.3 Perspectives of Austria

A couple of years ago, the German author Hans Magnus Enzensberger published an enjoyable book with the title '*Ach Europa*'. In this text, he used the immensely quotable phrase '*Ein gutes Klischee ist eine wahre Gabe Gottes*' - a good cliché is a true gift of God. On this basis, Austria is a blessed country, because there are a good many clichés and preconceived notions about it in circulation, and doubly blessed because the majority of them are vaguely true and also mostly rather positive.

First, Austria is seen in the world as a country of music - true, music plays an important part in the life of Austria and the Austrians. Many famous composers who are part of world heritage were born or lived there and musical events and festivals abound. Second, Austria is a country of culture - true again. For a medium-sized country with a population of 8 million, Austria can proudly count a relatively high number of writers, painters and scientists among its famous citizens. Some Austrians who lived in your hospitable country gained great recognition, like Ludwig Wittgenstein, Sigmund Freud or Sir Karl Popper. Third, Austria is a country of sports and a prime vacation choice and so '*gemütlich*' - true, and rather evidently so, given the beauty and the variety of our landscape with its mountains and lakes, so inviting for summer as well as for winter sports. Sitting in a café, reading newspapers, talking, taking out time for friends and family is still very much part of our lives and part of that specific way of life that gives a country its characteristic flavour.

But there are also many other aspects to Austria which are not so much part of this vague, but widespread image that people have of our country, but which are also worth knowing. There is, for example, little awareness that Austria is a highly industrialised, very modern country with excellent research institutions and many successes in the development of cutting edge technology. There is also little awareness that Austria - having successfully emerged from the ruins and the hunger of the immediate post-war period is today amongst the wealthiest countries of the world and per capita income ranks among the highest in Europe.[1] There is little awareness that we are doing very well in competitive world markets and that, for instance, our exports to the United Kingdom have increased by over one third during the last year.

People tend to think of Austria's history and classical culture, but only a very few are aware of the highly creative avant-garde culture that finds its place next to the State Opera and the Vienna Philharmonic Orchestra. And, finally, it has to be said that despite all the '*Gemütlichkeit*' the Austrians are also a very disciplined and hard working people, who take work and achievement very seriously indeed.

5.4 Austria and the European Union

Austria will be the first of the new members of the European Union (followed by Finland and Sweden) to step into the role of the Presidency although I hasten to add that the long history of our close relations to the European Economic Community and now the European Union has us quite well prepared for assuming the tasks which await us. After all, Austria's decision to join the European Union was the logical conclusion to a development which has over recent decades brought Austria into ever closer co-operation and partnership with European institutions.

Since regaining our full sovereignty and independence in the aftermath of World War II, Austria has been continuously involved in European politics. By virtue of our membership in the Council of Europe, the European Free Trade Association and the Conference for Security and Co-operation in Europe, political and economic co-operation between Austria and her European partners grew steadily stronger and more comprehensive. Joining the Union was therefore the logical and culminating step on a road upon which we had embarked long before.

Permit me also to point out that our decision to join the Union was primarily based on political motives. Though there is no doubt that the economic advantages were very important, they were always only a secondary argument. There was never any doubt in our minds about the political dimension and the political importance of the European integration process for peace and stability on our continent, which has suffered so many dramatic upheavals and conflagrations in this century alone, not to mention the constant confrontations of our long history.

But there were other arguments as well. It is important to remember that, while Austria is indeed a country with a very long tradition and has in fact only in 1996 celebrated its millennial

---

[1] One should not forget that in 1948, the UN High Commissioner for Refugees wrote a report to the United Nations which said that at that time, of all the countries in the world, Austria was the one most threatened by hunger and starvation.

existence, in its present form as a modern European nation state Austria is still rather young. Our history and our self-definition has always been a supranational one, whether you put it into the context of the Holy Roman Empire of the German Nation or into the context of the Austro-Hungarian Empire. Thinking and living in a larger European framework and in supranational structures is therefore not an alien concept to us. There is, one would say in today's language, a kind of genetic predisposition, and the historic memory is still alive.

Secondly, we have come to the conclusion that national sovereignty and its exercise under today's circumstances demand a different definition than applied in previous times. In our view, sovereignty today is no longer defined by proud autonomy, by standing alone and regulating one's own affairs. Sovereignty today means being there with a voice and a vote where decisions that affect one's country and its well-being are being taken. In that respect, joining the European Union has not infringed upon our sovereignty, but - through the concept of shared sovereignty - has actually increased it.

The third element which I would like to mention relates perhaps more to geography, although it also has strong political implications. As a landlocked country, surrounded by eight neighbours of a very different hue and orientation, one very quickly becomes aware of the natural limitations of the nation state to solve problems.

Many of the acute questions which confront us today, be it the imperative protection of our environment, the steadily increasing impact of heavy traffic, be it law enforcement, border control or measures against massive and uncontrolled migration, peace-keeping, peace-making, preventive diplomacy, demand co-operation with others, and require the framework for problem solving which the European Union provides us.

5.5 Priorities of the Austrian Presidency

5.5.1 Introduction

I hope that my presentation of the Austria of today will help you better understand the basis from which Austria will approach its first Presidency of the European Union. We have to face up to several top priorities in Europe, six of which I will now outline.

5.5.2 European Monetary Union

The first priority is European Monetary Union. The success of a common European currency will be essential, if Europe wants to meet the economic challenges of the 21st century. The Euro will develop the potential of the single market and make Europe fit to meet the challenges of globalisation. Strengthening the competitiveness of European companies, the Euro will in the long run also have positive effects on the job market.

At the same time, the Euro constitutes a major step in the political process of European integration and a source of confidence in Europe's future. With the successful launch of the single currency during the British Presidency on 2 May 1998, a 'Euro Zone' has been created that comprises eleven member states. Who would have thought one or two years ago that eleven member states comprising some 290 million people in European states would really fulfil the criteria?

Let me add a personal remark in this context: It is your decision, of course, in Great Britain, but it is my sincere hope that the United Kingdom will eventually choose to join us in this fascinating project of European integration. While it is my firm belief that the Euro will be a strong and stable currency from the beginning, it is also evident that Economic and Monetary Union will not be perfect before its borders and those of the European Union merge.

During its Presidency, you can be sure that Austria will do its utmost to contribute to good and harmonious co-operation between 'the eleven and the four' Union member states. It will be our main task to oversee the final preparations for the introduction of the Euro on 1 January 1999. Issues will include the passing of secondary legislation on the European Central Bank, preparing the external representation of the Euro Zone, and enhancing economic co-ordination.

5.5.3 Employment

Our second priority is employment and I think we share with many the feeling that employment is a top priority. With over 18 million people currently out of work in the European Union, the fight against unemployment remains Europe's top priority. The Union needs to show that it can contribute significantly to overcoming this problem and deliver results. According to a recent survey, this is what the people in Austria most want the Union to do.

It is important to know that Austria has been able to offer 95 per cent of its workforce a safe and secure job. Perhaps even a bit more important is that we were able to offer 95 per cent of our young people either a good education, apprenticeship, or good job. Let me point out that it was on the basis of Austria's initiative - Austria as a champion of high employment at home - that the Amsterdam Treaty for the first time included a chapter on employment, with the aim of producing a more co-ordinated strategy to fight unemployment, and to give the European Investment Bank a clearer role in promoting job-creating investment.

The special European summit in Luxembourg was the necessary first step. Work under the British Presidency has gone in the right direction. We look forward to an additional impetus from the European Council in Cardiff, which will give us an opportunity to scrutinise the National Action Plans for Employment and agree on 'best practices'.

It will be the main task of the Austrian Presidency to secure an effective follow-up. In particular, the Vienna European Council in December of this year will be an opportunity for a critical evaluation of the fifteen National Action Plans of the European Union member states and to decide on the EU-employment guidelines for 1999, never forgetting that it remains a national responsibility and will not become *acquis communautaire*. Yet co-ordination and co-operation on the European level is of paramount importance for us. Areas of special emphasis during our Presidency will include equal opportunity for women and men, as well as improving employability through education and training in skills and technology.

5.5.4 Enlargement

Our next priority is enlargement. This is a decisive period in the history of European integration. The Union finds itself on the brink of fulfilling the dreams of its founders and friends: of expanding to include the new democracies to its east in a united, prosperous and stable Europe.

Enlargement is by far the best and most effective instrument to strengthen security in the region. It keeps the nationalist demons at bay. It reinforces the civil society in these countries and stimulates economic and political reforms. It helps to stabilise societies and thus reduces the risks of organised crime and illegal migration. In the long term, the Union will either export stability towards the applicant countries, or it will import instability. No other country has a higher stake in this than Austria.

Yet the road to enlargement will be a bumpy one; it will not be easy. Many difficulties will have to be overcome. The sheer number of applicants and the great differences in economic and social development which they represent, are a far greater institutional and political challenge to the European Union than it has ever seen before. Some of the concerns voiced - also in Austria - seem quite legitimate, as there are major discrepancies between the fifteen and the applicant countries in terms of salaries, in social and in environmental standards.

Nevertheless, the solution will not be to slow down the enlargement process, but to find ways and means to soften possible negative side-effects, or to remove their causes altogether. The unique opportunity to establish a unified Europe must not be missed! Enlarging the Union will rank high on the agenda of the Union and of member states in the years to come. The British Presidency secured a good start of the enlargement process at the end of March and, in particular, of the implementation of the pre-accession strategy. It is of paramount importance that the accessions are adequately prepared, so that the best possible results for all can be achieved.

As the only member state to share half of our borders with four applicant countries, Austria is particularly interested in a successful enlargement process. During our own Presidency, we will endeavour to continue the effective implementation of the pre-accession strategy. It will also be our aim to move the negotiations into their substantive stage and open political negotiations on the first chapters. Furthermore, the European Council in Vienna will have an opportunity to discuss the Commission's first report on the progress of the eleven applicant countries and of fine-tuning the enlargement process accordingly.

5.5.5 Agenda 2000

Enlargement requires not only major preparations by the applicant countries. The Union itself is not yet prepared for the accession of new members. It needs to reform itself to get ready for the future and to be able to meet the challenges of an enlarged Europe. In order to do so, the Union has set itself an 'Agenda 2000', which includes such internal reforms as a new Common Agricultural Policy, a new structural policy and what is probably the most difficult question: a new financial framework for the period 2000 - 2006. Detailed drafts for the new regulations were presented by the Commission earlier this year.

The British Presidency has structured Council work on the Commission proposals and we can expect the European Council in Cardiff to give further guidance on the handling of this crucial dossier and probably a clear timetable for us. To fulfil the Agenda 2000 step by step, and to advance negotiations in the many different fields involved, will not be an easy task. Austria is ready to take over the baton on 1 July. We shall do our utmost to make headway and strive to make substantive progress in the Agenda 2000 negotiations in time for the European Council in Vienna.

5.5.6 Environment

There is growing awareness of environmental problems in the Union and in the world at large. This is particularly gratifying to a country like Austria, which has always kept the environment topic high up on its national agenda. The Union must make continued efforts if we are to achieve lasting protection of the environment.

Like the British Presidency, we will - as a further example of our parallel approach - pursue a 'green agenda', which will include, amongst others, the following priorities: improving the ecological standards in the Union, strengthening the principle of sustainable development and enhancing the Union's leading role in international environmental negotiations.

5.5.7 Youth and children

We must not overlook the fact that children represent the most valuable, but probably also the most vulnerable part of our society. They need all the help and protection we can provide in order to be able to handle the challenges and problems of the next century. We must therefore demonstrate on the European level our firm commitment to the fight against sexual abuse of children. We must prevent child labour on a global level and secure their education.

One of the major initiatives of our Presidency will also relate to the prevention of violence, the fight against Aids and drugs affecting children. Furthermore, we would like to discuss with our EU partners models for making family life and the demands of our professional lives more compatible.

5.6 Conclusion

Austria's EU-Presidency thus comes at a time of great challenges for the Union. The tasks of managing the agenda of the Union, of steering the negotiations and of acting as the Union's representative in the Common Foreign and Security Policy are formidable indeed, particularly for a new member state of the Union. But so are the opportunities. We see the Presidency as a unique opportunity to work towards a strong and united Europe, a Europe that serves the people and enjoys their support.

Let me perhaps end on the note of subsidiarity, which fits so well in this context. It is with great interest that we Austrians have been following the process of devolution initiated by the British Government. Coming, as I do, from a federal republic with a long-standing tradition of taking into account and supporting the provinces and regions, I would like to stress how much importance we Austrians attach to the principle of subsidiarity and how positive our experiences are.

The regional and local communities have an important part to play in the process of integration. People tend to identify with where they come from. Therefore, subsidiarity is a viable means for bringing the Union closer to the citizens and for augmenting their acceptance of a Europe in change. I am therefore grateful to the organisers that part of this conference is devoted to the subject of 'Regionalism and Citizens' Participation in European Integration Policy' which will allow my fellow countrymen to share their experience with you. Chances are good that we will have a discussion of this important topic at the European Council in Cardiff. I look forward to that discussion and I count on my British friends and their support on this issue.

Before closing, I would like to ask you to join me on a brief historical excursion. It was 184 years ago, at the famous Congress of Vienna, that a British and an Austrian statesman co-operated closely and succeeded in bringing a long period of stability and peace to European politics. Now, I do not have much in common with Chancellor Fürst Metternich, and I very much doubt that my friend Robin Cook would choose Lord Castlereagh as his role model. Moreover, both of them eventually failed in their respective missions, as the former US Secretary of State Henry Kissinger pointed out rightly in his fascinating analysis of this period: "A World Restored". But nevertheless, a very important message remains: in spite of their different approach to politics and many different positions and historical experiences, they managed to create a political order in Europe which served it well into the later part of the 19th century. I hasten to add, however, that Austria is preparing itself for an efficient and hard-working Presidency and that all comparisons with and references to the 'Dancing Congress of Vienna' will be totally out of place! We are building a Europe of shared sovereignty, totally different from the one envisaged by Metternich and Castlereagh, based on equality of all partners of the Union.

****

Questions and Press Conference

Question 1:

In what ways might Austria promote minority rights in applicant states to the European Union, as well as the human rights agenda?

Schüssel

The question of a positive treatment of minorities is included in the partnership agreements with the applicant countries. I think it is very important to keep in mind that countries can only become members of the European Union if they accept the highest European standards for treating their minorities not as an enemy or threat, but as an enrichment by virtue of the variety and diversity they bring to the Union and to the countries themselves. There are problems in that respect and they will be tackled during the negotiations. You can be sure that under my Presidency, all the relevant issues will be mentioned during talks with Hungary and Romania, with Slovakia and with Czechia and with the Slovenes and the Estonians. And of course the situation in Cyprus is well known. I think it is very important to need to keep in mind that this is an ongoing priority for future years.

As for the human rights issues, this is very important. In December 1998, that is to say, during the Austrian Presidency, we will celebrate the 50th anniversary of the Human Rights Declaration. I intend to mark the importance of that occasion by hosting a commemorative celebration in Vienna on the afternoon before the European Council of Vienna. Yet we want to commemorate not only the history of the Declaration, but to see it as an heritage for present and future times. So this is why we are interested in discussing human rights issues with Turkey, keeping in mind that Turkey is an important strategic partner, but you can only have a good partner if you speak the truth and can mention all relevant issues and I think human rights issues are very important to tackle with Turkey. We are interested in the human rights situation in the Middle east and we are interested to discuss human rights issues with our Chinese counterparts, with whom we will speak about Tibet. We shall also be talking about the situation in other parts of the world; let us, for example, not forget Algeria and the Mediterranean situation. So I think that is a very important question you mentioned and you can be sure that Austria shares the same view on human rights and minority issues as the British Presidency and Robin Cook.

Question 2:

You spoke about foreign and security policy challenges. Ought there perhaps to be more European discipline when crises arise, such that European countries perhaps first try to co-ordinate their own position? Among the things that are likely to arise during your Presidency are the issue of whether to start lifting sanctions on Iraq and what to do about the Middle East peace process. In each of those cases, individual major European Union members have in the last six months been taking positions that have been different from those of other individual major European Union countries. How are you planning to deal with that?

Schüssel:

I think it is important to understand how a Presidency works. It is not an opportunity to play your own hobby horses and pursue your own priorities. I think a good and professional Presidency has to keep in mind that it is a co-ordinative process. You have to co-ordinate the fifteen member states and to speak with one voice - with a strong voice - and to give Europe a face during the six months of the Presidency. I think it is important to co-ordinate the European strategies, the different national strategies, and this is sometimes difficult, because there are different points of view. I think a good and efficient Presidency co-ordinates. What I have in mind is that we need a step-by-step approach. When European Monetary Union was initially conceived some ten years ago, it was a vision, a project, a dream. In a lot of expert circles and professional watch groups concerned with European policy, people smiled at the prospect. Today it is reality. And I think the same could emerge in Common Foreign and Security Policy. We are now planning the planning cell in the Council Secretariat to integrate for the first time a real professional and competitive branch of political experts surveying CFSP and supporting the Presidency. The next step will be a more co-ordinated link between the political and the military branch, as enshrined in the Amsterdam Treaty. As you know, there is a proposal that Petersburg actions could be decided by the European Council and fulfilled by the West European Union - not forgetting that NATO is the most effective European and transatlantic security organisation, and bearing in mind that there is no need for a parallel approach and doubling costs and structures, but using the relevant organisations that are already there. So I think it is my goal to co-ordinate and to use the most effective channels to come to a European voice and European strategy.

Question 3

The Minister has envisaged an enlargement of the European union to possibly 26 members, but has not mentioned institutional reform as one of his priorities. Is it the view that the Amsterdam Treaty effectively puts a lid on that - we don't need any further change - or is that going to recur on the political agenda? And does Mr Schüssel really feel confident that he can resolve all of the problems of Agenda 2000 by unanimity?

Schüssel

I agree that the institutional questions are important, but most Europeans do not really understand the present institutional framework. You should therefore not expect that you can gain more support for the European project by always talking about power, institutional questions and weight of votes. I have now been in the General Affairs Council for three years and I remember only one time when we counted the votes. So this is in my mind a purely hypothetical question and has nothing to do with reality.

I take now a personal step forward: you know the Austrian position during the Amsterdam negotiations was quite clear: never touch the minimum of one Commissioner per country. I would stick to that, because it is a principle of the Union that every member state is represented in the relevant institutions. At that time, the Austrians also said never touch the weight of votes. In my mind, there should be more flexibility in the next round. But this is my personal position. I say it very openly.

On the other hand, I think we should concentrate on the next important steps: first is ratification of the Amsterdam Treaty. The Austrian Parliament will ratify the Treaty on 17 June 1998 and the Second Chamber will do so at the start of July. I would find it a tactical mistake to start the discussion on institutional reform before all the member states have even ratified the Treaty of Amsterdam. Second, I think the next priority after that is Agenda 2000. I think we should complete the Agenda 2000 and concentrate on this very important and ambitious issue and then we could start discussions on institutional reforms. And by the way, I fully agree that a Union of say 20-26 member states needs more majority voting; there is no doubt about it. It may go in favour of one's own national position sometimes, or it could be disadvantageous, but all-in-all, everybody would win. So in my mind, this is an important - and probably the most important - issue. It would be much easier to solve the problems of the size of the Commission. Don't forget that we have national governments with, in our case, 13 fully-fledged ministers with a portfolio and other countries have more than 30 ministers. Why should the European Commission not have 26 members with a reasonable participation in portfolios? This is possible. The most important and delicate question is majority voting and I am in favour of majority voting.

Question 4:

In view of the Balkan problem, will the fact that Austria is not a member of the Contact Group pose a problem and should room be made on it for the Austrian Presidency? Second, to what extent does Austria share Germany's concerns about Turkey?

Schüssel

First, we intend to participate in the Contact Group and have received information that this is possible. I think this makes sense, because there is a need for good co-operation amongst the

Contact Group members and the European Union Presidency. This was the case during the Dutch Presidency; it was the case during the Luxembourg Presidency. Both countries were not members of the Contact Group, but during their Presidency they attended the meetings and I think this is very important.

As for Turkey, I fully share Robin Cook's assessment of the strategic importance of having good relations with Turkey. There are only two models for the Arab-Islamic world: one is a theocratic model as in Iran; the other is a more secular model as in Turkey. You can be sure that Austria will do its utmost to bring Turkey into the European network. A month ago, we had a European Democratic Union meeting in Salzburg, which we organised as the host country. The present Turkish Premier Minister attended the meeting. I had a long private discussion with him. It lasted more than two hours and concerned how we can co-operate to move ahead. The result was a document on the European strategy presented at the press conference and agreed between us word-for-word. It avoided any negative mention of Germany, or any individual member states. It underlined the importance of Turkey being eligible for European Union candidacy. We hope that at the European Council in Cardiff, this importance of having Turkey as an eligible candidate according to progress in the Copenhagen criteria and according to the association agreement will be stated. And we expect that Cardiff will make a next step forward and that during the Austrian Presidency we will continue the work. I think we should calm down a little bit and not exaggerate the differences, but underline that both Europe and Turkey need to co-operate and need each other.

Question 5

What will Vice-Chancellor Schüssel, as chair of the EURO-XI, do about British participation?

Schüssel

I understand the concerns raised by some British politicians about differences in the economic cycle and about the exchange rate. I think these are good and reasonable arguments. On the other hand, this is not a project for the next six months. I think the Euro will be there for the coming decades. As I pointed out previously, nobody really expected a few months or years ago that eleven countries would be part of the first round, that three more would be able to fulfil the criteria and that the fifteenth country is approaching the criteria. So it did prove possible to create a common framework and real European convergence towards a common goal. This gives us trust and hope that this European strategy and vision could be strengthened.

On the issue of co-operation between ECOFIN and the EURO-XI Council, as I pointed out during my speech, I think it is and should be our ambition to integrate the four countries who are not members of the first round as much as possible. This is very important and I think the decisions reached at Luxembourg gave us enough substance, so that all matters of common interest have to be raised and discussed at the ECOFIN Council. On the other hand, there is the opportunity to talk about problems concerning the eleven in the European Eleven Council. I think this needs some '*Fingerspitzengefühl*' (finesse) and I think this is possible and we have to learn how to handle it. You can be sure that Austria is an integrative country and our Presidency and will keep the herd together.

THE PRIORITIES OF THE AUSTRIAN PRESIDENCY

Question 6

Dr. Schüssel said that one of his priorities would be to move on to the substantive stage of the negotiation process. But on the other hand, we hear from Brussels that nothing important will be happening until July next year, when the screening process finishes. So what will in fact be happening during the Austrian Presidency? Second, how does he reconcile the priorities of environment and enlargement, because if one insists on the strict application of environmental criteria, most of those countries will simply not qualify?

Schüssel

That nothing will happen until July 1999 is pure nonsense and based on misunderstood reports and rumours from Brussels. The real situation is that after the enlargement process commenced at the end of March 1998 under the British Presidency, we immediately started with the *aquis* screening, which the Commission took up. We expect that by July, a substantial number of chapters could have been screened by the Commission. In September/October 1998 we then intend to have two rounds at the COREPER level to discuss relevant chapters with all the six countries that are in the inter-governmental conferences and in parallel the Commission will screen the rest of the chapters. We will therefore not wait until July 1999. Perhaps the Commission will need until then to screen all the relevant chapters; this is possible. But in the meantime, we will start real political talks and expert talks with the applicant countries. I think this is a very reasonable and pragmatic approach and was agreed between Robin Cook and I.

Second, it is true that there is a possible contradiction between environment and enlargement, but knowing that, we created a pre-accession strategy with a lot of money. Half of the money is more-or-less reserved for environmental purposes in the relevant candidate counties. We know of course that whilst accession negotiations are underway, there will of course be no standstill on the environmental policy front within the Union in respect of, for example, car emissions and endangered fish species. The latter will clearly not constitute a problem for the applicant countries, but we know that there could be problems in the industrial area. We have therefore reserved a lot of money for the candidates to catch up in respect of their environmental standards. We also expect that in the interim phase those countries will - for their own sake and in support of their quality of life and environment - themselves do a lot.

Question 7

Will the Austrian federal government resist calls from border regions within Austria - notably the Burgenland - to slow down enlargement and how is it going to deal with these concerns?

Schüssel

Pursuing a good policy means you have to stand up and say what you think is right or wrong. From my point of view, enlargement is the right and only reasonable strategy to export stability and the latter is of course in our interest. Of course we have concerns in Austria. The Hungarians too have concerns; they have a lot of politicians who play the populist card against Hungary's participation in the European Union. That is they way it is. There is never 100 per cent unanimity regarding a political strategy. We have the same in Austria. There are fears and concerns. Good policy takes account of the concerns, listens to the people and does not sweep the concerns under the carpet. On the other hand, one has to stand up and say what one thinks is right. There were the same fears and concerns when the Iron Curtain fell. The difference is, as I said earlier, when I entered government in April 1989, we had an equal trade balance with all the Central and Eastern European countries. Today we have a huge trade surplus. At that time, the part of Austria I represented was a dead-end, with no links, no contacts across the border. Today we have 15,000 joint ventures in the neighbouring countries and a really flourishing economic, political and cultural scene.

On the other hand there are dangers and fears, but with care they can be handled in the right way. So you can be sure that we from the Federal Government in Austria will stick to enlargement and I know there are a lot of politicians in in the Austrian provinces that border on the applicant states (i.e. Lower Austria, Burgenland, Styria. Upper Austria and Carinthia) that share the same feeling. But I would never say do not take seriously what the average citizen thinks. Yet it is our obligation to listen to them and to say publicly what we think is right and what is wrong.

Question 8

Could you close by giving another brief summary of the main issues during the Austrian Presidency?

Schüssel

Wir erwarten, oder nehmen uns vor, daß vieles geschieht, aber nichts passiert. Das ist ein wichtiger Satz. Wir hoffen, daß wir vieles weiterbringen, aber daß nicht unvorhergesehenes, negatives passiert, obwohl wir uns natürlich auf vieles - auch Krisensituationen - vorbereiten müssen; daß ist keine Frage. An positiven Dingen ist für uns ganz wichtig die Einführung des Euro, das muß eine starke, glaubwürdige Währung werden, die am Ende der österreichischen Präsidentschaft im Jänner 1999 Wirkung hat und von der Bevölkerung geglaubt und angenommen wird. In der Beschäftigung wollen wir weiterkommen. Vor allem der Wienergipfel soll ja auch die Koordination der fünfzehn nationalen Beschäftigungspläne bringen, und wir hoffen, daß wir am Ende dieses Jahres eine Million Jobs mehr zur Verfügung haben in ganz Europa als Ende 1997. Dann gehört die Agenda 2000 dazu: soweit kommen wie irgendwie möglich, so daß wenige Monate später ein Abschluß unter deutschen Vorsitz möglich ist; und natürlich die Erweiterungsfrage wird unter österreichischem Vorsitz in die ersten politischen Verhandlungen münden. Daß sind, wenn Sie so wollen, die wichtigsten Vorhaben, die wir und vorgenommen haben. Aber wir hoffen, daß nichts passiert.

Translation[2] : It is our expectation, or at least our intention, that a lot will be done, but that nothing will happen. That is an important statement. We hope, that we will make advances on many fronts, but that nothing unexpected, or negative, will occur. However, we will of course have to make preparations for many eventualities, including crisis situations; of that there is no question. On the positive front, the introduction of the Euro is very important for us; it must be a strong, credible currency, that comes into force at the end of the Austrian Presidency, in January 1999, and which the people believe in and accept. We want to make progress in employment. Indeed, it is above all at the Vienna Summit that the fifteen national employment policies are to be co-ordinated, and we hope that by the end of this year we will have a million more jobs available throughout Europe than at the end of 1997. Next, Agenda 2000 must also be mentioned: we must get as far as we possiblly can, so that a mere few months later, it will be possible to finalise matters under Germany's

---

[2] Subsequently undertaken by the editors

chairmanship; and Austria's chairmanship will of course see the enlargement question move into the phase of initial political negotiations. These are, as it were, the most important tasks we have set ourselves. But we hope that nothing will happen.

6

THE CHALLENGES OF ADMINISTERING THE

AUSTRIAN PRESIDENCY *

Gregor Woschnagg

6.1 Introduction

I would like to outline the problems which the Austrian Presidency is going to face and to share with you our expectations regarding the challenges we will face in chairing the administration of EU business from 1 July to 31 December 1998. I shall concentrate my remarks on three aspects: Agenda 2000, enlargement and third country relations. Before embarking on this task, however, I would like to make some preliminary remarks about the challenges of what will be Austria's first Presidency.

This will be, as I say, our first Presidency of the Union, of which we have been members for only three years. When we took over the preparatory work for the Presidency, we had an internal discussion about the demands of taking on the Presidency after such a short membership period. There was some debate about whether or not we ought to follow the example of the Portuguese, because when Portugal joined, they would have had to take over the Presidency after merely two years of membership. They felt that this would be too much for them and therefore decided that it would be best to wait for another six years, and to use the intervening period to prepare themselves for the task. So the Austrian government looked into the possibility of also delaying its Presidency. However, it then started to calculate that if it were to do so, Austria would have to wait not six years, but at least eight. Moreover, were the European Union to enlarge, we might in fact have to wait ten years. We therefore decided to take the advice proffered by experienced colleagues, like my opposite number in the British Foreign and Commonwealth Office, Dr. Emyr Jones Parry, Director of European Union Affairs, and to take up the Presidency and enjoy it. The first Presidency is always a very difficult one, but something one will always remember, rather like one's first kiss. Our British friends are already a bit blasé, because they have engaged in several

---

* This chapter comprises two elements. The first is based upon the speech delivered by Ambassador Dr. Gregor Woschnagg in London on 3 June 1998, on the occasion of the conference on 'Austria and the European Union Presidency', on which this volume is based. The second consists of extracts from the subsequent question-and-answer session and press conference. There have been relatively minor editorial changes to both elements.

kisses during recent years. For them, kissing has become quite a routine, but for us, the intimate relationship with the Union which the Presidency involves is still a very exciting prospect.

The second introductory point I wish to make is that we shall be taking over the Presidency in the second half of the year, which is arguably a much more difficult period to hold it. Our outgoing British friends thus have the benefit of the alphabet. The reason for the second part of the year being more difficult is that it includes the month of August, which seems to be a holy month in the European Union: nobody wants to work in August. We found this out during our membership negotiations, when the then Austrian Foreign Minister Alois Mock, suggested in the course of our membership negotiations that, should the latter not move ahead very rapidly, we ought to organise an additional meeting in August. It was fascinating to see that when he made that suggestion, everyone in the room was petrified and decided that this was impossible. Eventually, the chairman said 'Well, this is an interesting proposal from our Austrian friends, but in August we actually all wanted to take our holidays in Austria'. In this way, we learnt that one never has meetings in August. In effect, this means that the Presidency of the second part of the year is a much shorter one, though the workload is more-or-less the same as in the first half of the year.

Third, preparing to assume the Presidency has caused those of us who were involved in Austria's membership negotiations to change our attitudes to 'Brussels'. When we were negotiating, it was always with 'Brussels' and sometimes 'Brussels' was our enemy. Yet now we are about to take over the Presidency ourselves, we have to change our perspective and understand we are the Union. It is not 'them' in Brussels, but us. I think this will be a very healthy development for Austria. We will identify with the Union in a much stronger way than hitherto. We have in particular to learn that the Presidency of the Union we will retain our national interests, but it will be our task to guide all the deliberations in a neutral manner; we will be responsible for steering all the negotiations among the fifteen partners and preparing all the common positions. This of course involves quite a lot of work; we calculated that, during our Presidency, we will have to organise fifty ministerial meetings and one thousand, four hundred meetings on civil service level. As these figures make clear, this is an immense operation and requires a considerable degree of integrated organisation. The big lessons we have learned during our preparations for the Presidency is that integration starts at home. If one is not able to integrate the different ministries and interest groups at home, one will be unable to present oneself coherently in Brussels. We learnt this lesson the hard way and I think that, as a result, we are now quite prepared. We do not have as easy a task as our British friends. For one, they have been able to draw on their long experience. Second, they are also not faced with a coalition government, a situation that can cause some difficulties.

Nevertheless, we think we have prepared things well. Our preparations currently look rather like an iceberg: 90 per cent of what we have done is underwater and only 10 per cent is visible. After the European Council of Cardiff, we shall come out with our Presidency programme. What we will do is re-write the existing draft, taking into account our assessment of how far our British colleagues have been able to pursue the various dossiers. We shall then take up the reins from the British Presidency and continue to promote the interests of the Union.

In our opinion, small member states are sometimes able to pursue quite effective Presidencies. Big member states sometimes think they can do everything themselves and they do not need to draw upon the support of the people in Brussels. By contrast, small member states, with more modest administrative resources of their own, soon learn how to work as part of a team with the Commission, with the Council Secretariat and with the other member states. What we have learnt from our colleagues in, for example, Ireland and Luxembourg, is that small member states are somehow more flexible in cutting through red tape because they have smaller, flatter (i.e. less hierarchical) bureaucracies at home. I think this is perhaps one of the secrets of how to achieve speedy decisions.

Having made my introductory remarks, I now wish to move on to the first of the topics which I propose to discuss.

6.2 Agenda 2000

The biggest headache we will have is the question of the Agenda 2000. One reason for that is because there is an intervening variable which nobody can influence, namely, the German general election of 27 September 1998. Until that election is behind us, discussion of reform of the CAP will be as it were petrified in Germany. Nobody knows what the outcome of the election will be and it may be that even after the election, the Germans will need still more time before they can reach any decisions, since it may be necessary for a new coalition government to be formed and for it to establish its policy position regarding European integration.

A second factor likely to make matters difficulty during our Presidency is that we are likely to experience at European-level a problem analogous to that which has been widely experienced at the national level: a conflict of interests between on the one hand the Ministers of Agriculture, who want more money to be spent on farmers, and on the other hand the Ministers of Finance, who say we should spend less. At the European level, a similar conflict is likely to emerge between the Agricultural Council and ECOFIN, which are likely to have different positions on how Agenda 2000 reforms ought to be implemented with respect to agricultural issues. It will then be for the foreign ministers of the Union to try to find a compromise between those different interests. That is extremely difficult, because the time-frame for completing those negotiations is very limited. The window of opportunity we shall have to undertake this task will close in about October, or November 1998, at a time when the Vienna summit will already be on the horizon. The Germans are now planning the timetable of their Presidency, which follows on from ours. Initially, it was planned to hold a summit on Agenda 2000 in Köln at the end of the German Presidency in June 1999. However, they now think that it may well be necessary to organise an extraordinary summit at a much earlier date (on 24-25 March 1999, since the European Parliament's elections are due in June 1999, and this means that holding a summit in the same month on Agenda 2000 would be impractical and undesirable. These considerations reinforce my point that the window of negotiations will be very short. Under the Austrian Presidency, negotiations will need to be concluded by something like October/November 1998. During the German Presidency, only up to January/February will be available for this task. Everything will by then have to be more-or-less wrapped up and the compromise will have to be established, because it will then have to go to the European Council and to the European Parliament before the MEPs leave Strasbourg to start their re-election campaigns. All this makes planning extremely difficult to plan from the Presidency perspective, but we will have to do it, and shall need the help of all our colleagues to do so.

6.3 Enlargement

Austria's interest in enlargement has already been discussed in Foreign Minister Schüssel's contribution to this volume. The enlargement process started very well under the British Presidency and now it is our duty to continue it. Our ambitions are as follows. We will receive from the Commission its report on what is referred to as the '*acquis* screening'. The intention is to undertake this with reference to 12 of the 31 chapters under negotiation, and to produce the report by the end of the British Presidency. This means that the task of the Austrian Presidency will be to continue with the process from that point forwards. We could perhaps open negotiations on some chapters that have been dealt within this *acquis* screening. Because the EU does not yet know what direction the reformed CAP will take, we cannot open negotiations on these matters. Instead, we could commence negotiations on other matters, including small and medium-sized enterprises, education, science and research - in other words, things in respect of which the *acquis* is quite clear.

Since the Union is very likely to evolve during the period in which negotiations with applicant countries take place, the latter will be faced with having to accommodate themselves to ever-changing conditions that will have to be addressed in the revised *acquis*. In short, the applicant countries will then have be faced with what might be described as a moving target. For this reason, no aspect of the negotiation can or will be closed until all chapters, including new *acquis* where necessary, are closed. One condition is that the results in one chapter may not be allowed to pre-judge another, this whole procedure will be quite complicated.

The Commission will also produce a report on the status of all eleven applicant countries. It will try to find economic data to assess the extent to which those countries have been able to implement the *acquis communautaire*. It is hoped that it will be possible to start this report at some stage during the summer, though political and human rights issues will only be reported on a little bit later. It may of course be the case that the German elections of September 1998 might delay matters, such that the report may well not come out until October. Whatever the case may be, the Commission report will then be tabled at the European Council in Vienna, and perhaps that will offer an opportunity for a broader examination of the status of the applicant countries. As the applicant countries are of course all keen to be at the front of the membership queue, this process is of course important.

The other matter is the European Conference, which has been successfully opened under the British Presidency and as a result we now have a group of experts, the Kohl group, charged with looking at the 'third pillar' and the fight against organised crime and drug trafficking. The first meeting of this group will be on 10 June 1998, and we have decided that we should organise another foreign minister-level meeting during the Austrian Presidency to discuss these matters further. It is currently scheduled to be on 6 October 1998.

6.4 Third-country relations

An important dimension of EU-third country relations is that covered by the Barcelona process. There have in this connection already been meetings between the Union and the Mediterranean countries, followed by meetings in Barcelona and then Malta. On task of the Austrian Presidency will be to prepare another meeting ('Barcelona Three'), which will be held during the German Presidency in April 1999 in Stuttgart. The aim of that meeting would be to conclude association agreements with the relevant countries. Negotiations with Egypt and Lebanon have yet to be launched, but once that is done it should be possible to continue this process. The Austrian Presidency will also have to address the significant problem of the role of the European Union in the Middle East. The contribution made by the EU in this region is predominantly financial. Notwithstanding the scale of that contribution, the Union's involvement has to date benefited from considerably less visibility than that of, for example, our American partners. I think our task is to provide assistance to enable the stalemate in the peace process to be overcome, a goal that is in all our interests. Furthermore, our goal would be to pursue what one might call confidence-building measures in the economic and political realm.

Another matter that we shall apply ourselves to during our Presidency relates to the questions concerning the transatlantic partnership. On 18 May 1998, there was of course a summit in London, at which declarations on political and economic co-operation were signed. It was a very difficult task for British diplomacy to achieve these agreements and I really must congratulate our British colleagues for all the hard work they undertook behind the scenes. The task of the Austrian Presidency will be to ensure that the agreed measures are implemented. We have to, as it were, breathe life into the new transatlantic partnership. We need much stronger co-operation with our American partners - including in foreign policy matters - and we should try to nip in the bud any disputes we may have with them concerning economic issues, since these often tend to spill over into the political realm. During our Presidency we shall also have a face-to-face meeting in Vienna on 2-3 October 1998.

6.5 Human rights

In his contribution, the Foreign Minister also briefly touched upon the Austrian position in the area of human rights. We would like to enhance the visibility of the European Union's contribution to democratisation and promoting human rights. We have a meeting on this topic planned in Vienna on 10 December 1998, the eve of the European Council in Vienna, and we will also continue a dialogue with relevant countries - in particular, for example, with China. To this end, we will organise a foreign ministers meeting in Vienna on 10 December 1998, one day before the start of the European Council and the proposed human rights seminar to be held from 26-30 October 1998 in Beijing.

6.6 Environment

As for the environment, it has already been noted that in this respect, Austria's position is amongst the most ambitious in the European Union. During our membership negotiations, we were able to ensure that the considerably higher standards that we had achieved in several dimensions of environmental policy were maintained for a period of four years. Unfortunately, that four-year period comes to an end at the end of our Presidency, when we shall be obliged to abandon those higher standards and operate on the basis of the lower ones that pertain elsewhere in the EU. For Austrian politicians and diplomats alike it would, as you can imagine, be a nightmare scenario if, for example, the Austrian Parliament were to require us to attend a hearing convened to explain why the only result of the Austrian Presidency was apparently a lowering of our high environmental standards to the 'bad' European level. This will hopefully not happen and we shall have to work very hard to prevent this nightmare coming true.

6.7 Treaty of Amsterdam

Finally, there is the matter of implementing the Amsterdam Treaty. We have had a positive referendum in Denmark, where in view of the unpredictability of the Danes there had been some concern. Yet this time they surprised us all in a positive way. Assuming that all the other member states all ratify the Treaty, the Austrian Presidency will then have the task of implementing its various provisions. That will of course include taking forward the important steps the British Presidency has undertaken in respect of the envisaged policy planning and early warning unit. There will also be a discussion of the higher representatives of the CFSP in the second half of the year.

6.8 Conclusion

Austria's EU Presidency thus comes at a time of great challenges for the Union. The tasks of managing the agenda of the Union, of steering the negotiations, and of acting as the Union's representative in the Common Foreign and Security Policy are formidable indeed, particularly for a new member state of the Union. But so are the opportunities. We see the Presidency as a unique opportunity to work towards a strong and united Europe, a Europe that serves the people and enjoys their support.

****

Questions

Question 1

Were any Austrian diplomats seconded to the Foreign and Commonwealth Office during the British Presidency and are there any such plans now?

Woschnagg

Yes, as a learning exercise, we had an Austrian diplomat working in the Irish Foreign Office and also in Luxembourg's. We are also very glad that one Austrian diplomat was able to work in the Foreign and Commonwealth Office, where he learnt a lot. We are also willing to receive a British diplomat in our team. We have at present already a German and Dutch diplomat working in our team. This is very helpful, because they have already experienced several presidencies and we are very grateful for this support.

THE CHALLENGES OF ADMINISTERING THE AUSTRIAN PRESIDENCY

Question 2

Will the Austrian Presidency take on board colleagues from the associated countries and to what extent?

Woschnagg

In view of Austria's efforts to meet the Maastricht criteria, the Austrian civil service was on a strict savings regime and we were thus unable to increase staffing levels in preparation for the Presidency in the way we had wanted. The assistance we receive from the foreign ministries of other members states is thus a way in which we get additional help and excellent native speakers. This helps the work on all the various dossiers. For a short period, we had some diplomats on one or two week placements from applicant countries, but they were not with us for long placements of, say six months duration. Since ours will be a very hard-working Presidency, we have decided we can only accommodate diplomats on secondment from EU members countries. At the moment, our priority is to undertake all the necessary work for the Presidency, for which we value the support of the diplomats from members countries. We would be willing to consider placements from colleagues in applicant countries once the Presidency is concluded.

Question 3

What are Austria's economic priorities? During the British Presidency a lot of emphasis was put on economic reform and are seeing new fora for co-operation and peer review on employment, etc. There will be quite a lot of important dossiers during the Austrian Presidency, not least on tax. In addition, there will be a new forum of discussion in the EUROXI. How will the Austrian Presidency rank economic priorities compared to other priorities?

Woschnagg

At the beginning of the Presidency, we will have a seminar with a wide range of experts on tax legislation. It seems to us appropriate to start with this type of solid academic discussion, since we know that once the single currency is introduced, the next big debate will be on taxation and we will need to be well prepared for it. Taxation differentials between member states are clearly an important factor taken into account by those considering investment decisions. We have very different tax systems in the EU and many tax loopholes. We are also faced with the fact that citizens are making increasing demands upon their governments, whilst at the same time demanding lower taxes. We think we should have a more balanced way of financing such activities. This is something which, in his capacity as chairman of EUROXI, the Austrian Minister of Finance has started to examine and it is an issue he wants to pursue during the Austrian Presidency. Once the single currency has been introduced, it will be much easier to compare the taxation systems of the member states, and to see the disparities between them. Questions will then inevitably be raised about differences in efficiency, about why some countries have much higher tax rates, why some have much higher proportions of civil servants, and so on.

As for questions regarding the implementation of EU directives and regulations, there have been very long and detailed discussions in Austria and considerable efforts to improve the country's record in this respect. Some of the reasons why Austria and Germany had problems in this regard relate to their status as federal states. This means that it has often been difficult to implement EU policies, because the state governments (Länder) have to approve them. But progress has been made and Austria now ranks in the middle of the league on implementation rates. We want to see the remnants of the work necessary for the single market completed by the end of our Presidency.

Question 4

First, when does Dr Woschnagg expect a high representative for foreign and security policy to be appointed and will the appointee be a person whose background is in politics or a civil service person? Second, how does he plan to approach the issue of lifting sanctions on Iraq and how does he think the EU might be able to reach agreement on that?

Woschnagg

The issue of the appointment of a high representative is linked with the implementation of the Amsterdam Treaty, which has still not been ratified in all member states. There is clearly now some public discussion on this issue, and a need to appoint the representative in late autumn 1998, not least because (s)he will have to participate in the selection of his/her team (of ca 20 persons). However, the General Affairs Council has yet to discuss whether the person appointed should be a civil servant, or a politician; someone from a big or a small country. Once the Council's view as to the character of the appointee has become clearer, we shall have to start the process of finding appropriate candidates. Once appointed, the high representative should enhance CFSP and should help the Union adopt a more unified position towards the Third World.

Question 5

First, how does Dr Woschnagg envisage the relationship between EUROXI and ECOFIN, and how does he intend to deal with British pressure to be party to any kind of political decision-making in that body? Second, Herr Schüssel said that the EU must not let Kosovo develop like Bosnia. Does Austria have any ideas as to how to deal with Kosovo, especially since Austria is not a member of NATO?

Woschnagg

One of the longest discussions in the Luxembourg Council was to do with the relationship between ECOFIN and those member states that have joined single currency. As I recall, it was a very heated discussion, though the outcome was a typical EU compromise, containing both what the French call *ambiguité destructif* and *ambiguité constructif*. The Austrian Presidency will now try to make something workable out of those very vague words. We will chair the EUROXI Council, the membership of which we hope will in due course be increased to 12, 13, 14 and 15. That would then mean that ECOFIN would be able to return to its normal role. In the meantime, EUROXI is a Council that has in the first half of 1998 had to be headed not by the British Presidency, but by the following Presidency, since Britain will not be participating at the start of monetary union. Accordingly, it has been the task of the Austrian Minister of Finance to call and chair this meeting. We know it is a difficult and delicate meeting. It will hopefully not be conducted with undue publicity and we hope that we will be able to have the British Chancellor participating for the opening procedure. In short, we have the blessing of the British Presidency for our role in EUROXI, and will continue our work. It is important work, because it will help ensure that the new currency will be very stable and this will be necessary in order to persuade people to switch from their own currencies to the Euro.

THE CHALLENGES OF ADMINISTERING THE AUSTRIAN PRESIDENCY

The Kosovo question is most difficult. There are many unforeseable developments in foreign policy. This happened also to the British Presidency, which at the outset did not know it was going to have to deal with Kurdish refugee problems, or with Algeria. One of the unforeseen crises will of course be Kosovo, which is why we are trying to enter our Presidency with something like 10% free 'capacity', to enable us to undertake good crisis management. We cannot at the moment really predict what we will do about Kosovo. The signs are, for example, that the elections in Montenegro may show Milosevic that he has limits within which he has to operate, but this is not certain, because in this part of the world there is a lot of emotional and not very logical thinking. The former type is very difficult to calculate, so we need to be prepared for negative developments in this area and will then have to react.

Question 6

Given the conflict in the Austrian coalition government over foreign and security policy and specifically re NATO expansion, what risk is there of the Austrian Presidency being unable to respond on behalf of the EU in the event of a conflict arising between EU and NATO enlargement?

Woschnagg

I do not see any problem in the Austrian coalition that might indicate a conflict between NATO and EU enlargement. These are two different organisations. EU enlargement is a much longer process, which we have started and will continue. NATO enlargement is much faster and a process which we will not deal with during our EU Presidency, since the EU Presidency only concerns EU matters.

Question 7

The forthcoming financial settlement appears to suggest the maintenance of the status quo, but we know there are more net contributors than in the past and that Austrian, Swedish and Dutch Finance Ministers have written asking for rebates akin to those granted to the British. Is this going to lead to conflict between Austria and GB on how the budget is resolved, or what shape of budget deal is anticipated?

Woschnagg

The Commission is a very clever organisation. All proposals regarding CAP & structural policy reform have been tabled, but not the proposal concerning the EU's 'own resources', i.e. 2000-6 budgets. The Commission are waiting until after the German elections before putting these proposals in front of the member states, since they do not want to inflame the discussion in Germany. We shall have to look into all these matters during our Presidency. The financial perspective is a very troublesome area, because it is at heart a distribution battle. Everyone wants to get more from and pay less to Brussels, but if everyone does this, the EU will no longer be able to function. On the other hand, there is one idea of creating a budgetary ceiling of 1.27 % of GNP average, but we do not yet have a consensus on this. Spanish diplomats maintain that enlargement will be much more costly, and that we cannot live with the ceiling of 1.27 %. I think the Irish are also not very happy, but all the others think that we should have this kind of ceiling up to the year 2006 and perhaps beyond. A consensus is already emerging about the whole budgetary matter. This means that below this ceiling we have to arrange priorities in areas such as CAP and structural policy in such a way that we can also digest enlargement. But this distribution battle amongst the fifteen member states is of course intense and the Commission is as it were leaning back and observing the battlefield and is awaiting the outcome. We know that Britain has a privileged position, as for that matter do the Germans, who also have a discount, since they only pay two thirds of their nominal share into the fund which provides the British rebate. It is now clear that some countries have been able to achieve more advantageous results than others. Newcomers like the Austrians, who are net contributors, are in a difficult position, because we are very careful not to inflame the debate concerning the whole distribution issue, since we know that at the end of the negotiations we will have to find a compromise such that the EU will be able to function in the period 2000-6 and beyond. Even the farming community, who may not like the CAP reforms at all, know that their position will improve once the EU has a longer-lasting agreed budget.

There is, however, one additional matter I would wish to raise: whenever we are discussing the EU's 'own resources', we need to be aware of, and take account of, the whole range of different EU funds. One fund which we have been of late been examining is the cohesion fund, from which, countries such as Spain and Ireland have to-date been substantial beneficiaries. Yet, Ireland is now an economic success story and perhaps it should therefore now leave the Objective 1 area and in view of its greatly enhanced economic performance should henceforth play in the 'upper league'. The same argument can be applied to Spain, since Spain has also made very considerable progress. The improvement of the Spanish situation is illustrated by the fact that Spain is now able to participate in the single currency and so we have suggested to our Spanish friends that in future they ought perhaps not to be recipients of cohesion fund resources. The Spanish diplomats answered that the two matters were not only unrelated, but were covered in different chapters of the Maastricht Treaty. This response is perhaps indicative of the difficult discussions which will have to be conducted during the Austrian Presidency in the autumn.

Question 8

The effectiveness of the co-decision procedure depends on a close working relationship between the Presidency and the European Parliament. The British Presidency made a big effort at the outset to establish a good relationship. Through the optic of achievement, how does Dr Woschnagg propose to tackle that relationship?

Woschnagg

Relations with the EP could be difficult, but one of the most important tasks of our Presidency will be to ensure that this is not the case. Accordingly, we have been working on improving relations with all MEPs. For example, Austrian ministers have in recent months all visited the EP, where, in preparation for our Presidency, they have held discussions with all the committee chairmen and party groups in the EP. This has of course been a very time-consuming process, but it is necessary, since the EP is keen to have a bigger say in the discussions on Agenda 2000. To this end, they have been putting pressure on member states on the Council of Ministers, making it clear that they would like to have a first reading of Agenda 2000 as early as the autumn of 1998. These concerns will have to be reflected in the Agenda 2000 compromise proposals, and I think this is very welcome. Though the Amsterdam Treaty is not yet in force, the EP would like Agenda 2000 matters to be subject to the procedures outlined in that Treaty. We are therefore now trying find a way to accommodate those demands as well as those of the Council of Ministers. I am confident we will find a compromise.

Question 9

What is Austria's attitude to the development of social dialogue & particularly to the provisions under the Amsterdam Treaty, which effectively mean that trade unions and employers are able to propose legislation to the Council?

Woschnagg

Social dialogue is very close to our hearts. Our experience of social dialogue (or what we call 'Social Partnership') within Austria has taught us that this approach is extremely important for our industrial success. It has enabled us to be amongst the countries with the lowest level of strikes and this in turn has helped ensure that Austria has benefited from considerable inward investment. Firms knew that if they established a factory in Austria they would not have a strike and this is important for companies who need to be able to rely on delivering their goods on time. Given this experience, we have been enthusiastic advocates of social dialogue, and would like to have it at the European level too, where we feel confident it would promote harmonious relations. In short, we have had good experiences with it and think we should also extend the befts of this to the European level in the same way.

7

AUSTRIAN SOCIAL AND ECONOMIC

PARTNERSHIP: A MODEL FOR EUROPE ?

Harald Ettl

7.1 Introduction

One of the principal features that characterises Austria's domestic political system is the manner in which social and economic policy is made. Indeed, Austria has for many years figured as a prime example of neo-corporatist decision-making. In this chapter, I will examine this system of social and economic partnership and the political role of the organisations that represent business and labour interests. I will also outline the principal objectives and strategic instruments that comprise the Austrian experience and the implications that Austria's membership of the European Union may have for the future of those instruments. Finally, I will consider the desirability or otherwise of the European Union adopting elements of the Austrian system of social partnership in its own decision-making procedures. Of particular relevance in this context is a possible strengthening of the role in European Union policy making of the Economic and Social Committee (as the forum of 'European Social Partners').

7.2 The Austrian system of social and economic partnership

7.2.1 Introduction

Social and economic partnership is a system of co-operation between government and the bodies representing business and labour interests in the economic and social policy decision-making process. This system does not mean that there are no conflicts of interest between labour and business. But it means that both sides are prepared to solve such conflicts in peaceful negotiations rather than resorting to measures of industrial action, such as strikes and lockouts.

A mechanism of collective bargaining and a functioning system of industrial relations are both essential elements of any social and economic partnership system. But 'social and economic partnership is not an incomes policy in the restricted sense of the concept', according to the OECD. Much rather it has to be viewed 'as a system functioning on a broad basis, with a long historical tradition, encompassing most aspects of economic policy' (OECD, 1982).

We can only appreciate Austrian social and economic partnership fully if we regard it as a result of Austria's historic development, a process in which economic, social and political factors all played important roles. This partnership was not established according to a schedule drawn up by authorities or legislative bodies, but it is the culmination of a long process of trial and error, of compromises between conflicting economic and social interests, of constant adjustments to changing domestic and international environments. It evolved in a small country whose economic and political structures are sufficiently small in scale to enable them to be 'comprehensible', and where the numbers of actors in economic and social policy are limited. Austria's system of social and economic partnership is thus not amenable to being simply transferred to other countries with different economic and social backgrounds and different cultures. Nonetheless, some of the lessons learnt in Austria may be of interest (and applicable) to other countries as well.

From the re-creation of Austria as an independent state in 1945 onwards, both workers and employers - the social partners - played a very central role in the difficult economic and social policy decisions that had to be taken by the governments of the early post-war period. Although there were more social conflicts in those days than in the 1960s and 1970s, it was in those early days that 'social peace' was established as a common goal, equally valued by the two major political parties as well as by the big bodies representing the social partners. All of them considered the preservation of 'social peace' as a necessary precondition for Austria's endeavours to catch up with the standard of living of her economically more advanced western neighbours.

Agreement among the social partners on the essential goals of economic and social policy is another precondition of social and economic partnership. This agreement was first laid down in writing in 1957. It has constantly been adapted to meet changing requirements and has been applied flexibly. Global economic development and political change in Europe made the social partners redefine their agreement on 23 November 1992 - a redefinition that addressed their common goals and means of co-operation. Some of the major objectives and strategic instruments that this agreement outlined are:

- the 'augmentation of affluence and social standards by qualitative growth which should be as compatible as possible with ecological concerns and create the resources for rehabilitating the environment.

- joint efforts to achieve full employment; specific labour market problems require special consideration and support of problem groups such as elderly employees, the young, and women.

- safeguarding overall economic stability by suitable policies with regard to income, competition and currency

- to attain this end, it is necessary to ensure international competitiveness for the Austrian economy. This requires in particular constant efforts toward achieving high investment levels, extending research activities, persistently improving productivity and quality, and an excellent infrastructure.

- broad participation in international and in particular European integration by joint and active co-operation within the scope of objectives and conflict management strategies as developed by the social partners, in which efforts they expect to be supported by the federal government.

- support for increased internationalisation of the Austrian economy.

- promotion and development of human skills and talents in Austria. In this, the social partners perceive a special challenge with regard to education and training.

- maintenance and improvement of a humane working environment and continued development of a well-balanced social structure in Austria.'

Compared to previous agreements, the most recent one reflects a shift in emphasis towards a more international orientation and greater competitiveness on the part of the Austrian economy. Greater emphasis is also placed upon labour market and education policies.

7.2.2 Interest associations

The Parity Commission - a central institution in the Austrian system of social partnership - was established in 1957 on the basis of a solid structure of already existing interest associations for the major socio-economic groups. The Austrian Economic Chamber (*Wirtschaftskammer Österreich* - dating back to 1848 and originally called the 'Chamber of Commerce') is the oldest of these associations. By law, all business enterprises, small shops, big joint stock companies, private firms, subsidiaries of foreign companies, and state-owned corporations are members of the Federal Economic Chamber. It is entrusted with the task of representing the economic and social interests of the business community. For farmers, the Chambers of Agriculture (*Landwirtschaftskammern*) function on a similar basis.

On the side of labour, there are two associations. The first is the Chamber of Labour (*Kammer für Arbeiter und Angestellte*), which operate ona system of compulsory membership for all Austrian workers and employees, except some groups of civil servants and workers in agriculture. The second labour association is the Austrian Trade Union Federation (*Österreichischer Gewerkschaftsbund*), which is a voluntary association. Despite the existence of the Chamber of Labour, trade union membership in Austria is relatively high (over 50% of the labour force). Trade unions and the Chamber of Labour do not compete, but they co-operate very closely. Collective bargaining, for example, is reserved for trade unions, while the Chamber of Labour provides services for individual members and acts as a 'think-tank' employing a considerable staff of experts with a university training in economic and social policy matters. Besides these 'big four', there are numerous smaller voluntary interest associations ('lobbies'). Except for the Federation of Austrian Industry (*Vereinigung der österreichischen Industrie*), none of them plays a major role in Austria's economic and social policy.

7.2.3 The Joint Commission for Prices and Wages ('Parity Commission')

When government and interest associations decided to establish the Parity Commission in 1957, the commission was not founded by statute, but on an agreement between the participants. Hence, participation was - and still is - strictly voluntary. Theoretically, any one of the participants could withdraw at any time, and then the Parity Commission would cease to exist. Although this was not originally the intention, this turned out effectively to put pressure upon all participants to compromise on workable solutions for the problems brought before the Commission. If such a body were established by law, there would be no such pressure, because if no compromise were found, the commission would still continue to exist.

The Parity Commission consists of the Federal Chancellor, who acts as its chairman, as well as three other cabinet ministers and the top representatives of the interest associations. It has several subcommittees, such as the Subcommittee on Wages (established in 1961) and the Advisory Council for Economic and Social Affairs (*Beirat für Wirtschafts- und Sozialfragen*; established in 1963). The Council for Economic and Social Affairs Board has been dealing with a growing number of economic and social policy questions. Its studies and expertise cover such diverse fields as capital markets, fiscal policy, industrial policy, the regulation of working hours, environmental protection, the financing of social insurance, agricultural policy, and the question of European Union membership, to mention but a few.

7.2.4 Collective wage bargaining

Collective agreements are concluded between one of the fourteen trade unions and one or several divisions of the Federal Economic Chamber. The role of the Parity Commission in collective bargaining is very discreet. When a contract expires (duration: generally one year), it has to agree to the start of negotiations for a new contract - which it by convention always does. When the negotiations have come to a conclusion, the commission is notified of the result. By means of this procedure, the central federations always have a complete overview of what is happening in collective bargaining between their various divisions.

The trade unions pursue a wage policy which is productivity oriented, 'solidaristic', and also takes general economic conditions into account. Productivity orientation means that, in the medium and long term, real wages should grow at the same rate as GDP per person employed. 'Solidaristic wage policy' means that all workers and employees should get the same wage increase in the medium and long term, no matter whether they work in sectors with high or low productivity increases, in sheltered or exposed sectors, in the private sector, or in the public sector. 'Taking into account general economic conditions' has a variety of implications, depending on which of the objectives of economic policy is most difficult to deal with at a given moment, for example, if unemployment is rising, or if there is an exogenous price shock . Within the framework of a fixed exchange rate of the Austrian Schilling to the stable currency block - a framework which the trade unions have always accepted and supported - close attention must be paid to the competitiveness of Austrian goods and prices in international markets. This is resolved by a sequence of bargaining rounds: the metal workers union, which covers the most important sector for Austria's international competitive performance, traditionally opens a new round of wage bargaining in early autumn each year. The metal workers 'set the pace' for the other unions which enter their bargaining processes in the following months. In general, all wage settlements are agreed upon within a narrow range of only one to two percentage points difference from the average wage increase. There are no rigid wage guidelines and the government never intervenes in the bargaining process in the business sector. Should the negotiations reach stalemate, the presidents of the central associations (Trade Union Federation and Federal Economic Chamber) usually act as intermediaries.

Industry is by far the most important sector of wage bargaining. However, collective agreements for industries do not always fully exploit the scope for wage increases. Hence, depending on the situation in the individual firm, workers' representatives at enterprise level may bargain with their employers for additional wage increases. The 'Labour Constitution Act' provides for workers' councils in every enterprise with more than five employees. Moreover, in joint stock companies (and also in limited liability companies) workers' councils are represented on the supervisory boards.

7.2.5 The significance of social and economic partnership for economic stability

A high degree of price stability and the practice of wage bargaining must be seen as integral components of an overall system. In the 1960s and 1970s, firms and trade unions in different sectors could be reasonably sure that the same degree of restraint and self-restraint was practised on all sides. A social contract of this kind is possible only within a comprehensive network of interest representation, of truly 'comprehensive' associations, and requires a considerable amount of mutual confidence.

The Austrian type of social and economic partnership is of course not the only possible version of such a system, but it provides a structure that has proved to be both viable and reasonably effective under changing conditions. In the 1960s and 1970s, inflation was successfully contained within narrow boundaries. This was a major contribution to the rapid and sustained economic growth through which Austria gradually approached western European standards of living. In the 1970s, the system helped the economy come to terms with only a slight rise in unemployment until 1981. Since then, unemployment has been increasing, but at 4.5 per cent in 1998, Austria's unemployment rate is still less than half the European average.

If there is rapid inflation - as was the case several times in the 1970s and 1980s - the appreciation of the currency relative to countries with higher inflation rates becomes a prerequisite for the maintenance of price stability. The relevant decision was taken in 1973, when Austria decided to side with the DM-block and to actually peg its currency to the DM.

Since Austria has never relied on devaluation to recover a loss in international competitiveness, her determination to participate from the outset in the single European currency project was a logical consequence of previous policy. Economic and Monetary Union therefore does not require any fundamental changes in the focus of Austria's incomes policies.

7.2.6 Other areas of co-operation

The social partners also have control of other areas, such as pensions and health insurance and the administration of essential parts of agricultural production and protection. In other policy areas, bodies representing the social partners participate in an advisory capacity, for example as advisors on labour market policies, the promotion of investment and innovation, on environmental policies and consumer protection. The role of the social partners in the provision of economic and social statistics is also important, as experts from the interest associations are members of the various advisory committees of the Federal Central Statistical Office. Their participation ensures that there is a commonly accepted statistical data base to refer to in virtually all questions of economic and social policy.

The representative bodies also have the legal right to comment on draft legislation which the government intends to submit to parliament. Moreover, in many matters relating to industrial relations, the government asks the social partners to discuss and propose draft bills or parts of such draft bills. Due to their involvement in so many policy areas, the social partners have developed a strong sense of political responsibility, which affects not only their members, but the economy and society as a whole.

7.3 The social partners and the European dimension

With the acceleration of the process of European integration, especially after the adoption of the Internal Market Programme by the European Community, Austria had to reconsider her position in the integration process. The domestic debate started in 1986, and all social partner organisations played a very active role and submitted detailed position papers. At the Austrian government's request, the Council for Economic and Social Affairs analysed the various aspects of membership, reported on possible benefits and disadvantages of alternative integration strategies, and accordingly made recommendations.

On the basis of this study, the social partners concluded that full participation in the integration process could be ensured only by full European Union membership. The study and the recommendations, jointly supported by all social partners, were published in 1989. They played an important role in the controversial debate on membership that took place in Austria before the accession referendum in June 1994. The fact that more than 66 per cent of those who voted were in favour of membership can at least partly be attributed to the firm position taken by the social partners.

Since Austria's accession to the European Union, the Austrian social partners have been facing new and far-reaching challenges. Like the country itself, the Austrian social partners do not only wish to adapt to European policy; they also want to play an active role in formulating that policy. Their basic objectives are to strengthen the international competitiveness and stability of the European economy, to maintain and advance social standards and to safeguard the ecological basis of life.

Citizens' support for, and participation in, European integration is essential for its future. In order to achieve this, credible approaches to rising unemployment have to be offered, as this is currently probably the most urgent problem in the eyes of European Union citizens. This means that all measures will have to be regarded in the light of their effects on employment, especially as regards the implementation of Economic and Monetary Union, where an austerity policy aimed at meeting convergence criteria can endanger employment, as well as enlargement to the East, where excessive differentials in living standards can result in unsustainable migration pressure on the labour market.

At the Intergovernmental Conference (IGC) in June 1997, the social partners submitted a position paper on selected topics of European integration. With regard to Economic and Monetary Union, the position paper's main task was aimed at the realisation of all potential advantages, while at the same time securing the stability of the new currency. During the 1980s, Austria was - as a small open economy - twice affected by sudden exchange rate changes. They either aggravated an existing recession (1992/3), or interrupted an economic upswing (1995). In view of this experience, the principal benefit from Economic and Monetary Union is the elimination of the risk of exchange rate fluctuations within the European economy. Hence, the participation of eleven countries in the 'first round' of Economic and Monetary Union, with the prospect of the other countries joining sooner (by 2002) rather than later, must be seen as a major achievement in the European integration process.

In their position paper, the social partners argued that, for the future conduct of economic policy, indicators of the 'real' economy must be given due consideration.

> Although real economic factors such as integration of markets and current account are not 'official criteria' for joining Economic and Monetary Union, according to the Maastricht Treaty, they must be considered in the decision whether to allow a country to participate in Economic and Monetary Union. For the co-ordination of national economic policies, general goals, especially employment, should also be given due attention. In the long run, only those economies whose fundamentals are in order will remain stable. Provisions must be made, therefore, to ensure that the Europe-wide consolidation programme does not overburden the labour markets. The social partners point out the importance of an appropriate economic policy for maintaining real stability.

> The fiscal convergence criteria impose considerable constraints on national fiscal policy as an instrument for cyclical, distributive and regional convergence. Yet when a country must deal with economic shocks, a certain degree of fiscal autonomy is necessary. For this reason, the budgetary and indebtedness criteria should be made to apply as an average over a period of several years so that at least the automatic stabilisers can take effect. (Beirat (1996: 3f))

In view of this less-than-satisfactory situation in European Union labour markets, the Austrian social partners were of the opinion that employment policy should become a central focus of European economic policy. In this respect, the fact that the Amsterdam Treaty explicitly includes employment policy in the European agenda of economic policy constitutes a significant step forward. The social partners have also actively participated in the elaboration of the first Austrian National Action Plan of Employment.

7.4 Social and economic partnership on the European level

Against the background of the Austrian experience of social and economic partnership, the Advisory Council for Economic and Social Affairs recommended further development of both Social Dialogue and the Economic and Social Committee (ESC), but also strengthening the bodies representing interests themselves, in order to optimise co-operation and negotiations between European-level social partners. Ther argued as follows:

> For this it is necessary that the agreements concluded in the Social Dialogue become binding on all fifteen member states. This is absolutely essential for legal security, but also from the point of view of competition. This requires the integration of the Protocol on Social Policy in the revised Treaty. The problem regarding the distribution of negotiating mandates and the implementation of negotiation results can only be solved by the gradual establishment of a special

culture of negotiation as it exists, for example, in Austria. Such a culture is necessary for the maintenance of the European social and welfare system

The current 'fragmentation' of the Social Dialogue into a plethora of individual topics is counterproductive. The Austrian Social Partners therefore support the prospect of future European negotiations over problems of transnational dimensions with the goal of developing a European system of labour relations. The existing problem of representativeness in the Social Dialogue must be solved. If acceptance of results is to be ensured, ... the small and medium sized enterprises [in particular] must be adequately represented.

The ESC's role as monitor of the Single Market should be reinforced. Within the framework of the multilateral supervision of the member states, it should be granted the right to information. A central issue is that of the binding nature of the ESC's recommendations. The Commission and the Council should be obliged to report to the ESC on how its recommendations are taken into account.

From the Austrian point of view, the Social Dialogue should encompass all economic and socio-political topics and not be restricted to classic industrial relations issues. Only then can the dialogue partners assume full responsibility for larger issues. The extension of the consultation procedure to all areas of social and economic policy would thus be an important step toward the development of a social and economic partnership on the European level.

It is absolutely essential that the European interest groups become stronger from within, in order to allow the formulation and implementation of a European policy. This development should be supported by the European Union through organisational assistance, for only strong European umbrella organisations (in contrast to lobbies) representing broad regional and professional interests are in a position to represent interests and take responsibility comprehensively.

If the European social partners want to play a more appropriate role in the future, they must develop an independent profile as 'policy advisors' for the European institutions. (Beirat (1966: 5f))

Reducing public sector deficits to required levels is seen as a precondition of overall economic stability in the European economy as well as in member states. This should also include a certain stabilising effect of fiscal policy on GDP and employment in the recession phase of the business cycle.

7.5 Conclusion

It is very likely that the picture which I have tried to sketch of social and economic partnership in Austria is too harmonious and suggests too much perfection - too much 'rationality' in particular. Hence, two things remain to be emphasised. Firstly, changing conditions require constant adaptation and reaction, which also means a good deal of improvisation and 'making do' - our neighbours think Austrians have a special talent for living with such imperfections.

Secondly, the conflict of interests between different social groups cannot be eliminated, but has to be tackled in a constant endeavour to find a consensus, or a compromise. I believe that this also means a good deal of frustration on the part of all participants, which they must be prepared to accept. They will do so as long as they can be reasonably sure that the outcome of this constant endeavour is better than that of alternative systems. Criticism notwithstanding, most Austrians - politicians, businessmen, trade unionists, economists, workers and employees - are convinced that theirs is still a most satisfactory system, and hence Austria will continue to work with it in the foreseeable future.

In sum, Austria's system of social and economic partnership has proved to be an effective method for the country to resolve complex economic disputes in the domestic arena. It has also been a key factor in the facilitation of domestic political consensus. Membership of the European Union provides Austria with both challenges and opportunities: Austria needs to adapt to a transnational political and economic environment which may have an impact on existing institutions and practices; I would also argue that the European Union may be able to import elements of the Austrian model to achieve a similar degree of consensus on socio-economic questions at the European level

Bibliography

Beirat für Wirtschafts- und Sozialfragen, (1989) *Österreich und die Europäische Integration*, Vienna.

Beirat für Wirtschafts- und Sozialfragen, (1995) *The Austrian Way - The State, The Associations, The Social and Economic Partnership*, Vienna.

Beirat für Wirtschafts- und Sozialfragen, (1996) *Positionspapier zu ausgesuchten Themen rund um die Regierungskonferenz 1996*, (with English summary), Vienna.

Beirat für Wirtschafts- und Sozialfragen, (1998) *Wirtschaftspolitische Handlungsspielräume / Marges de manoeuvre de la politique économique / Room for Manoeuvring in Economic Policy*, (full text in 3 languages), Vienna.

Beirat für Wirtschafts- und Sozialfragen, (1997) *Beschäftigungspolitik*, (with English summary), Vienna.

Bischof, G. and Pelinka, A., (eds.), (1996) 'Austro-corporatism: Past, Present, Future', *Contemporary Austrian Studies*, Vol. 4, New Brunswick: Transactions Publishers.

Chaloupek, G., (1994) 'Die Rolle der Sozialpartnershcaft in der Stabilisierungspolitik', *Wirtschaftspolitische Blätter*, Vol. 41, No. 3, pp. 318-323.

Farnleitner, J., (1993) 'Sozialpartner gemeinsam zu neuen Zielen', *Wirtschaftspolitische Blätter*, Vol. 40, No. 1, pp.122-127.

Karlhofer, F., (1997) 'Arbeitnehmerverbände im politischen System Österreichs', in H. Dachs, *et al.* (eds.), *Handbuch des politischen Systems Österreichs. Die Zweite Republik*, Vienna: Manz, pp. 389-404.

OECD, (1982) *Economic Surveys Austria 1982*, Paris.

Prisching, M., (1996) *Die Sozialpartnerschaft. Modelll der Vergangenheit, oder Modell für Europa? Eine kritische Analyse mit Vorschlägen für zukunftsgerechte Reformen*, Vienna: Manz.

Tálos, E. and Falkner, G., (eds), (1996) *EU-Mitglied Österreich. Gegenwart und Perspektiven: Eine Zwischenbilanz*, Vienna: Manz.

Tálos, E., (1997) 'Sozialpartnershcfat. Koperation - Konzentierung - politische Regulierung', in H. Dachs, *et al.* (eds.), *Handbuch des politischen Systems Österreichs. Die Zweite Republik*, Vienna: Manz, pp. 432-451.

8

SOCIAL PARTNERSHIP AND BEYOND:

THE EU PRIORITIES OF

THE FEDERATION OF AUSTRIAN INDUSTRY

Peter Mitterbauer

8.1 Introduction

The aim of this chapter is threefold. First, it will briefly identify the peculiar historical roots and the post-war record of Austrian social partnership (*Sozialpartnerschaft*). Second, it will outline the future role which social partnership ought to play both within Austria and at the level of the European Union. Finally, this chapter will briefly enumerate some of the main proposals of the Federation of Austrian Industry (*Vereinigung der Österreichischen Industrie - VÖI*) regarding the priorities that ought to be pursued by the European Union during Austria's Presidency and beyond. As will become clear, whilst we agree that Austrian social partnership has served Austria well in the past, we disagree with the arguments articulated elsewhere in this volume by Harald Ettl and widely shared within the Austrian Trade Union Federation (*Österreichischer Gewerkschaftsbund*), namely, that it constitutes a model that could usefully be transferred to the European Union level. Instead, we believe that greater emphasis should in future be placed upon flexibility (not least in the labour market) and upon greater international competitiveness.

8.2 The roots of Austrian social partnership

Since World War II, Austria has developed what constitutes a unique system of social partnership. It has been based upon close, voluntary co-operation between four institutions. By law, membership in three of these institutions is obligatory for all the relevant persons. The three are the Austrian Economic Chamber (*Wirtschaftskammer Österreich*), the Chamber of Labour (*Bundesarbeitskammer*) and the Chambers of Agriculture (*Landwirtschaftskammern*). The fourth institution that is formally a constituent social partnership actor is the Austrian Trade Union Federation. The Federation of Austrian Industry (VÖI), which represents about 80 per cent of Austrian manufacturing industry and is currently presided over by the author of this chapter, is not a formal member of Austria's system of social partnership, but it is *de facto*, involved in all major activities of the social partners.

There are two specific features of social partnership in Austria that deserve special attention here. First, its activities are not restricted to labour relations and collective bargaining, but cover a large range of economic, social, environmental, educational and other policy areas. The involvement of the social partners in these policy fields takes various forms, from counselling, to participation in advisory or policy-making committees and commenting on draft bills for legislation. Second, the social partners have established a so-called Advisory Council for Economic and Social Affairs (*Beirat für Wirtschafts- und Sozialfragen*), where experts from all the institutions involved in the social partnership processes elaborate commonly agreed studies and analyses on a broad range of policy issues. This enables them to establish an undisputed factual basis for further discussions.

Social partnership *à l'Autrichienne* is the result of a number of very specific historical circumstances. The first of these are the traumatic experiences of the inter-war period, which was characterised *inter alia* by the outbreak of civil war and the annexation of Austria by Nazi-Germany. During the period of Nazi rule, leading figures from both of Austria's major inter-war political parties - the Christian Social Party and the Socialdemocratic Workers' Party[1] - met in the concentration camps. It was there that they decided never again to engage in armed combat against each other, but instead to solve their problems at the negotiating table. The Austrian consensus model was born, reinforced last but not least by the fact that between 1945 and 1955, Austria was subject to occupation by the four victorious Allied powers. An appreciation of these roots of Austria's system of social partnership is essential for an understanding of why it became what it is today and why this model cannot be easily transplanted to other countries.

8.3 The record of social partnership in Austria

Overall, the historic record of social partnership has been positive. The major accomplishment of social partnership was to achieve a firm and lasting commitment to economic growth on the part of the representative bodies of both labour and of employers. The motto underpinning this commitment was: let us bake as large a cake as possible and only then discuss how we are to divide it.

Amongst the most obvious positive effects of social partnership were the nearly total absence in post-war Austria of strikes, as well as a relatively moderate wage policy, which was geared to maintaining the international competitiveness of Austrian industry. Together, these consequences of social partnership have contributed to the Austrian economy undertaking an impressive catching-up process. For many years, the Austrian economy delivered higher rates of economic growth and lower rates of inflation and of unemployment than did most other industrialised countries. Today,

---

[1] These parties are the forerunners of Austria's two major post-war parties. Thus the *Christlichsoziale Partei* (Christian Social Party) became the *Österreichische Volkspartei* (Austrian People's Party, or ÖVP), whilst the *Sozialdemokratische Arbeiterpartei* in 1945 reconstituted itself as the *Sozialistische Partei Österreichs* (Socialist Party of Austria). In 1991, it renamed itself the Socialdemocratic Party of Austria (*Sozialdemokratische Partei Österreichs)*.

Austria belongs to the list of the ten richest countries in the Western world and Austrian industry has reached levels of productivity that match those of Germany. Social partnership is clearly one of the explanatory factors for this economic success story.

However, social partnership has also brought many drawbacks. During the 1990s, when the processes of European integration and globalization have accelerated, Austrian companies have come to perceive such drawbacks as a growing burden. The price which labour organisations have demanded for their constructive co-operation in Austrian social partnership has been a dense net of regulations governing the labour market, as well as the development of what is an excessive net of social welfare protection. There were also undesirable developments on the part of non-industrial employers. These included devices aimed at protecting Austrian domestic markets from outside competition. As international competition remained moderate and international capital and investment flows were restricted, this system worked surprisingly well.

Yet with the opening up of national markets pursuant to European integration and globalization, social partnership in many instances became an obstacle to what Austria badly needed, namely, enhanced flexibility and adaptation of its companies and corporate structures. Furthermore, a growing number of other European countries embarked on policies designed to secure stable overall framework conditions, thus reducing strikes and stabilising their currencies. Overall social, political and monetary stability ceased to be Austria's unique selling point.

As a consequence of these developments, Austria's deficiencies in respect of other policy fields came to be felt more and more painfully. Examples include Austria's lack of flexibility regarding working hours; its compensation schemes; the regulatory overkill in respect of workers' protection; environmental policy; business start-ups; permits for opening factories; the operation of new machinery, and so on.

To be fair, things have of late improved and Austria constitutes an attractive location for foreign direct investment. But the impetus for change hardly came from the system of social partnership. Instead, change was forced upon Austria by the European Union and by competitive pressures from globalised markets. It should also be mentioned that unions responsible for the exposed sectors of Austrian industry have shown considerable flexibility in their day-to-day policies vis-à-vis companies. However, they have not given up on their demands for the maintenance of a strict regulatory framework expressed in statute and binding collective agreements.

Notwithstanding some minor corrections implemented recently, Austria's very costly social security and protection schemes are still sacrosanct. And with the business cycle further strengthening, trade unions are again starting to voice demands for higher wage increases in order to stimulate aggregate demand. At the same time, they express their reservations about an early enlargement of the European Union in view of possible labour migration and the ensuing pressure on the level of wages and salaries in Austria.

8.4 The future of social partnership in Austria

Austria's social partnership arrangements have been an undeniable success. Yet the contextual conditions under which they flourished have in recent years changed dramatically. Accordingly, unless we wish to risk damaging effects on the Austrian economy and on the quality of Austria as a business location, the manner in which social partnership operates must in future be different.

To ensure that Austria's social partnership system survives and continues to serve the country, two major adjustments are imperative. On the one hand, much more flexibility has to be introduced into labour markets as far as working time and remuneration schemes for workers are concerned. Legislation and collective agreements should stipulate only a broad framework and some minimum standards. Meanwhile, individual companies should be allowed considerable flexibility to pursue - in consultation with their employee representatives - arrangements that suit their peculiar situation. Our point of reference in this process cannot of course be the quite different framework conditions in developing countries, or emerging markets; it has to be the regulatory framework in comparable industrial countries like the United Kingdom or the Netherlands.

On the other hand, the participants in Austria's social partnership system must put their full weight behind the political decision-making process designed to promote forward investments into the longer-term future of the country. These investments concern predominantly research, development and technology, education and infrastructure. This obviously implies a shift away from current expenditure and transfers in public budgets towards more spending in the areas mentioned.

In future, the focus of social partnership must be upon a joint effort geared at making Austria more competitive internationally. It is this that will secure high rates of growth and employment. In the past, an important function of social partnership was to achieve what was perceived to be an equitable division between 'capital' and 'labour' of the benefits of economic growth. That function should be firmly relegated to the past. Nowadays, it is important that we employ these gains in a productive manner; we need to invest in our economic future and to ensure that in our country, capital is rewarded as well as it is in our competitor countries.

At the European level (and especially in the social field), business representation has developed on the basis of voluntary and highly representative employers' organisation. This European system does not, however, correspond very well with the Austrian system of *Sozialpartnerschaft*, which is based mainly on non-voluntary, mandatory membership in three of the four organisations concerned.

8.5 Social partnership at the level of the European Union

How social partnership ought to operate at the level of the European Union is a matter of some debate. There are different views between not only the European Trade Union Confederation and the Union of Industrial and Employers' Confederations of Europe (UNICE), but also between member countries of the Union. Indeed, traditions of and experiences with social partnership differ widely among European Union-member states, and so do attitudes as to the role of the social partners on the European level.

Nevertheless, it should prove possible to agree on a number of basic principles. First, the social partners' participation in the European decision-making process should remain restricted to topics brought up in the framework of 'Social Dialogue' and to those relating to industrial relations.

Both sides, employers and unions, should be free to decide whether they wish to take up a topic in the Social Dialogue process.

Second, as far as subjects such as, for example, economic, social and environmental policy are concerned, the social partners as they are presently defined at the level of the European Union should be accepted by the Commission as privileged discussion partners. They should not, however, be involved in any decision-taking process.

Third, the Economic and Social Council should not be seen as a substitute for consultations with the social partners. Indeed, the membership and staffing of the Economic and Social Council prevent this organisation from being the voice of the European social partners.

Fourth, the European social partners should not seek to be involved in European monetary policy. This is a matter for which the European Central Bank bears sole and exclusive responsibility.

Fifth, it makes sense for the social partners to take over some responsibility for employment policies at the national level, as suggested by the Guidelines of the Commission. However, this should be done with considerable care and taking into account the strongly varying national conditions that pertain in the member states of the Union.

Finally, ideas of harmonising European national wage and incomes policies should be rejected from the outset. This has to remain a national responsibility. Only at the national level can all the relevant and widely differing special factors and conditions be taken into account. Examples of such factors include productivity levels; the tax burden on labour; the non cost-related dimension of competitiveness, as well as sectoral-specific and regional realities.

8.6 VÖI priorities for the Austrian Presidency and beyond

8.6.1 Introduction

Earlier this year, the Federation of Austrian Industry produced a lengthy document setting out its proposals regarding the priorities which the European Union should pursue during the Austrian Presidency.[2] Some of the VÖI's concerns have already been alluded to above. This section, however, will provide further details of the selected demands contained in that document. These relate to three key thematic clusters: enlargement of the European Union, economic and monetary policy and above all internal policy and the completion of the single market.

The Austrian Presidency of the European Union comes in a period which could be decisive for the future of the Union. Top priority will be given under the Austrian Presidency to the final preparatory work for the timely start of the third stage of the European Monetary Union (EMU) on 1st January 1999. The Federation of Austrian Industry is convinced that for political, security and economic reasons, an early integration of the Central and Eastern European Countries and Cyprus must take place. These countries will constitute an important potential market for the European economy. At the same time, early integration could help to avoid the possible political

---

[2] See Mandl (ed.) (1998).

destabilisation of some of these countries. In order to meet these challenges, the EU has to simultaneously implement all the necessary internal structural improvements (as outlined in the Agenda 2000), namely the reforms of the structural policy, the common agricultural policy (CAP) and the future financing of the Union's activities.

8.6.2   Enlargement

For both economic and political reasons, Austrian industry is especially interested in the integration of the Central and Eastern European Countries (CEECs) and Cyprus into the EU at the earliest possible date. There are at least three important prerequisites for this. The first concerns reform of EU agricultural and structural policies, of the financial perspective as well as modification of specific institutional features of the Union. the second relates to the ability of the candidate countries to meet the criteria set out at the Copenhagen Summit. The third is the finding of mutually agreeable solutions for the negotiation process.

Austria should use its Presidency in order to pursue these reforms and negotiations for enlargement. From the perspective of Austrian industry, the goal of these negotiations should be the extension of the four freedoms of the Single Market, as well as the existing standards of the EU. Interim arrangements should only be granted in exceptional cases, where it is necessary to smooth entry into the Single Market. In order to ensure the credibility of the Austrian position inside and outside the EU, the Austrian people should be kept informed of the opportunities an expanded Europe will bring.

8.6.3   Economic and monetary policy

The Austrian Presidency of the European Union is the last one before the start of the third stage of Economic and Monetary Union. Both the participant countries and the bilateral exchange rates have been identified during the Presidency of the Unites Kingdom. The Austrian Presidency will therefore be responsible for the preparations of the Euro exchange rates as well as for the final arrangements preceding the full operation status of the European Central Bank. From the perspective of Austrian industry, all decisions and signals to the market must assign top priority to achieving confidence in the new currency and the prevention of any kind of speculation and rising interest rates.

8.6.4   Internal policy / completion of the Single Market

a)Employment - 'The future of work'

The inclusion of the new chapter on employment into the Amsterdam Treaty and the formulation of the various 'National Action Plans for Employment' must not lead to unrealistic expectations in the member countries. The best way to increase the level of employment is the creation of a legal framework whereby the available potential can be realised. To this end, attention during the Austrian Presidency, might usefully be focused on three aspects in particular.

The first is in-depth analysis of global structural changes (discontinuities), concentrating in particular on the impact of concomitant phenomena on the labour markets, on the chances of finding work, and on the risks incurred. Second, we need in-depth analysis of the influences of qualifications, types of work organisations (including virtual entrepreneurial structures), costs of labour, application of high technology (information highway) to educational and employment systems and the implementation of policy recommendations. Finally, it would be most helpful if we could seek to devise new high-quality criteria for fund allocation for industry and surrounding structures derived from the European Social Fund. This would guarantee that this important instrument would be at the disposal of industry for the purpose of restructuring and as a means of combating unemployment in the future too.

b) Environmental policy

In the second half of 1998, some important measures should be undertaken in the environmental sector at EU level which would not only considerably improve the ecological situation in Europe, but would also have a positive impact on the position of the economy in terms of international competition. The Austrian Presidency should therefore have as its general aim the following five goals. First, it should develop the harmonisation of environmental standards in Europe at a higher level. Second, it should work out a clearly defined schedule with deadlines for the Central and Eastern European Countries on the grounds of competition, so that they can adapt to EU environmental law not only in terms of production norms, but also as environmental standards for industrial plants. Third, when dealing with the Auto-Oil Programme, the Austrian Presidency should take into consideration the specific interests for the mineral oil and car industries. Fourth, during Austria's accession negotiations, it was agreed that Austria's stricter environmental be maintained for a transitional period, which comes to an end on 31 December 1998. Instead of merely trying to extent that transition period, Austria should strive to ensure that the European Union's lower environmental standards are elevated to match the higher standards that pertain in Austria. Finally, the Austrian Presidency should determine the criteria for the use of the flexible instruments which were agreed on at Kyoto (Emission Trading, Joint Implementation, Clean Development Mechanism) at the fourth UN-Conference on Climate Protection in Buenos Aires in November 1998 in a way that will not only avoid distortion of competition for European industry, but also open the way for a cost effective policy of green house gas reduction

c) Tax harmonisation

From the point of view of the Federation of Austrian Industry, the Presidency's tax harmonisation efforts ought to relate in particular to corporate taxes, value-added tax and energy taxes. As regards the first of these, there are at least four goal the Federation would like to see realised. First, double taxation of cross-border business transactions ought to be ended. Second, within the territory of the European Union, losses of subsidiaries and branches should be taken into account when calculating corporate tax liabilities. Third, barriers arising from tax and company law should be removed, so as to promote the cross-border restructuring of groups and particularly cross-border mergers. Finally, the tax regime for small and medium-sized enterprises ought to be simplified.

The Federation of Austrian Industry believes that the Austrian Presidency should fully support the measures proposed by the European Commission for a common VAT system throughout the Union. In order to ensure fair competition, efforts directed at harmonising energy taxes should be continued. This should be done in a way which will not put further strain on energy-intensive industries.

d) Research and development
From the point of view of Austrian Industry, the Fifth Framework Programme on Research and Technological Development is the key starting-point for the improvement of European competitiveness. The Federation of Austrian Industry expects the Presidency to adopt this framework and its specific programmes in order to aid the smooth running of research and development. Important aspects are efficient and unbureaucratic development, converting research results into marketable products, and the inclusion of small and medium-sized enterprises.

e) Education and training
Since the European Training and Mobility Programmes (LEONARDO and SOCRATES) are due to expire in 1999, new arrangements will have to be made for the future. This will require renewed efforts before and during Austria's Presidency. The Austrian education system has some very special characteristics which are recognised by the EU and could be helpful in the creation of European training initiatives. Of particular attraction are Austria's dual system of vocational education and training; the country's specialised vocational schools and the co-operation which exists between schools and the business sector.

f) Small and medium-sized enterprises
The dominant position that small and medium-sized enterprises maintain within the European economy shows the importance of this key area for economic growth and employment. For the EU and the member states, an effective policy to help these small and medium-sized enterprises suggests improvement of the framework conditions and intensification of their job-creating potential. Benchmarking and analysis of best prices would be the most appropriate instruments toward this end.

Strategies therefore have to be developed and measures taken to lift bureaucratic barriers for these enterprises; to provide for simplification in the legislative and administrative environment in order to reduce costs (especially by providing a simplified VAT system); to facilitate easy access to all EU research and development programmes for small and medium-sized enterprises; to improve the financial conditions for these enterprises by means of , for example, access to venture and equality capital and low-interest loans.

g) Energy
One of the most important objectives of the European Energy Policy has to be completion of the Single Market in this sector. This requires the implementation of the Single Market Directive for electricity into the law of all member states, as well as the adoption of the Single Market Directive for gas. Together, these measures will strengthen the European economy on a global scale and reduce distortion of the markets within the EU.

Progress could also be achieved within the area of energy-saving and the efficient use of existing energy. Possible means to this end include reviewing building regulations (e.g. heat insulation); the development of leaner-burn engines for cars; the use of waste heat and waste materials in industry and the construction of co-generation plants.

h) Competition factors

In order to ensure the success of enterprises within the Single Market, clear and up-to-date competition rules are necessary. With the simplification of the regulations concerning mergers and acquisitions, the Austrian Presidency's aims should include the following. First, to be more liberal in the implementation of the suggested European Commission policies on competition concerning vertical and horizontal agreements and to apply European law only to those cases which are of importance to the EU as a whole. Second, as regards the future regime of state aid supervision, the Austrian Presidency should take into account the Commission's proposals to enhance the transparency of state aid, and to protect the remedies available to third parties who wish to dispute such allocations. Finally, in order to achieve a complete and effective implementation of EU regulations in the field of public procurement within the Single Market and the opening up of this sector, the Presidency, in co-operation with the Commission and the other member states, should seek to modernise and simplify the regulations of the EU, with a mind to improving the key elements of modern public procurement, including the examination of electronic transactions which speed decision-making.

i) Consumer policy

The Federation of Austrian Industry is not in favour of consumer protection within the EU moving in the direction of improving the regulation of important civil rights matters, e.g. the question of guarantees. This may be deemed as being less functional or beneficial to consumers. In our opinion, such topics are subject to the principle of subsidiarity and room should be given for the development of legal standards in the free market. What is necessary is on the one hand a more effective enforcement of current national regulations and an improvement of information to enterprises and consumers. On the other hand, there should be a stop on all further bureaucratic conditions in the area of consumer goods purchase and consumer goods guarantees which make business relations between consumers and enterprises unnecessarily more expensive.

j) Legal framework as a location factor

The Austrian Presidency is charged with the task of speeding up the positive impact of the Treaty of Amsterdam in order to achieve more a transparent and accessible legal framework in the European Union. This will ensure that private individuals, as well as those who are engaged in trade and commerce, will become more familiar with EU laws. There are a number of measures that must be achieved in order to attain higher quality in this area. These include continuous simplification of legal texts, codification; re-announcement and a prohibition of retroactive legislation.

At a time of intensified economic competition and increased integration of the markets, an optimal legal framework will be a very important location factor for international competitiveness. This could be achieved by the examination of the efficiency and more efficient functioning of the administration of the member countries, particularly through the use of benchmarking.

k) Judicial co-operation

In order to safeguard the European economy, we urge the Austrian Presidency to create the framework for a common EU policy on immigration and asylum. Particular attention must be given to the possibility of free movement for business purposes as well as combating organised crime and major international fraud. Instead of introducing new legislation, this should be achieved by the co-operation of the judicial executives of the member states. The improvement of the Convention on Jurisdiction and Enforcement will also improve the functioning of the Single Market.

8.7 Conclusion

In light of the points made in this chapter, it is clear that the dream of an extension of the Austrian system of social partnership to the European level is bound to remain a dream. Austria's model of social partnership may have been successful in the past, but it remains a model of and for the past. It is not an answer to Europe's urgent need to modernise its economic and social systems and to prepare Europe's industry for the challenges of the 21st century.

Instead, the European Union needs to respond to the demands of rapid technological change and globalization by providing the framework most conducive to promoting the international competitiveness of European Union companies. That is the underlying rationale of the programme advanced by the Federation of Austrian Industry, which is designed to help secure prosperity both within Austria and the wider Union.

Bibliography

Abele, H. *et al.*, (1989) *Handbuch der österreichischen Wirtschaftspolitik*, Vienna: Manz.

Bayer, K. (1996) 'Industrie: Zwischen Marktchancen und Anpassungsproblemen', in Tálos, E and Falkner, G. (eds), (1996) *EU-Mitglied Österreich. Gegenwart und Perspektiven: Eine Zwischenbilanz*, Vienna, Manz, pp.131-47.

Breuss, F., Kratena K and Schebek, F. (1994) 'Effekte eines EU-Beitritts für die Gesamtwirtschaft und die einzelnen Sektoren' *Monatsberichte*, Special Issue.

Keuschnigg, C. and Kohler, W., (1996) 'Austria in the European Union. Dynamic gains from integration and distributional implications', *Economic Policy*, 157-211.

Mandl, C., (ed.) (1998) *Austrian EU-Presidency 1998*, Vienna: Vereinigung der Österreichischen Industrie.

Traxler, F. and Zeiner, E., (1997) 'Unternehmerverbände', in H. Dachs, *et al.*, (eds.), *Handbuch des politischen Systems Österreichs. Die Zweite Republik*, Vienna: Manz, pp. 371-388.

9

EMPLOYMENT, EMU AND

THE SOCIAL AND ECONOMIC DIMENSION

Gertrude Tumpel-Gugerell[1]

9.1 Introduction

Significant progress has been made on the path towards European Monetary Union (EMU). The prospective EMU members' efforts in recent years to achieve monetary and fiscal convergence have been successfully completed. The same may be said of technical preparations for EMU. These achievements are, however, clearly in contrast with developments in the labour market. In many countries, the 1993 recession caused unemployment to rise again and to reach levels that even exceeded those of the mid-1980s. For the EU as a whole, unemployment stood at 10.8% in 1997, i.e. somewhat above its peak of 10.0% in 1985. Only a few European countries (notably the United Kingdom, the Netherlands and Denmark) have achieved a substantial decline in unemployment.

The high level of unemployment that persists in many European countries has to be seen as the main contemporary economic and social threat to the European Union. At the same time, European unemployment also poses a key challenge for both the start and success of EMU, especially with regard to the public's necessary acceptance of the new institutional economic policy framework. More than 18 million Europeans are formally out of work, and probably much more are informally engaged in special training schemes. Being out of a job is not only a catastrophe for the individuals affected, but unemployment also implies a waste of economic resources and a burden on public budgets. Persistent high unemployment may erode social cohesion in the EU and may contribute to xenophobia and a rise of nationalism.

As a consequence, unemployment – together with EMU and EU enlargement – will be among the central economic policy topics in the upcoming months and years. It also ranks at the top of the agenda of the Austrian EU Presidency. In fact, in the eyes of the public, monetary union and European unemployment are closely interrelated. At least part of Europe's recent labour market and employment problems are attributed to the foremost goal of European governments – achievement of the convergence criteria stipulated by the Maastricht Treaty – that has of late dominated their economic policies. The success of EMU will most likely be measured to a

[1] I would like to thank M. Schürz and G. Rünstler for their valuable assistance in writing this chapter.

significant extent by the developments in European labour markets in the immediate future. Unfortunately, compared to the views and expectations shared by a large majority of the population and the media, the relationship between EMU and employment is not at all that clear from an economic point of view. The prospect of a single European currency no doubt gives rise to a number of questions related to labour markets and employment. Important interrelations notwithstanding, a direct relationship between changes in unemployment and the creation of EMU may not be established that easily.

Of course, treatment of this issue cannot be exhaustive in this article. This contribution therefore highlights selected topics, and it is divided into four parts. First, the European unemployment problem is briefly discussed from various angles, including an assessment of the role which monetary policy plays in reducing unemployment. Second, this article deals with several issues related to the creation of EMU and its implications for labour markets. Third, as Austria's unemployment is one of the lowest in Europe, it may be worth taking a look at its achievements from an Austrian point of view. Austrian economists, in general, attach great value to policy co-ordination and centralised wage bargaining. Finally, the article deals with economic policy co-ordination and its role in growth and employment.

9.2 Demand and structural factors of european unemployment

The European unemployment problem may be traced back to the recession of the early 1980s. Between 1980 and 1985, unemployment in the EU-15 area rose sharply, from 5.8% to 10.0%. It reached similar levels in the United States in 1982 and 1983. However, while the United States succeeded in substantially reducing unemployment again, the decline in European unemployment was, at best, moderate during the expansion that followed in the late 1980s. Since then, unemployment rates would apparently jump during slumps and exhibit only moderate reductions during expansions. More recently, the rise in European unemployment was very much concentrated over the period from 1990 to 1994. This general pattern made economists reach the conclusion that either structural unemployment had increased sharply, or negative demand shocks virtually had a permanent impact on the unemployment rate.

The extent to which the rise in unemployment should be attributed to demand and structural factors raises a number of questions and has been discussed at length in the literature. Some researchers (e.g. Layard *et al.*, (1993); OECD (1994)) have argued that the rise in equilibrium unemployment rates took place in response to structural changes in labour markets largely independent of demand conditions. This approach focuses on labour market frictions due to the institutional characteristics of national labour markets. Researchers have argued that a number of factors have made labour more costly, such as the expansion of the benefit system and the interrelated increase in labour taxation, hiring and firing costs due to employment protection, the wedge between consumer and producer prices due to changes in import prices, union power, and so forth. It follows therefore that according to this view, unemployment mostly lies outside the reach of macroeconomic policy.

Following the seminal work by Blanchard and Summers (1986), however, a number of authors stressed the relevance of various mechanisms that make temporary changes in labour demand have a longer-term and - in the extreme case - virtually permanent impact on unemployment. This so-called hysteresis in unemployment suggests, therefore, that aggregate demand policy matters. Major economists have taken up this view in several recent articles (Ball (1996); Nickell, (1997); DeGrauwe (1998)). There is, indeed, econometric evidence that demand shocks might have contributed to the rise in unemployment (e.g. Ball (1996); Jäger and Parkinson (1994); Rünstler (1998)).

What are the mechanisms proposed in order to explain hysteresis in unemployment? The literature (e.g. Layard *et al.*, (1993); Bean (1994); Wyplosz (1994)) essentially points to a combination of three effects: insider wage setting, skill deterioration of the long-term unemployed and capital-labour substitution. First, wages may be set in order to maintain current employment levels rather than in response to the unemployment rate. So-called insider wage setting thus results in a pronounced increase in wages in response to stepped-up labour demand, largely preventing the creation of jobs during expansions. Efficiency wage considerations suggest a similar effect (St. Paul (1996)). Second, the deterioration of skills seen among the long-term unemployed clearly reduces their employability given the prevailing wage structure. Third, it is well-known that the capital-labour ratio in Europe has constantly been on the rise, very much in contrast to the United States and Japan, where it has largely remained unchanged. The public often ascribes this increase to labour-saving technical progress. However, it may also be a consequence of wage setting, since firms might adjust the capital-labour ratio according to relative factor costs. In recent contributions, Blanchard (1997) and Caballero and Hammour (1998) come to the conclusion that real wage pressure had significantly contributed to capital-labour substitution up to the mid-1980s. From that period on, its role has, however, become less apparent.

Let us bear in mind though that demand and structural explanations for the rise in unemployment complement each other. In fact, it appears that a variety of factors may have contributed to the rise in unemployment. Unfortunately, a discussion of the contribution made by each factor would exceed the scope of this chapter. Yet, in the present context, some remarks on policy considerations should be made. The main question from the monetary policy standpoint is therefore: Could restrictive policies possibly result in permanently higher unemployment or, in turn, could expansionary policies permanently reduce unemployment?

Monetary policy may help reduce unemployment, but it is very unlikely that it does so by itself. Demand conditions may affect unemployment in the longer term due to hysteresis effects; nevertheless, this is certainly not solely the responsibility of monetary policy. One main lesson that can be learned from the literature on hysteresis is that expansionary monetary policy – even under the assumption that it fosters investment growth – does not necessarily increase employment. It will only do so if certain conditions are met, such as, in particular, the requirement of wage moderation. Moreover, job creation may be supported by greater labour market flexibility and suitable training programmes for the long-term unemployed. Hence, even if demand conditions impact upon unemployment in the longer term, it is beyond the capacity of central banks to influence many determinants of these underlying processes.

Monetary policy could, however, help combat unemployment in two ways. First, hysteresis effects are likely to be asymmetric. Recessions may lead to a longer-term increase in unemployment, while expansions contribute little to a longer-term decrease. Monetary policy could therefore weaken the effects of labour market frictions by taking the edge out of recessions. Several pieces of empirical evidence (Elmeskov and McFarlan (1993); Ball (1996)) corroborate this view.

Based on cross-country regressions, Ball (1996), for instance, argued that two main factors had affected the rise in unemployment, namely, the length of disinflationary policies and benefit duration. He further identified an important interaction between those two variables, indicating that the impact of disinflation was particularly pronounced in cases where benefit eligibility had been available for a prolonged period.

Second, a balanced monetary policy may support job creation. Several countries have succeeded in reducing unemployment, namely the UK, the Netherlands and Denmark. All three countries had undertaken reforms that brought about a much more flexible labour market, and all three countries experienced a strong economic expansion at the same time (the question arises, however, to what extent labour market reforms themselves, acting as a positive supply shock, have induced these expansions).

This suggests that both commitment to growth and appropriate wage setting processes may be necessary to bring down unemployment. In a recent article, DeGrauwe (1998) argues that a combination of structural and demand factors ought to be regarded as the root of high European unemployment. He points out that in the United States and Europe, the conduct of monetary policy in response to the most recent recessions has displayed important differences, which might have contributed to differing labour market performance. DeGrauwe proposes that labour market reforms be combined with balanced demand management to solve the European unemployment problem, and he concludes by offering a quite pessimistic view on what the prospects of such a policy mix would be.

9.3 The implications of EMU for labour markets

The beginning of the Third Stage of Monetary Union will mark a fundamental change in the economic policy framework of the EU. Right from the outset, EMU will eliminate exchange rate fluctuations among the participating countries and centralise monetary policy decisions within the European Central Bank (ECB) to conduct a single monetary as well as exchange rate policy for the Euro area. An assessment of how this substantial change in the institutional setup of European economic policy might influence European labour markets very much depends on the fundamental understanding of how monetary transmission affects the real economy.

Putting the focus on monetary transmission means, at the same time, to touch upon an old and controversial debate in economics. Our understanding and assessment of the mechanisms through which monetary policy may affect the real economy is still very limited and far from undisputed. Transmission mechanisms include, among others, interest rate effects, exchange rate effects, other asset price effects and the so-called credit channel. Clearly, different positions taken on the relative importance of these various mechanisms may lead to very diverse conclusions as to the extent to which transition to EMU will affect the conduct of monetary policy within Europe. The fact that transmission mechanisms cannot be expected to work symmetrically throughout the Euro area - at least not at the beginning of a single monetary policy - further complicates this issue. This is especially true of the exchange rate channel and, given the existing differences in financial market structures, of all kinds of credit channel effects. In light of this high degree of uncertainty, it becomes rather obvious that - whatever the specific conditions for economic policy from 1999 on - the establishment of EMU should not be generally expected to solve the unemployment problem.

EMPLOYMENT, EMU AND THE SOCIAL AND ECONOMIC DIMENSION

Here, we should take a look at a few more specific issues that can tell us something about our understanding of the interrelationship between EMU and the labour markets and related policy requirements.

It is generally agreed that the new monetary regime should be more favourable to economic growth and employment, as exchange rate turbulences within the Euro area and the countries with a derogation in ERM2 will be ruled out. EMU is expected to create a European zone characterised by macroeconomic stability, low inflation and low interest rates and to support the deepening of the single market. Monetary union will thus open up a variety of new investment opportunities. Investment activity should, first of all, benefit from the stability context mainly in the sense that it will not be disturbed by stability conflicts or monetary turbulences. In addition, reduced volatility in financial variables and economic activity should lower the required rate of return on investment decisions. Declining inflation rates and convergence at low levels of long-term interest rates all over Europe already bear testimony to the progress made in this respect in the run-up to EMU. Second, EMU is seen as an important complement to the deepening of the single market by reducing transaction costs, as well as establishing broader and more efficient financial markets. For these reasons, the stability provided by the EMU regime should help overcome a key element of 'eurosclerosis', i.e. insufficient growth of productive capacity.

Apart from its impact on capital formation, there are several other channels through which the credibility of the ECB in delivering price stability could be of importance for creating a favourable climate for employment. It could, for instance, exert a positive influence on price and wage setting processes by reducing nominal uncertainty. The extent to which nominal surprises contribute to rising unemployment is clearly related to the degree of persistence in price and wage setting. Proponents of structural explanations for European unemployment generally conclude that the effect of nominal surprises should have been small (Bean (1994)). Indeed, they should be quickly corrected in the wage bargaining process. This, however, is not entirely true in cases of strong persistence effects in wage setting, as discussed above. (See section 9.2.) One may thus conclude that, although the benefits of increased price stability for the bargaining process may not be particularly pronounced, the net effect ought to be rather positive. It should be stressed, however, that increased price stability can only provide a better framework for appropriate incomes policies and is not an instrument in itself.

Moreover, it has often been argued that EMU, while supporting integration and stability, bears some risk for employment prospects due to country-specific asymmetric shocks. EMU will reduce the relative importance of domestic shocks in the participating countries. Demand shocks are likely to become more synchronised owing to the single monetary policy. However, monetary shocks, in particular due to their effects on the external exchange rate of the Euro, will still affect EU countries and regions to various degrees, due to differences in trade and production structures. The same applies to supply shocks. Yet, EMU member states will lose their interest rate and exchange rate instruments for adjusting relative prices to asymmetric shocks. It has therefore been argued that there is a substantial need for higher wage flexibility in order to adjust to changes in the internal and external environment.

In principle, labour markets may also adjust to asymmetric shocks in other ways, e.g. through migration. In this context, it is often argued that labour mobility in EMU will be limited, due to Europe's differing languages and cultures and that this would involve substantial costs in terms of unemployment in the case of asymmetric shocks. Many studies comparing the United States and Europe have come to the conclusion that there will be less labour mobility, lower wage flexibility and weaker fiscal stabilizers. Most of these comparative studies thus strike a rather sceptical view on EMU (e.g. Bayoumi and Eichengreen (1993); Decressin and Fatas (1994); Peters (1994)).

Again, these worries might be overstated. During the 1980s and, to a lesser extent, in the run-up to EMU, many countries experienced disinflation and used fixed exchange rates as an anchor in order to achieve price stability. Subsequently, their competitiveness temporarily deteriorated at the same time. It thus appears that during the last two decades exchange rate devaluations aimed at restoring competitiveness took place with long delays. This implies that in the past, the exchange rate was often simply *not* used for competitive purposes. Besides, labour mobility in Europe is not only low between countries, but also within them. If it is true that labour mobility promoted concentration of industry, it would therefore also increase the potential for asymmetric shocks. In terms of policy, this may imply that European labour markets might have to be reorganised along the lines of regions.

Nevertheless, it cannot be emphasised enough that wage moderation and high nominal and real wage flexibility are *sine qua non* to securing competitiveness and employment. With EMU member states having lost the exchange rate option, inflationary wage-price spirals at national levels would necessitate subsequent disinflation, which would be even more painful than during the 1980s. The best monetary policy at the EMU level can do is to create a stable monetary environment to support capital formation and thus also long-term growth. To fight regional and national unemployment, other instruments have to be employed, however. Enhanced wage flexibility is a precondition for monetary policy to gain the leeway necessary for supporting long-term growth.

Wage setting should thus be oriented towards national developments in labour productivity and competitiveness and be committed to the goal of price stability. This suggests a certain need for policy co-ordination. Austria fortunately has one of the highest estimated degrees of real wage flexibility among the OECD countries. Co-ordinated wage bargaining structures proved to be helpful in this respect.

9.4 The Austrian experience

It may thus be instructive to take a brief look at Austria, the country with the lowest unemployment rate within the EU-15 area (Luxembourg aside). This section starts out with some general characteristics of the Austrian economy and then focuses on Austria's labour market.

The Austrian economy was highly integrated into Europe even before the country's accession to the European Union in 1995. At 37%, Austria's export share was among the highest within the EU-15 area in 1994 and has been steadily increasing since then. About two thirds of Austrian exports are directed to the EU. Though it initially started from a lower level, during the last three decades, the country has experienced a continuous catch-up in industrial productivity, when compared to its European competitors. Labour productivity in manufacturing now appears to have reached German levels. Cyclical fluctuations are closely related to those of Germany (Rünstler

(1993)), yet in general, they have been substantially less pronounced. This seems to be due to several automatic stabilizers, including fiscal policy.

Most importantly, from 1973, Austria maintained a close peg to a currency basket, and as of 1979, the Austrian schilling has been linked to the Deutschmark. In this way, Austria managed to avoid a number of depreciations and, in turn, painful disinflation, which afflicted some other European countries during the 1980s. Indeed, Austrian inflation has consistently been among the lowest within Europe. Moreover, as indicated by a sustained small interest rate differential *vis-à-vis* Germany, the credibility of the currency peg has never wavered. Unemployment rose during the 1983 recession, albeit substantially less than was the case in many other European countries. Since then, it has been on a slight upward trend. In 1997, the Austrian unemployment rate amounted to 4.3%, which corresponded to the second lowest rate of the EU-15 area.

Why has Austria been able to maintain a relatively stable macroeconomic environment and low unemployment during the turbulent 1980s? From the Austrian point of view, the key to its success mainly lies in policy co-ordination and, in particular, in centralised wage bargaining. Corporatist structures have played an important role in the Austrian institutional framework. From the very beginning, the currency peg has been supported by broad consensus among the social partners. Wages have been - and still are - set in a centralised bargaining process that is closely geared towards export competitiveness and labour productivity trends. The fact that German and Austrian labour unit costs nearly move in tandem reflects this, as do various studies that typically rank Austria among the countries with the highest real wage flexibility (e.g. OECD (1994); Roeger and int'Veld (1997)). While it is often argued that great union power leads to low wage flexibility, the high degree of centralisation appears to have had just the opposite effect.[2]

Table 9.1 Austria's Macroeconomic Performance from 1961 to 1997

	1961-73	1974-85	1986-90	1991-95	1996-97
GDP per capita (growth)	5.0	1.6	2.2	1.3	2.1
Private consumption deflator	4.1	5.9	2.1	2.9	1.6
Unemployment rate	1.8	2.5	3.4	3.7	4.4
Public deficit (% of GDP)	0.8	-2.4	-3.2	-3.9	-3.6
Public debt (% of GDP)	17.5	50.5	57.7	60.6	67.8

Source: Eurostat (1997); data from 1996-97: national sources.

Real wage adjustment thus figured prominently when it came to adapting to external shocks. This, in turn, enabled monetary policy to maintain the currency peg to the Deutschmark with high credibility. At the same time, fiscal policy aimed at countercyclical policy, stabilising demand through the promotion of public and private investment during economic downturns. Austrian economists frequently argue that the specific policy mix of:

---

[2] For a discussion of the role of centralisation in wage bargaining structures, see e.g. Calmfors (1993).

- maintaining price stability through a currency peg,

- fiscal stabilisation and

- the social partners' commitment to adequate wage and price policies,

all its imperfections notwithstanding, has significantly contributed to the relative success in fighting unemployment by creating a stable macroeconomic environment. In particular, in light of the contributions by Ball (1996) and DeGrauwe (1998) discussed above, one could maintain that the Austrian policy mix, in mitigating insider effects through centralised bargaining and stabilising demand through fiscal policy, might have considerably contributed to the absence of hysteresis in unemployment.

It may be added that, following Austria's accession to the EU, some of the relevant circumstances have changed, due to stepped-up competition in domestically-oriented sectors. So far, nominal wages in these sectors have mostly been set in line with manufacturing wages, while prices have been established so as to bring real wages in line with sector-specific productivity developments. Hence, real wage flexibility in domestically-oriented sectors may have been partially achieved by price setting. Increased competition in the domestically-oriented economy increasingly puts constraints on price setting though. As a consequence, a greater degree of cross-sector flexibility in wage setting may be necessary in the future. It remains to be seen how these developments will impact upon the Austrian labour market.

Country experiences offer a wide range of different institutional arrangements for co-ordinating the main areas of economic policy. Austria's experience shows that over the long run, given the appropriate policy framework, there need not necessarily be a conflict between price stability and a high level of employment. Of course, one should be aware of the fact that individual country experiences cannot be easily transposed to a European level.

9.5 The importance of policy co-ordination

The interdependence of macroeconomic policies underlines the need for extensive co-ordination between policies in EMU. As the ultimate effects of measures taken in different areas of economic policy will depend on the way policies interact, it is essential to closely orchestrate these different areas of economic policy. In general, effective co-ordination makes it easier for policy makers to achieve their stated policy objectives in an efficient manner. Lack of co-ordination, in turn, might well result in a situation where one policy burdens another. A fundamental requirement for efficient policy co-ordination is the joint determination of objectives and policies by the monetary and fiscal authorities. A situation where the different policies are only made consistent by passive reaction of one policy to the commanding position of the other would certainly not assist in maximising the effects the various policies have. Policy co-ordination might cover the whole range from information exchange, surveillance, policy discussions and recommendations to joint policy actions.

In EMU, it will be essential to achieve co-ordination between the different areas of economic policy. The Treaty of Amsterdam formulated growth and job creation as the primary goals of economic policy in Europe. It also established the institutional, functional and financial independence of the ECB. The idea underlying the delegation of monetary policy to an independent institution is to limit the influence of short-term political considerations on monetary policy and to combat inflation more efficiently. In turn, the independence of the ECB entails a large amount of responsibility for economic and social developments in general.

However, if other economic agents do not contribute their share to the envisaged outcome, the ECB will have to impose costs on the real economy. The relationship between monetary policy and wage bargaining has been discussed above. A similar case can be made for fiscal policy: An unbalanced fiscal stance would force the ECB to keep the official interest rates higher than desirable, in order to offset inflationary pressures. The Stability and Growth Pact attempts to avoid *ex ante* any potential conflict between monetary and fiscal policy. It should, however, be stressed that a successful implementation requires more forward-looking fiscal behaviour and greater emphasis on using cyclically adjusted budget deficits as a measure for the fiscal stance. Loose fiscal policy in periods of expansion (even when the actual budget deficit stays below 3%) might well trigger restrictive measures in downturns. Fiscal authorities should therefore aim at keeping cyclically adjusted deficits well below 3% in order to leave some flexibility for countercyclical measures in recessions.

The co-ordination of monetary and fiscal policies also raises institutional and operational issues. Policy co-ordination encompasses the whole range from information exchange, surveillance policy discussions and recommendations to joint policy actions. Extensive discussions among ECOFIN, the EURO-XI, the ECB, the European Parliament and the Social Partners should lead to a balanced policy mix. Such a dialogue helps assess potential interactions between macroeconomic policies well in advance. Given the clear objectives set forth by the Maastricht Treaty and the Statutes of the European System of Central Banks, this does not conflict with the independence of the ECB. The requirement for the EU countries to submit National Action Plans on overall employment policy strategies that are presented and discussed on an international level is an obvious improvement in this respect.

The Maastricht Treaty left it up to the ECB to define the goal of price stability. There is no quantifiable numerical measure as to how price stability has to be interpreted. The belief that a central bank can control inflation perfectly is wrong. The real world of central banking is not that simple and mechanistic. Official interest rate changes affect inflation with long and variable lags, so inflation cannot be closely controlled in the short run. This underlines once more the need for policy co-ordination.

9.6 Conclusions

European Monetary Union will fundamentally change the economic policy framework of the EU. Right from the outset, EMU will eliminate exchange rate fluctuations among the participating countries. EMU can be expected to create a broad European zone marked by macroeconomic stability, low inflation and low interest rates. The new framework should be more favourable to investment and economic growth, reducing various risks and promoting an efficient allocation of resources.

Although a stable monetary framework will improve the longer-term underlying conditions for new competitive jobs, it will not provide a solution to the European unemployment problem by itself. EMU thus may be seen as stimulating job creation, but it will by no means be a sufficient condition for a reduction of unemployment rates. Balanced monetary policy that aims at stabilising both prices and demand might to some extent support employment. Such a policy, does, however, need to be complemented by a broad and coherent effort for policy co-ordination, which strives for a sound fiscal stance, wage moderation and structural reforms of product and labour markets. Opportunities to reduce unemployment to a sustainable level only present themselves during times of expansion. In light of this, it is of the utmost importance that the necessary discipline be maintained in good times, so as to prevent inflationary pressures, which would force fiscal and monetary authorities to pursue counteractive policies later on.

Policy co-ordination requires an intensive dialogue among European institutions, including the ECB, in order to formulate joint medium-term objectives for promoting growth and employment. The EU certainly cannot afford negative-sum policy games between fiscal authorities and the ECB. Negligence in this area might produce economic outcomes that will likely benefit no one. Developing adequate institutional structures for combining policies both at the European and national levels and establishing commitment to these structures will be the challenge of the years to come. Promoting this dialogue and initiating these structures is a primary responsibility of the EU presidencies. The Austrian National Bank looks forward to Austria's opportunity to play a central role in these processes, both during its tenure of the Presidency and thereafter.

Bibliography

Ball, L., (1996) 'Disinflation and the NAIRU', in: Romer C. and Romer, D., (eds.), *Reducing Inflation*, NBER Studies in Business Cycles, 30, Chicago: The University of Chicago Press.
Bayoumi, T. and Eichengreen, B., (1993) 'Shocking aspects of European Monetary integration', in Torres, F. and Giavazzi, F., (eds.) *Adjustment and Growth in the European Monetary Union*, Cambridge: Cambridge University Press, pp. 193-229.
Blanchard, O., (1997) *The medium run*, Brookings Papers on Economic Activity, 1997(2), pp. 89-157.
Bean, C., (1994) 'European unemployment: a review', *Journal of Economic Literature*, 32, pp. 573-619.
Blanchard, O. and Summers, L., (1986) 'Hysteresis and the European unemployment problem', *NBER Macroeconomic Annual*, NBER.
Caballero, R. and Hammour, M., (1998) *Jobless growth: appropriability, factor substitution, and unemployment*, NBER Working Paper 6221.
Calmfors, L., (1993) 'Centralisation of wage bargaining and macroeconomic performance: a survey', *OECD Economic Studies*, 21, pp. 161-191.
DeGrauwe, P., (1998) *European unemployment: a tale of demand and supply*, Paper presented at the World Economic Forum, Davos 1998.
Decressin, J. and Fatas, A., (1994) *Regional labour market dynamics in Europe and implications for EMU*, CEPR Discussion Paper 1085.
Elmeskov, J. and McFarlan, M., (1993) 'Unemployment persistence', *OECD Economic Studies*, 21, pp. 59-87.

Layard, R., Nickell, S. and Jackman, R., (1991) *Unemployment - Labour Markets and Macroeconomic Performance*, Oxford: Oxford University Press.

Jäger, A. and Parkinson, J., (1994) 'Some evidence for hysteresis in unemployment', *European Economic Review*, 38, pp. 329-342.

Nickell. S., (1997) 'Unemployment and labour market rigidities: Europe versus North America', *Journal of Economic Perspectives*, 11(3), pp. 55-74.

OECD, (1994) *OECD Jobs Study*, Paris: OECD.

Peters, T., (1994) 'European monetary union and labour markets: what to expect?', *International Labour Review*, 134, pp. 315-332.

Röger, W. and int'Veld, J., (1997) *Quest II: a multi-country business cycle and growth model*, Economic Papers, Brussels: European Commission DG II.

Rünstler, G., (1993) 'Technische Probleme von Konjunkturprognosen', *Wirtschaftpolitische Blätter*, 1993 (4), pp. 127-144.

Rünstler, G., (1998) *Some evidence for nonlinearities in unemployment persistence*, Institute for Advanced Studies, Vienna, mimeo.

St. Paul, G., (1995) 'Efficiency wages as a persistence mechanism', in Dixon, H. and Rankin, N. (eds) *The New Macroeconomics*, Cambridge: Cambridge University Press.

Wyplosz, C., (1994) *Demand and structural views of unemployment*, INSEAD Working Paper 94/57.

10

EUROPE AND THE REGIONS:

A REPLY TO PERNTHALER AND GAMPER

Katharina Krawagna-Pfeifer

10.1 Introduction

The relationship between the European Union and the institutions of its member states is the subject of much discussion and speculation. As the process of European integration gradually widens and deepens as a response to the implications of a globalised world economy and the end of the Cold War, there is an increasing tendency to seek regionalised solutions to economic and political challenges, and to use EU-level institutions, policies and programmes to solve common problems. The global and regional interdependence of states, individuals and economies has reduced the autonomy and relevance of 'traditional' forms of political organisation. The European Union itself is an attempt to provide an effective framework within which the peoples of Europe can co-operate and build structures that enable them to meet the challenges of this globalised, evolving world. However, membership of the European Union, and the concomitant acceptance that much economic and political activity is more effectively constituted at the EU-level, means that there must be a re-ordering of the institutional framework that has heretofore supported European states.

One of the central debates about the significance of membership of the EU, not least in Austria, but also in the other European states that are federally constituted, is the degree of relevance that domestic federal structures have, and even to what extent powerful sub-state units make sense at all in a Europe which is gradually growing into one, and in which 'Austria' is the logical sub-unit of governance. In their contribution elsewhere in this volume, Pernthaler and Gamper argue for an increased direct role for the Länder within the decision-making structures and processes of the EU as 'the only way to create a really democratic and federal European Union'. In this chapter, I will seek to provide a critique to this view: I will briefly examine their argument, review the current position in Austria, summarising some of the reasons why I take issue with their interpretation of this situation.

Pernthaler and Gamper provide two major reasons why the constituent sub-units of the member states should play a more central role in the European Union: that membership of the Union has not abolished *per se* federal structures in its member states (only modified them); and that the creation of a 'democratic' Europe requires the direct participation of those tiers of government closest to the people. This leads them, on the one hand, to point to the potential for the continuing involvement of the Länder - in direct representation in EU institutions and in the implementation of EU regulations - and, on the other, to argue for what they term 'asymmetrical federalism' as the solution to the differing traditions of governing structures within member states. Yet at the same time, they voice fears that Austrian accession to the EU has led to the loss of certain Länder competencies - the 'collapse of Länder autonomy'. As I have already made clear, I believe that the logic of globalisation, the recourse to 'regional' (i.e. European) solutions, and the requirements of efficiency mean that the time has come for a radical rethink of the institutional infrastructure that constitutes the member states of the EU, and Austria in particular. I will now outline the domestic Austrian debate.

10.2 The future of federalism - the implications of EU membership

Austria is formally comprised of nine independent provinces, according to article 2 of the Austrian Federal Constitution. The debate on the future of the Austrian Länder after accession and their continuing relevance was triggered off in the summer of 1997 by a surprising protagonist - a Styrian federal politician, Gerhard Hirschmann. Hirschmann proposed that the nine Länder be dissolved and replaced by three regions: the western, eastern and the southern regions. At a Graz symposium held in early summer 1998, Hirschmann admitted that he consciously formulated his proposal to provoke the public not only to take notice of him, but also to take this issue seriously. This deliberate 'provocation' led to a public outcry: one would have thought that Austrians believed that they were going to have to abolish the Republic! This was perhaps due to the fact that the Länder have always lived in the certainty that they were the ones who actually established or re-established Austria after 1945. However, I would argue that this timely reminder that membership of the EU, in a globalised world, reinforced the need to rethink the future of Austria's domestic political institutions: reference to historical merit does not tell us a lot about the appropriateness of structures and institutions for the future. I will now outline the major reasons why the role of the Länder must be revised.

Firstly, membership of the EU has, after all, already had profound implications for Austrian politics: more than 50 per cent of the laws and regulations with which the Austrians now have to comply are debated and decided in Brussels - and in the economic sphere, it is perhaps as much as 80 per cent. Thus, pivotal decisions are now taken at a higher (European) level, in an attempt to meet wider challenges to Austria. This undermines the relevance of the 'lower' levels.

Secondly, and just like other member states, Austria has had to give up a considerable amount of its legal autonomy and rights of sovereignty by the fact of membership. This also must affect the Länder, which are already subject to the federal authorities and not exactly equipped with a great amount of independent authority. Thus, crucial areas of competency are no longer located at the Länder or federal level.

Thirdly, whilst membership of the EU has profound implications in itself for the future of the Länder, other questions understandably arise as to whether the current Austrian institutional distribution is appropriate and, above all, whether it makes economic sense in the current global economic climate. In the form practised by Austria, federalism is a seemingly expensive affair. A country of merely eight million inhabitants, Austria is required to pay for 15 federal ministries, nine provincial governments and the same number of provincial parliaments. There are 78 Landesräte (provincial ministers) sitting in the provincial governments and 448 members of provincial parliaments. In addition to this, there is the national parliament (*Nationalrat*, or National Council) with 183 members and the 64 member Federal Council (*Bundesrat*). The latter constitutes the institution in which Austria's constituent Länder are represented and although it is often referred to as the 'uppper' house, in reality, it constitutes the lower chamber.

In total, therefore, around 800 top politicians are engaged in looking after the affairs of around eight million Austrians. On average, they each earn around 60 000 Austrian Schillings (ATS) per month (ca. £3,000) and when one includes the costs of the bureaucracy needed to support them, the total annual expense of this network of politicians runs to hundreds of millions of ATS (tens of millions of pounds sterling). It is perhaps instructive to compare this situation with that of Bavaria, which with its eleven million inhabitants has to support only one government and state parliament below the federal level.

Fourthly, accession to the EU and the process of progressive integration has not only had financial implications for federalism, but has also caused stresses within the balance of power within member states' domestic structures. These stresses extend from functional loss to the emergence of new, often cross-border regions, and may lead in time to the complete dissolution of the national states as we know them. When existing geographical units of administration are both losing their powers and are having their boundaries redrawn, it would be surprising if there were not a debate about rationalising lower tier institutions of governance.

10.3 The EU and federalism

Having outlined four main reasons why there must be a reassessment of the continuing relevance and future effectiveness of the Länder, I now wish to turn to some observations about the EU's structures that aim to incorporate local diversity and sub-state governments. There has been much talk about the implications of the introduction of the subsidiarity principle in the EU's legal regime through the Maastricht Treaty. It would however be a mistake to imply that this principle put Austrian federalism and subsidiarity within the EU on the same level. The Länder or regions do not actually have the subjective rights to demand subsidiary at the European Court of Justice; nevertheless, they may make demands of this principle in the event of a specific intra-state dispute. Thereby, this principle has a significant effect on the future development of internal state structures. I would argue that the specific structures of the EU make the influence of the sub-state units contingent on the member states; a position which further reinforces the need to refine their role.

In this context, I feel that the Committee of the Regions should not go unmentioned. This body, which was included in the Maastricht Treaty through a German initiative, is significantly dependent on the individual member states. The composition of these committees is, therefore, not homogeneous and confined to representatives of sub-state federal units like the Austrian Länder. Its members stem from federal organisations, as well as from regionalised, decentralised and unitary states. The fact that the Committee is not a real 'regional chamber' is made clear in the allocation of its 222 seats. This does not occur according to the actual size of the relevant regions but is distributed by a formula dependent on the size of the member states. In addition, the committee has not only been drafted as a forum of regions, but also as a forum of local government: around half of the seats are occupied by local authority representatives. Furthermore, the Committee only has the right to be consulted. Increasing the powers and scope of the Committee has been denied up to now and will probably not ever take place.

An acceptable definition of the regions that was independent of the specific position accorded them by the law of the respective member state would be very difficult. For example, the classification of statistical units which has been worked out and utilised by Eurostat defines three categories of administration. The German Länder belong, with the three Belgian regions, to the first group, whilst the Italian and French regions, and the Austrian Länder have been put into category 2 - a lesser category. However, if Austria were divided into three regions - for example, Eastern Austria (Vienna, Lower Austria and Burgenland), Southern Austria (Carinthia and Styria) and Western Austria (Upper Austria, Salzburg, Tyrol and Vorarlberg), in the manner that Herr Hirschmann proposed - then Austria would fall into category one as well, which would increase the salience of the Länder. The smaller the unit, the less relevant, it would seem.

In contrast to this, in its regional charter of 1988, the European Parliament defined the regions, despite their sizes as 'a complex of areas which represent closed structures and inhabitants who have common elements and who would like to hold onto and develop further unity to strive towards cultural, social and economic progress'. Thus, the European Parliament argues that the regions should take on a significant role in support of European integration and identification. The attempt to thus bring the idea of a united Europe nearer to the average citizen is focused on the image of a 'Europe of the Regions'. We are here at the interface between Austrian federalism and European regionalism. In this context, both are seen as an implementational variant of the subsidiarity principle. In my opinion, however, it would be wrong to consider regionalism as simply being synonymous with federalism. It is an independent principle, related to EU structure, and not to present state constitutions. For primarily, regionalism means a transfer of state (and thus Länder) executive power and legislative jurisdiction. The Länder should not be seen as limbs of the Austrian state - also not as an alternative to the state - but should simply complement it. In any case, a clear distinction between federal states and unitary states will get more difficult in the future, as the federal principle is getting less and less bound to its realisation in the federal state. Furthermore, in many ways the issue of the future of the regions such as the Länder is strongly connected to the future of the national states. Empowered again after the part loss of sovereignty through EU membership, new, cross-border regions will gain increasing significance and may come to replace existing regions as they are given a leading role within the EU structures.

However, this does not mean a displacement of the 'national state' by these new regions, as they are not in the position to offer a real alternative to the national state, and are on too small a scale to be an effective player in a wider European environment. Thus, the role of federal units should concentrate on giving disadvantaged groups the chance of more independence but should not lead to an 'egoism of small units' in the sense of provincialism. The return to smaller, more manageable regions may strengthen security and identity, but I doubt that the efforts around the regional 'garden fence' broadens the view towards a Europe without borders. It is this continuing need to examine the wider context within which Austria and the EU must operate, to be economically competitive and administratively efficient, that forms the core of my argument.

10.4 Conclusion

I have outlined why I believe that there is a fundamental requirement for us to re-examine the role, functions and scope of sub-state units within the European Union. I believe that those who propose, like Pernthaler and Gamper, an attempt to mirror Austrian federal structures and procedures at the EU level do not fully appreciate the new realities of the globalised post-Cold War world.

Not only should the existing structures of state necessities be taken into consideration, but it is also extremely important to meet the needs of the citizen, and this is the major argument for reform. The chances that the people will accept this are great - not only on a democratic political level, but also on an administrative level. The Länder or regions (this also counts to a greater extent for local authorities) are closer to the citizens than are the central governments. However, this does not mean that their primary duty is to replicate themselves at the European level. Indeed, this points towards a change of functions for the Länder: to get away from a struggle to gain authority as an expression of power in relation to the central state administrations towards a more meaningful reallocation of tasks, functions and competencies which are more appropriate for them in the new international environment, and are oriented towards the needs and interests of the people and the search for new possibilities of co-operation which goes far beyond all borders.

Comparison with other states shows that only regions of a certain geographical size will exist in European competition. As we enter into this competition, it will not be enough to refer back to earlier Länder independence. It is this which requires us to re-examine the role of Austrian federalism.

11

AUSTRIAN PERSPECTIVES ON EU ENLARGEMENT

Hannes Swoboda

11.1 Introduction

In recent years, Austria has moved into the centre of a free Europe and has derived clearly visible material benefits from this. Psychologically and politically, however, it has not yet fully come to terms with the new situation. Prejudices which have been fostered and nurtured for many years have prevented many from recognising and exploiting the chances and opportunities. Even the political groups that welcome Austria's new geopolitical situation have not yet translated it fully into political reality. In this chapter, I will seek to examine Austria's current relationship with the rest of Europe, to explore the nature of the domestic debates surrounding this relationship, to analyse the effects of EU enlargement on Austria, and to outline a potential strategy that Austria could employ to meet the challenges that such expansion implies.

11.2 Austria moves into the centre of Europe

To look at the specifically Austrian debate on questions of EU enlargement in terms of current analyses and discussions is undoubtedly an incomplete and unsatisfactory approach. One should really immerse oneself in the historical, sociological, psychological and linguistic aspects in order to throw light on the background to current arguments and attitudes. This was the opinion expressed, for example, by the Germanic and Romance philologist Luigi Reitani in his article entitled 'Multi-cultural or xenophobic State: the particular schizophrenia of the "Viennese psyche"': 'What does the concept of a foreigner really mean in a city whose character has been so much shaped by foreigners?' Everyone knows: the Viennese have the belligerent Turks to thank for their coffee, plump Bohemian cooks for their pastries; music and architecture were gifts of the Italian soul; courtly rituals came from Spain, the gentlemanly manners on which the Viennese upper classes modelled their behaviour from England. Everywhere in the city the signs of a foreign presence can be seen; even the Viennese dialect shows an openness to foreign words which is unusual in German. The Viennese Prater owes its name to the Spanish *prado* (a meadow), the word *Bassena* (the tap in the corridor of an apartment house) comes from French, *Beisel* (pub) comes from Yiddish. The Viennese do not call an envelope by the usual German word *Briefumschlag*, but instead talk about a *Kuvert*. A *seccatura* (nuisance) makes a Viennese, like an Italian, *rabiat* (furious). Viennese taking their leave are often heard to say *ciao*. Clothes shops have Italian names: *Per l'uomo, Tutti e due*, even *Belle scarpe da Ulrike* ('Nice Shoes *chez* Ulrike')! The Viennese press is characterised by a similar linguistic *mélange*. Foreign words, it would seem, are as much part of the city's character as foreign people.[1]

Reitani ends by saying, 'In almost no other city do xenophobia and foreign influences coexist in such proximity as they do in Vienna. Foreigners are called to Vienna, given all the honour due to them, and then kicked out: whether they are Burgtheater or opera directors or just asylum seekers, the treatment is the same. They are a part of the city which lives in a constant, conflictual and productive dialogue with the whole. The multi-racial face of the city of Vienna was shaped by foreigners, but is also set against them. Schizophrenia has its dwelling place here. But, there and again, is there such a thing as a healthy city?[2].

So far, of course, we have spoken only about Vienna as the federal capital, but there is hardly an informed observer of the Austrian scene who will dispute the strong, not to say dominant, influence of Viennese culture on Austrian society, or deny that there is wide agreement on this throughout Austria. Let us stay with Vienna for a moment.

As the person with political responsibility for urban development and planning in the Austrian federal capital, on 20 April 1990, only a few months after the upheavals in Eastern Europe, I opened a conference entitled 'Vienna 2010' with the following words: 'The people of Austria, and of Vienna in particular, are pinning great hopes on the events of the last few months in Eastern and Central Europe and the steps in the direction of a common market. Delight at these developments, however, is now increasingly accompanied and overlaid by practical concerns. The past few months have already shown the problems that await Vienna at a variety of levels: excessive demands on public and personal transport, a growth in the unofficial employment market and the black market, and a growing rejection of 'foreigners' by the 'resident' population, certainly not unconnected with the problems just enumerated, are phenomena that foreshadow future difficulties. The dichotomy between the hope of a new economic revival and the many fears about the uncertainties of the future reaches into all areas of social and personal life. First there is the psychologically rooted unease that arises from the encounter with the new and the unknown, the need for everything to stay as it always has been, for the future to be clearly and safely laid out as a continuation of the past and the present. To the many changes brought about by the technological revolution that go deep into individual lives and into the shape of both work and leisure there are now added the arrival of 'foreigners' and the 'pressures towards a multicultural society'. There is a great danger that all the aggression arising from a reduction in clarity and comprehensibility will be manifested against those who are most easily perceived as representing a threat to people's own lifestyle - the foreigners [3].

Very soon after the fall of the Berlin Wall and the disappearance of the Iron Curtain, it therefore became clear that the new developments so close to our borders were seen by many not so much as opportunities, but as dangers. Even when the positive effects could be statistically demonstrated, too little was done by the politicians, firstly, to make these positive effects (improvement in the balance of trade, more Austrian foreign investment, etc.) known and,

---

[1] Reitani, L., (1990: 112).
[2] Reitani, L., (1990: 117).
[3] Swoboda, H., (1990: 7).

secondly, to convert them into equally positive attitudes. And this although the changes were clearly visible.

So we find ourselves in the grotesque situation where the experiences and relationships, ranging from political to familial, that have survived from the Austro-Hungarian monarchy are not being used as a basis for the enlargement of the European Union. Sometimes one even has the feeling that the problems, quarrels and - ultimately - failure of this multi-racial state, this first Central or Eastern European union that was Austria, form the basis for a widespread scepticism about eastward enlargement. It is true that many businessmen are working hard at investing in Austria's neighbouring countries, but public opinion is not keeping pace with this move to the East. As Karl-Markus Gauß says, with a certain degree of exaggeration, but not without reason, 'The fear of perhaps not being seen as a civilized Western European, but as someone from the lawless East is deeply rooted in the Austrian psyche'. So Austria joined Europe in the firm hope that the European Union would finally wrench it free of those links that had bound it for so long to the Hungarians and Poles, the Czechs and Slovenians. In a way, the European Union, with its economic criteria, was expected to play the role that the Iron Curtain had played for more than a generation - the division of Europe into two blocs, with the EU bloc being the Europe of prosperity, order and security.[4]

11.3 The domestic debate - contributions from political parties and public opinion

So, these positive and external economic developments, which were clearly apparent a few years ago, were turned to almost no political effect. The deeply rooted and at best ambivalent attitude to the unknown and to foreigners, the country's hard-won independence - these things and much more contributed to the political reserve of the Socialdemocratic Party of Austria (*Sozialdemokratische Partei Österreichs* - SPÖ) and the Austrian People's Party (*Österreichische Volkspartei* - ÖVP) at least. The Freedom Party of Austria (*Freiheitliche Partei Österreichs* - FPÖ), of course, was even less eager to emphasise the successes and advantages of the opening up of the East. Whereas the conclusion of the Association and Europe Agreements passed off quite quickly and relatively unremarked in Austria and hardly even played any part in the pre-EU-accession discussions, the EU decision to enlarge made a more comprehensive examination of Austria's attitude to this question necessary. Within the SPÖ, the subject was discussed very soon after Austrian EU accession, and attempts were made to weigh its positive and negative effects.

The main thing at issue in these discussions was the link between widening and deepening and the importance of a common environmental and social policy. The EU is facing a twofold task: the process of integration must be intensified and the EU must be enlarged. In the medium and long term, the two processes must run in parallel, although the essential decisions about the manner and direction of the process of deepening must be made before the enlargement process is set in motion. This will make it possible for applicant countries to take account of these developments in the EU in their internal preparation phase. From the social-democratic point of view, two important areas must be stressed in this process:

---

[4] Gauss, K.-M., (1998: 119).

- basic social standards must be more extensively defined and implemented, an opting-out , as it is practised in Great Britain should not be possible over a longer period[5] and

- environmental standards, which are of underlying importance not least for transport policy, must also be more forcefully formulated and implemented.

In the autumn of 1997, before the adoption in December of the European Parliament and Council resolutions on Agenda 2000, the SPÖ's federal party executive planned to issue a statement on the same subject. Although the paper drawn up by a party working group under my chairmanship met with general agreement, some of its details were nevertheless discussed and amended by the party bureau on several occasions, so that no resolution was adopted until the meeting of 18 March 1998. It places the emphasis on the need to harmonise living conditions as far as possible before accession, the resolution of social problems and the gradual approach to accession, particularly with regard to freedom of movement on the labour market. The resolution says *inter alia*:

- The enlargement of the EU is a long-term task with important security, economic and social policy implications.

  Its chief purpose is to harmonise and raise the standard of prosperity in Europe in order to eliminate distortions of production and relocations. Both the enlargement itself and the whole decisive phase of preparing for a larger EU must be directed towards this end.

- The essential aim in our view is to overcome the division in Europe which is unsatisfactory from the economic, social and political points of view and, indeed, dangerous, with realism and moderation, but also with the vision of a strong Europe which can represent the interests of its people both within this continent and worldwide.

- The enlargement of the EU is not a zero-sum game in which one party wins what the other loses.

- In the light of the differences between the applicant countries themselves, which are still great and are only slowly being reduced, enlargement of the Union will be possible only in stages.

- The gradual enlargement of the EU with important preparatory steps being taken in both the East and the West should help to resolve these problems of adaptation in a way which is in the interests of employees. Social and employment conditions should be brought up to as high a level as possible all over Europe, and the creation of common labour markets can only happen after there has been a significant lowering of unemployment rates in the East and the West. In this context it would be desirable for marginalised regions to receive appropriate special aid during the transitional years.

- The European social model must form the basis of any harmonisation strategy for the applicant countries.

---

[5] Dr. Karl-Renner Institut, (ed.), (1995: 26).

- The gradual introduction of freedom of movement for workers should be made conditional upon certain conditions being met. Objectively assessable criteria must be defined for this purpose, which will be examined as part of a regular procedure, particularly unemployment rates and wage structures.

- Competent, legally secure, independent representatives are a sine qua non for participation in the European social dialogue and must therefore be present in the Central and Eastern European countries also.'

The draft of this resolution by the federal party executive was, however, already in use as the basis of the parliamentary work of the SPÖ members of the European Parliament. Partly with the support of other Austrian Members of Parliament, partly on the basis of similar or identical motions, the essential points of this paper found their way into Parliament's recommendation on Agenda 2000.

In December 1997, the European Parliament, in its report on enlargement - the so-called Oostlander Report (named after its Rapporteur) - gave strong backing to the intention of the Council and the Commission to enlarge the European Union. Nevertheless, the EP, which has to agree to every new member, placed some 'conditions' or 'prerequisties' on this enlargement. From the Austrian viewpoint, the social dimension of these conditions is the most important. If the accession of new member states - and the related transition period - are to go smoothly - and this is the common intention and desire - then it was the Austrian opinion that no economic or social disruption should result from enlargement itself. Yet there it is not intended that this condition should impede speedy enlargement. On the contrary, careful preparation of the accession process, as a result of this condition, is helping to enforce public support for enlargement, especially in existing member states.

Because of the Austrian initiative, therefore, the relevant part of the EP resolution of 4 December 1997 reads as follows:

The European Parliament

- Recognises that regions adjoining applicant countries are particularly affected because of their geographical position and that they therefore require special support in the shape of programmes and resources, aimed especially at promoting cross-frontier cooperation and preventing abrupt changes in the competitive situation;

- Insists that the *acquis communautaire* be included de jure and de facto in all social control mechanisms when the applicant countries accedes and also notes that it is absolutely essential for the applicant countries to adjust to the European social model if social peace is to be ensured; also takes the view that the basis for broad social acceptance in the question of enlargement is an institutionalised social dialogue between autonomous partners on the two sides of industry, who must be involved in all relevant government decisions and flows of information at the accession negotiations;

- Calls, with regard to the free movement of workers, especially in view of the phenomenon of commuting, for appropriate, flexibly applied transitional periods based on assessment standards to be agreed on, in order to:
- ensure an urgently needed, socially compatible integration process,
- reduce the pressure on the European social model,
- ensure continuous economic, social and regional upward development in the applicant countries;
- Notes with concern that the social question is listed in Agenda 2000 only as an issue to be considered, and that unfortunately no more than secondary importance is attached to the treatment of the social dimension itself; calls, therefore, for a White Paper on the social situation and social policy in the applicant countries to be drawn up as part of the pre-accession strategy, incorporating the following points:
- urgent consideration of a common employment strategy in view of the unemployment situation in the EU member states and the problems of the border regions,
- particular attention to the importance of initial and continuing training for social integration, and
- a broad approach to social concepts and consideration of such aspects as the social implications of regional development tendencies, socio-cultural effects of migratory pressures and social consequences of transformation processes in agriculture;
- Calls on the member states of the Union and the Commission to make every effort to combat unemployment effectively and thereby create the preconditions for the free movement of workers in an enlarged Europe.

The ÖVP has so far adopted no official position. However, most press communications from the ÖVP, particularly those from MEPs, stress the positive aspects of enlargement. Titles like 'ÖVP welcomes EU eastward enlargement' (ÖVP Press Service, 16 July 1997) and 'Eastward enlargement is the EU's greatest historic task' (ÖVP Press Service, 31 November 1997) testify to this positive attitude. Problems are not forgotten, but a general approach is usually taken, as the following statement shows: 'Eastward enlargement means more stability and more security, not only for the EU but also for Austria - but only under certain conditions: there must be a fair sharing of burdens among all net contributors within Europe, there must be no additional burdens for Austria and transitional rules must be made to ensure that this happens' (ÖVP Press Service, 31 November 1997).

The two governing parties thus take a generally positive attitude to EU enlargement. This does not yet mean, however, that all political mandate-holders assume the same need and the same timetable for enlargement. Yet it is clear that they see enlargement as the integration of the neighbouring countries into the Union, so that adaptation by the applicant countries to the *acquis communautaire* is placed in the forefront and disruptions to the market, particularly the employment market, are to be avoided.

While the Liberal Forum and Greens are more supportive of the enlargement of the Union , the FPÖ rejects it, at least for the foreseeable future. In a position paper issued on the occasion of a recent event in connection with the Austrian Presidency, it said: 'Another vital central task of a responsible Austrian EU Presidency must be to discuss openly the question of EU enlargement. The importance of this project is highlighted primarily by the unresolved areas of financing and of the consequences for the EU as a whole, but particularly for those member states bordering on the CEECs and the effects on them (e.g. on the employment market, immigration, security, nuclear safety, social standards, etc.). In this connection, and with regard to Agenda 2000 (reform of the CAP, reform of the structural funds, new financial framework), it is of vital importance not only to present vital Austrian interests, but also to implement them as far as possible. As examples, mention can be made of relief of Austria's burden as a net contributor, Austria's plea for special subsidies for border regions, the avoidance of income reductions which will be suffered by farmers as a consequence of the CAP reforms, or prevention of the disadvantages for rural areas which can be expected to result from reform of the structural funds.[6]

It can already be seen from this relatively 'cautious' position paper that the FPÖ attaches no value to the enlargement of the EU and that the opportunities it will bring for Austria are not mentioned even in passing. This shows up even more clearly in official party statements, which we shall not look at in any detail on this occasion, however.

The question now arises whether the attitudes of the major parties, ranging from cautious approval through scepticism to rejection, reflect the opinion of the public.

It is a well-known fact that, in opinion sampling, answers are often influenced by the questions that are asked. So it would be necessary to carry out a large number of opinion polls over quite a long period in order to form a relatively 'objective' picture of public attitudes. However, since its results have been roughly reproduced by a number of other polls, we will give the result of the latest telephone poll (April 1998), in which over 1 000 people[7] were questioned. According to this poll, 50 per cent 'personally reject the enlargement of the EU', while 39 per cent welcome it. The strongest rejection of enlargement is on the part of workers (62per cent) and by supporters of the FPÖ (71 per cent). Somce 52 per cent of those asked considered that accession by our neighbours would bring more disadvantages, whereas 26 per cent expect more advantages. The social and political background of those who oppose enlargement is the same as in the case of the first question. As far as age is concerned, most of those who oppose enlargement belong to the 40-59 age group. Young people between 16 and 24 have the most positive attitude to enlargement. A positive attitude also correlates heavily with levels of education! A positive strategy for enlargement could well be supported by young and better-educated people.

11.4 EU enlargement and the Austrian labour market

Both the opinion polls and the public political debates reveal people's fear of the mass arrival of cheap labour as being mainly responsible for attitudes among the population ranging from scepticism to rejection. Are there any grounds for these fears?

---

[6] Freiheitliche Partei Österreichs, (ed.), (1998)
[7] Österreichische Gesellschaft für Europapolitik, (ed.), (1998).

In a study by the *Österreichisches Institut für Wirtschaftsforschung* (Austrian Institute for Economic Research - WIFO), the authors say:

> In the past, opening up to the east has brought undoubted advantages for the Austrian economy: the balance of trade with the countries to the east promoted economic growth, and hence employment, in Austria. The advantages for businesses are undeniable: Austrian exports to Hungary, the Czech Republic, Slovakia and Poland rose from 18.9 billion schillings in 1989 to 58.9 billion schillings in 1996. They thus more than trebled. The increasing importance of the new labour market in Central and Eastern Europe can be seen in its share of Austria's exports of goods: this rose from 4.4% in 1989 to 9.6% in 1996; by 1997 it may well have risen to about 12%. Imports from Eastern Europe have also risen considerably. They have squeezed foreign, as well as domestic, manufacturers out of the market. The positive effects were significantly greater, however, as can be seen from the balance of trade: having been virtually neutral in 1989, by 1996 it showed a surplus of 13.2 billion schillings.[8]

However, much of the domestic Austrian debate has focused on the perceived threats implicit in eastward enlargement. E. Walterskirchen and R. Dietz, the authors of the WIFO report - commissioned by the Federal Chamber of Labour - came to the following conclusion:

> According to the Austrian Institute of Economic Research, in the event of an immediate eastward enlargement of the EU with no transitional periods, there would as a result of the high income differences and the accumulated supply be an additional offer of labour in the first year of around 47 000 people on the Austrian labour market. Of these, approximately 26 000 would be cross-border workers, 21 000 immigrant workers. It is, however, extremely unlikely that there will be very rapid accession of the Eastern European countries without transitional periods. It is more realistic to assume that accession by the Central and Eastern European countries will take place around the year 2005. If there are no transitional periods on the employment market, in 2005 there will, in view of the considerable difference in levels of prosperity, still be the probability of approximately 42 000 additional migrants and cross-border workers per year (with the rates decreasing gradually).[9]

How did the authors arrive at this number of migrant workers/cross-border workers? The major factors in their calculations were the population figures for the neighbouring countries, particularly near the Austrian border, and the difference between their prosperity and/or income levels and those of Austria. As far as population is concerned, the authors based their calculations on figures for Austria's neighbours contained in Table 11.1. The authors' assumptions regarding per capita income and wage trends are reproduced in Table 11.2, where they are compared to the Austrian standard.

These population figures, which are based on current experience and realistic assumptions about the gradual process of economic convergence and international comparisons regarding

---

[8] Österreichisches Institut für Wirtschaftsforschung, (ed.), (1998: 11).
[9] Österreichisches Institut für Wirtschaftsforschung, (ed.), (1998: 1).

migratory or commuting trends, lead to the abovementioned projected migratory and/or cross-border commuting patterns. As a calculation by the German Institute for Economic Research[10] came to a similar conclusion, and indeed even predicted greater migratory movements, the authors feel that their work is corroborated. The conclusions they draw from their calculations are correspondingly short and to the point: long transitional periods and criteria for the introduction of free movement within the labour market!

Table 11.1   Population of accession countries bordering Austria

	Population in millions	Proportion near border
Poland	38.6	-
Czech Republic	10.3	1.0
Slovakia	5.4	1.8
Hungary	10.2	1.0
Slovenia	2.0	1.4
Total	66.5 (27.9 without Poland)	5.2

Source: WIFO (1998: 42 and 56)

Table 11.2   Per capita income and wage trends in accession countries bordering Austria

	Per capita GDP (Austria = 100)			Wages (Austria = 100)		
	1996	2005	2015	1996	2005	2015
Poland	28	38	50	12	19	33
Czech Republic	52	61	73	13	19	34
Slovakia	37	48	62	10	15	27
Hungary	32	42	55	12	20	35
Slovenia	52	61	73	36	43	56

Source: WIFO (1998: 7)

---

[10] Deutsches Institut für Wirtschaftsforschung, (ed.), (1997: 89-96).

11.5   Towards a domestically and externally credible strategy

The primary task of the Austrian Presidency is not to continue the internal Austrian debate or to give it a new direction. But it can and, indeed, should be used to find a consensus within the EU with regard to enlargement and the justified concerns felt by Austria as a country which borders on four of the applicant countries. In this process, three currently apparent shortcomings could be corrected.

First, official Austria, through its approval of the EU strategy, has represented itself *vis-à-vis* the Union's member states as a definite supporter of enlargement. At the same time, however, various statements by prominent politicians, the content of which is critical of enlargement, have filtered through to 'Brussels'. The rather clumsy and unvoted-on calls for special subsidies for frontier areas which may be affected have not added to the clarity of Austria's position.

Second, our neighbouring countries also perceive Austria's attitude as being mixed, or schizophrenic. Our statements and debates are reported very extensively, if not always accurately, in the neighbouring media. Perhaps our friends across the border are also oversensitive in some of their reactions, but a clear position, which must not hide any of our concerns and interest, could make the dialogue with our neighbours and future EU colleagues very much more fruitful.

Third, and above all, however, our own population should see things more clearly. They must know that EU enlargement will come and that it is in Austria's clear interests, politically, economically, socially, environmentally and so on. But our citizens must also have the feeling that their fears and anxieties are being taken seriously and that the government, in cooperation with the European Commission, is developing instruments to deal with any possible dangers.

During its Presidency, Austria could take its own sceptical, hesitant, delaying attitude and the misleading promises of some Western European statesmen and, in some instances, of the Commission, and turn the mixture into a realistic approach. Realism is absolutely necessary if we wish to avoid great disappointment. Neither the illusion that enlargement of the Union is nothing more than a pleasant 'stroll round the East', nor the belief that enlargement can be indefinitely delayed contribute anything to the great task - in terms of economic policy and of peace - that faces us.

In fact the term 'enlargement', which we use for the enlargement of NATO and that of the EU, is misleading. Membership of NATO does, of course, call for adjustment, but nothing like such comprehensive or thoroughgoing adjustment as membership of the EU. This is not yet fully understood by all the applicant countries either, particularly by those large sections of the population who naturally do not concern themselves with the details of EU membership. A large-scale information campaign is still needed here.

In any event, Austria should bring to the enlargement debate the measure of realism that is needed if we are to move forward without stumbling. The following principles and objectives could be borne in mind in this process.

1.   Accession is a process which brings the applicant countries ever closer to the various EU standards. Reducing the differences in standards brings the applicant countries

greater prosperity and increases the chances of the existing EU member states to maintain their standard of living. So it is a matter of <u>integrating our neighbours in the EU system or systems.</u>

2. Depending on the progress made in this process, transitional periods will be set. The main purpose of transitional periods is to avoid disruptions to the market. This is true both of the applicant countries and the present EU member states. Criteria and indicators must be developed for <u>market disturbances,</u> on which the transitional periods, which must be as flexible as possible, and/or their duration should be based.

3. Integrating our 'neighbours' in the EU will, even if transitional periods are applied in particularly sensitive areas, involve problems of adjustment. Transitional and adjustment aid is planned for those sectors, or areas. This principle must apply both to applicant countries and to existing EU countries.

4. In the particular case of border areas, cross-border activities should be the focus of aid measures, so that the population can prepare itself economically, socially and mentally for 'life without frontiers'.

5. Austria should, without tabling a formal resolution, put the idea of more realistic accession dates into circulation. Unfortunately, the dates mentioned by many leading statesmen were quite unrealistic and are now more unrealistic than ever. It is becoming increasingly apparent that a first round of accession should be scheduled for about the year 2005. This is most particularly the case if internal reform of the EU, including institutional reform, is rightly deemed to be a prerequisite for the first round of accessions.

6. Precisely because the enlargement process, at least for some countries, will be a long-drawn-out one, the status of the European Conference should be raised. The Conference, originally conceived as a sop for Turkey, should be used to bring the countries of Europe gradually closer, particularly on questions of internal and external security. It would provide a way of learning about and experiencing membership of a united Europe at an early stage. Neither the accession negotiations, nor the incorporation of the *acquis communautaire* would be invalidated by this, but an improved European security partnership would be developed.

11.6 Conclusion

So Austria has every possibility of bringing more realism into the enlargement debate during its Presidency without being 'unmasked' as a covert opponent of integration by our neighbours. Such realism could also take the wind out of the sails of the undoubted opponents of enlargement who exist in Austria.

Karl-Markus Gauß says of Austria's role:

> The European Union discovered the East long ago, but Austria did not play the role of guide, of knowledgeable teacher or of bridge-builder in this process. With our minds fully taken up with integration in the West, we forgot that the West has a crucial interest in the fragmenting East; a crucial interest, but only minimal knowledge, and instead of helping it with our knowledge and helping ourselves and the East in the process, we continued the desperate attempt to

hide the fact that we are the ones who are geographically and historically closest to the East[11].

In conclusion, Austria is very close to the East, geographically and historically, and maybe that is what makes it so difficult for us to act as travel guide and bridge-builder. But with a great enough effort it is possible to change even historically rooted and apparently firmly entrenched attitudes and opinions. This does, however, require courage and a vision of a better world, or at least of a better Europe.

If, into the bargain, this vision can be combined with direct economic advantages it should not be too difficult to take the necessary real steps towards it. If Austria were to fail seriously to do this during its Presidency, it would be missing out on great opportunities.

Bibliography

Deutsches Institut für Wirtschaftsforschung, (ed.), (1997) *Europäische Union: Osterweiterung und Arbeitskräftemigration*, DIW-Wochenbericht, 5/1997.

Dr. Karl-Renner Institut (ed.), (1995), *Österreichs Zukunft in Europa*, Vienna.

Freiheitliche Partei Österreichs, (ed.), (1998) *The Austrian Presidency - From the Point of View of the 'Austrian Freedom Party'. Stellungnahme zur Konferenz 'The Austrian Presidency of the European Union'*, Vienna, 15-16 May, 1998.

Gauss, K.-M., (1998),'Warum Österreich die Osterweiterung verschlafen mußte', *Europäische Rundschau* 98/2.

Österreichische Gesellschaft für Europapolitik, (ed.), (1998) *Das Meinungsklima in Österreich zur Osterweiterung der Europäischen Union. Umfrage unter wissenschaftlicher Leitung von Dr. Christian Haerper*, Vienna, April 1998.

Österreichisches Institut für Wirtschaftsforschung, (ed.), (1998) *Auswirkungen der EU-Osterweiterung auf den Österreichischen Arbeitsmarkt*, Vienna: WIFO.

Reitani, L., (1990) 'Vielvölkerstaat vs. Ausländerfeindlichkeit: Über eine besondere Schizophrenie der "Wiener Seele"', in Swoboda, H., (ed.), *Vienna. Identität und Stadtgestalt*, Vienna, Cologne, p. 112.

Swoboda, H., (1990) 'Besondere Planung', in: Magistrat der Stadt Wien and Institut für Wirtschafts- und Sozialforschung, (eds), *Vienna 2010, Stadtentwicklung bei Bevölkerungswachstum und offenen Grenzen*, Vienna.

---

[11] Gauß, K-M., (1998: 121).